Change Is Required

AMERICAN ASSOCIATION *for* STATE *and* LOCAL HISTORY

About the Series

The American Association for State and Local History Book Series addresses issues critical to the field of state and local history through interpretive, intellectual, scholarly, and educational texts. To submit a proposal or manuscript to the series, please request proposal guidelines from AASLH headquarters: AASLH Editorial Board, 2021 21st Ave. South, Suite 320, Nashville, TN, 37212. Telephone: (615) 320-3203. Website: www.aaslh.org.

About the Organization

The American Association for State and Local History (AASLH) is a national history membership association headquartered in Nashville, Tennessee, that provides leadership and support for its members who preserve and interpret state and local history in order to make the past more meaningful to all people. AASLH members are leaders in preserving, researching, and interpreting traces of the American past to connect the people, thoughts, and events of yesterday with the creative memories and abiding concerns of people, communities, and our nation today. In addition to sponsorship of this book series, AASLH publishes *History News* magazine, a newsletter, technical leaflets and reports, and other materials; confers prizes and awards in recognition of outstanding achievement in the field; supports a broad education program and other activities designed to help members work more effectively; and advocates on behalf of the discipline of history. To join AASLH, go to www.aaslh.org or contact Membership Services, AASLH, 2021 21st Ave. South, Suite 320, Nashville, TN 37212.

Change Is Required

Preparing for the Post-Pandemic Museum

Edited by Avi Y. Decter,
Marsha L. Semmel, and Ken Yellis

ROWMAN & LITTLEFIELD
Lanham • Boulder • New York • London

Published by Rowman & Littlefield
An imprint of The Rowman & Littlefield Publishing Group, Inc.
4501 Forbes Boulevard, Suite 200, Lanham, Maryland 20706
www.rowman.com

86-90 Paul Street, London EC2A 4NE

British Library Cataloguing in Publication Information Available

Library of Congress Cataloging-in-Publication Data

Names: Decter, Avi Y., editor. | Semmel, Marsha L., editor. | Yellis, Ken, editor.
Title: Change is required : preparing for the post-pandemic museum / edited by Avi Y. Decter, Marsha L. Semmel, and Ken Yellis.
Description: Lanham : Rowman & Littlefield, [2022] | Series: American Association for State and Local History book series | Includes bibliographical references.
Identifiers: LCCN 2022014896 (print) | LCCN 2022014897 (ebook) | ISBN 9781538161654 (cloth) | ISBN 9781538161661 (paperback) | ISBN 9781538161678 (epub)
Subjects: LCSH: Museums—Social aspects—United States. | Museums—United States—Management. | COVID-19 Pandemic, 2020—Social aspects—United States.
Classification: LCC AM7 .C478 2022 (print) | LCC AM7 (ebook) | DDC 069.0973—dc23/eng/20220422
LC record available at https://lccn.loc.gov/2022014896
LC ebook record available at https://lccn.loc.gov/2022014897

♾™ The paper used in this publication meets the minimum requirements of American National Standard for Information Sciences—Permanence of Paper for Printed Library Materials, ANSI/NISO Z39.48-1992.

For my son, Eliav Decter, my daughter, Alyce Callison, and my grandsons, Joshua and Nathaniel, who give me hope for the future.
A.D.

To my son David, who represents hopes and possibilities for the best of our collective futures.
M.S.

To Jo Yellis, My Life's Companion.
K.Y.

Contents

Foreword   xiii
Gretchen Sullivan Sorin

Acknowledgments   xvii

Introduction   1

Part I: Confronting the Crisis   13

Chapter 1   A Wake-Up Call   17
             Kristin Leigh

Chapter 2   Making Lemonade: Learning from the Pandemic   21
             Judy Gradwohl

Chapter 3   Beyond Command and Control: Inclusive
             Leadership in a Crisis   25
             Su Oh

Chapter 4   Getting Lost on Purpose   29
             Andrea Jones

Part II: The Turn to Digital   33

Chapter 5   The Virtuous Circle: From Local to Global
             and Back Again   37
             Robin White Owen

Chapter 6   Expanding Museums into Digital Spaces   43
              Lath Carlson

Chapter 7   I Went to a Bar for Time Travelers   49
              Michael Peter Edson

Part III: The Turn to Community   **53**

Chapter 8   Beyond the Handshake: Effective Steps in
              Community Engagement   57
              Armando Orduña

Chapter 9   Notions of Permanence, Visions of Change   63
              Darryl Williams

Chapter 10   Slaves Lived Here [Esclavos Vivieron Aqui]   69
              Meredith Sorin Horsford

Chapter 11   We Are Each Other's Harvest: Prospering
              through Partnerships   75
              LaNesha DeBardelaben

Chapter 12   Communities over Collections: Three Principles
              for Partnership   79
              Nafisa Isa

Part IV: The Turn to Equity   **85**

Chapter 13   Speaking Truth to Power Begins Internally:
              Confronting White Supremacy in Museums   89
              Kayleigh Bryant-Greenwell and Janeen Bryant

Chapter 14   What Keeps Me Awake at Night: A Letter
              on Decolonization   95
              Brandie Macdonald

Chapter 15   Museums, Disability, and "Uncertain Afters"   101
              Izetta Autumn Mobley

Part V: Rethinking Stewardship   **107**

Chapter 16   Caretakers of Our Histories   111
              Sven Haakanson

Chapter 17   The Collective Collection: Active, People-Centered,
              and Collaborative   117
              Mariah Berlanga-Shevchuk

Chapter 18   Broadening the Institutional Purpose of Zoos
              in the Post-Pandemic Era   123
              Scott Carter

Part VI: Rethinking Visitors   127

Chapter 19   On Bearing Witness   131
              Erin Carlson Mast

Chapter 20   Holding the Space We Make   137
              Beck Tench

Chapter 21   Discovering Connections: Supporting the Quest
              for Meaning and Well-Being   141
              Dawnette Samuels

Part VII: Rethinking Leadership   145

Chapter 22   Self-Worth, Trust, and Wonder: Leadership Lessons
              from Fred Rogers   149
              Mariruth Leftwich

Chapter 23   Protect People, Not Things   153
              Franklin Vagnone

Chapter 24   Courageous Imagination   157
              Nannette V. Maciejunes and Cindy Meyers Foley

Part VIII: Rethinking Structures   161

Chapter 25   From Silos to Social Networks   165
              Christian Greer

Chapter 26   Equity and Collaboration: Transforming Structure
              and Narrative to Center Community   171
              Brian Lee Whisenhunt

Chapter 27   Collaborative Knowledge Production for the
              Twenty-First-Century Museum   177
              Juliana Ochs Dweck

Chapter 28   Hitting Reset on Hiring and Advancing in Museums   181
                Sam Moore

Part IX: Redefining Success   **187**

Chapter 29   The (Unfulfilled) Promise of Evaluation   191
                Cecilia Garibay

Chapter 30   Word Processing   197
                Joanne Jones-Rizzi

Chapter 31   Measuring Our Value(s): Let's Start with Structure   201
                Ben Garcia

Part X: Expanding Purpose   **207**

Chapter 32   Museum Relevance in the Context of the
                Earth System   211
                Emlyn Koster

Chapter 33   Social Justice: Framework for the Future of Museums   217
                Elena Gonzales

Chapter 34   Are We Serious about Changing the Equation?   223
                Deborah F. Schwartz

Chapter 35   Purpose Is the Only Thing   229
                Dorothy Kosinski

Part XI: Voices from the Future of American Museums   **235**

Chapter 36   Thoughtful Agility   237
                Marcy Breffle

Chapter 37   The Unredeemable Museum   239
                Rebekka Parker

Chapter 38   Museums, Aesthetic Experience, and Design Justice   241
                Rina Alfonso

Chapter 39   The Water We Swim In   243
                Tramia Jackson

Chapter 40   More Show, Less Tell   245
                Rachel E. Winston

Chapter 41   The Optics of Museum Equity   247
              Karen Vidangos

Chapter 42   Will We Lose the Love to Labor at Museums?   249
              Shivkumar Desai

Chapter 43   Make Me a History Museum I Actually Care about   251
              Emma Bresnan

Chapter 44   Collapsing Enclosures   255
              Qianjin Montoya

Chapter 45   A Constellation of Interpretation: Object Labels
              in the Polyphonic Museum   259
              Sara Blad

Chapter 46   "If an Object Sits on a Shelf in a Dark Warehouse,
              Does It Make an Impact?"   263
              Jonathan Edelman

Chapter 47   Change and Opportunity: Resilience in a
              VUCA World   265
              Dejá Santiago

Chapter 48   Co-designing the Future   267
              Kirsten McNally

              Postscript: What We Have Learned   269

              Further Reading   273

              Index   277

              About the Editors   289

~

Foreword

A great department store, easily reached, open at all hours, is more like
a good museum of art than any of the museums we have yet established.

—John Cotton Dana, 1917

I was particularly fond of the writings of the Newark Museum's visionary director, John Cotton Dana, when I was in graduate school for museum studies
in Cooperstown. After all, as a girl from New Jersey, the Newark Museum was
the place that inspired me to think about a career in museum work, and my
parents often took my brother and me to its galleries and art programs when
we were children. Despite Cooperstown's progressive program, as their first
African American graduate student, occasional comments and questions indicated that there were individuals who had no experience with difference and
little understanding of African American history and culture. "You fit in really well with us," a fellow student "complimented" me the first week or so—a
comment I never forgot. I certainly wanted to change attitudes like that.

I identified immediately with Dana's comments in *The Gloom of the Museum*. Although penned in 1917, they seemed prescient. Except for its sometimes flowery Victorian language, his description of museums as stagnant,
elitist, and inaccessible could sadly have been written in the 1970s when
I was in graduate school. Today, a little more than one hundred years after
Dana declared department stores much more visitor friendly than museums,
we are still urging museums to break out of their colonial pasts, to make
themselves more relevant to their communities and less beholden to the

whims of wealthy board members and donors, and certainly to face the white supremacy inherent in their collections and histories.

Since the 1970s, dozens of the best museum thinkers and writers have been ringing the clarion, warning of the consequences for museums of doing nothing as the nation becomes more diverse. But most museums have simply been tinkering around the edges of diversity, inclusion, and real systemic change, and visitors remain about the same. *Excellence and Equity*, the profession's landmark statement of the public service and education role of museums, was completed in 1992; it marked recognition of the shift from museums that primarily collect and preserve objects to institutions centering people and learning. Perhaps most importantly, *Excellence and Equity* stated unequivocally that there could not be excellence in our institutions without equity. Although some museums took it as a renewed statement of purpose, others either ignored it or handed the report to their educators and told them to "handle it."

Over recent decades, other writers also pressed for sweeping changes in museum practice. Stephen Weil, former Deputy Director of the Smithsonian's Hirshhorn Museum and Sculpture Garden, expanded the conversation by urging museums to transform themselves "from being about something to being for someone," in his compelling article published in the museum edition of *Daedalus* in 1999. "Change by itself is so uncomfortable that institutions do not do it voluntarily or for noble reasons," wrote Elaine Gurian, former Deputy Director of the United States Holocaust Memorial Museum and international museum consultant. "They change because they fear the consequences of not doing so, and only then are willing to override the cries of anguish from the discomforted."

Lonnie Bunch, Founding Director of the National Museum of African American History and Culture and now Secretary of the Smithsonian, sees a grand vision for museums as places that can show Americans how much we share despite our differences, places that can help us to understand one another by courageously tackling the things that divide us, from climate change to race. A variety of increasingly loud voices agree. Movements like MASS Action and Museums Are Not Neutral, the push to unionize museum workers, and the demand to decolonize museums all demonstrate that museums can and should be more than just places that collect things and must become more focused on the people they serve. The tendency to center objects, their collection and preservation, rather than center humanity has at times made museums tone deaf to the purpose for which we protect these objects—to delight and enlighten the visitors we serve. Instead, we have treated the objects with greater care than we have treated our visitors and museum staff.

This is an important book. It is different. If you work in a museum or want someday to work in a museum, this is worth reading. To be sure, a steady stream of books and blogs outlining proposed changes to American museums are valuable and thought provoking. But this book goes further. At the outset, it offers the sage wisdom, experience, experiential common sense, and compassion of some of our profession's most talented individuals—museum colleagues who have always been unafraid to speak the truth. Some of the authors have been leaders and thinkers for decades; others are just now ascending to leadership positions. But most importantly, this book includes the voices of those who are rarely heard or whose voices have been ignored. They are the upstarts, the agitators, the innovators, the people of color, and the emerging museum professionals who, if we let them, will push our profession forward in positive ways in the future.

The confluence of events during summer 2020 brought about a reckoning in American museums, the result of which is yet to be realized. The murder of George Floyd in the midst of a global pandemic illuminated injustices in the American justice system but also made us recognize injustices elsewhere, including within our own cultural institutions.

Making the changes that are needed will not only enable museums to be relevant and meaningful to broad public audiences and equitable places to work, but they will also ensure their very survival. This task is going to take the concerted effort of all of us at every level, from board members to frontline staff. Reading this book is a great place to start.

Gretchen Sullivan Sorin
Director & Distinguished Professor
Cooperstown Graduate Program—SUNY Oneonta

~

Acknowledgments

It takes a community to write a book. In this case, many members of that community are here to speak for themselves. We want, therefore, to acknowledge and thank the fifty colleagues and friends who contributed essays (and editorial comments) to the completion of this work. A special word of thanks to Gretchen Sorin for her kindness in contributing the foreword to this book—a perfect grace note in every way.

Many other colleagues contributed to our thinking, either through participation in one or another of our virtual conversations or through helpful counsel and encouragement. The first, critical boost came from our editors, Charles Harmon at Rowman & Littlefield and Aja Bain at the American Association for State and Local History: Their willingness to push for early publication made it possible for us to complete our work quickly and without a lot of wasted motion.

Thanks also to the three (anonymous) reviewers whose critical comments were both encouraging and helpful. We are grateful to the staff at Rowman & Littlefield for their good work in translating the manuscript into a handsome volume. Thanks also to Bill Brookover, who was kind enough to give permission to reproduce one of his powerful *Dissonance* prints GRAND DISSIDENCE for the book cover, and to Arc Indexing, Inc. for their fine work on the index.

Other thoughtful and encouraging colleagues include Gail Anderson, Swarupa Anila, Horace D. Ballard, Christy Coleman, Sophie Don, Benjamin Filene, Karleen Gardner, Barbara Henry, Yael Horowitz, Sandra Jackson-Dumont, Gretchen Jennings, Jessimi Jones, Deborah Krieger,

Hanna Leatherman, Tori Lee, Kelly McKinley, Porchia Moore, Melissa Nunez, Jenny Sayre Ramberg, Lisa Sasaki, Averie Shaughnessy-Comfort, Carl Siracusa, Jasmin Tabatabaee, and Charles Wood. We thank them all!

Last, but by no means least, we want to acknowledge our families and our companions for their patience and support as we pressed forward with our work.

A.D., M.S., K.Y.

~

Introduction

This is a book about the future of American museums. Like other institutions, museums and zoos, science centers, historic sites, and arboreta, were powerfully affected by the nested crises of the pandemic. In 2020, climate change and natural disasters, the plague of coronavirus disease (COVID-19), social protest, and divisive politics hit the United States like a perfect storm. Businesses, schools, and community organizations shut down. Hospitals, medical services, and health centers were overwhelmed. Social protest, fueled by the killing of Black people by police officers, erupted in rallies and sporadic riots. In the midst of a bitterly contested national election, lies and disinformation proliferated. And then, on January 6, 2021, would-be insurrectionists stormed the Capitol of the United States, seeking to overturn the results of a free and fair election. The fate of civic life and culture, the destiny of American democracy, seemed to hang in the balance.

Each and all of these national crises called for responses from our institutions. But for more than a year, the situation was unprecedented: No one in our nation's history had lived through a convergence of cataclysms even remotely similar. For leaders and for communities, there were no playbooks, no tried-and-true solutions, no precedents, on which to rely. Adapting to novel circumstances and uncertainty became the order of the day; improvisation in society, economy, culture, and polity the new norm; restoration of health and healing the new American Dream.

Museums, as integral components of our social system, were compelled to respond and adapt. Virtually every American museum—from small historic

1

houses to vast universal museums—shut down for lesser or greater periods. Admissions and earned income declined suddenly and speedily. Furloughs and layoffs decimated museum staffs—among larger museums, an estimated 20 percent fired staff and 40 percent instituted furloughs. For many museums, the challenge was survival, plain and simple. Addressing the distress and needs of nearby communities became mostly a secondary consideration, though here and there museums stepped forward to offer neighbors immediate assistance as sites for clinics, voter registration, food distribution, or emergency day care.

Throughout the pandemic, most museums have focused on restoring the old normal. But even amid upheavals and disruptions several American museums have charted new directions for themselves and their communities. A large number of museums have taken a decisive turn to digital: Even as they were closing their doors to in-person visitors, museums across the country began to ramp up virtual tours, webinars, blogs, and other digital programs, reaching out to regional, national, and even global users.

As virtual audiences expanded and the needs of local communities persisted, a substantial number of museums have taken a turn toward community. Some museums have found new uses for their grounds and exterior walls; others have developed new kinds of collaborations with local neighborhoods; and still others have created new online resources and activities for homebound individuals and families. And, in yet a third turning, some museums have moved issues of equity and justice—internally and in the world—to the center of their institutional concerns.

Each of these strategic turns—to digital, to community, and to equity—has deep implications for museums' values, policies, and practices, as well as their missions and sense of purpose. The turn to digital, for example, raises important questions about online access, service area, public participation, and the collection of born-digital materials in sharp contrast to the usual collection of physical objects.

The turn to community speaks of a willingness to abandon traditional go-it-alone mindsets and suggests possibilities for new kinds of partnerships, alliances, and collaborations with museums and other local organizations. As museums seek to become more diverse and inclusive, the turn to equity can affect almost everything, from hiring practices to core narratives. Above all, these kinds of strategic choices represent an embrace of experiment and risk-taking, based on the premise that standing pat or returning to the old normal will sooner or later lead to a loss of vitality and relevance.

Embracing change and adapting to novelty also come with consequences and costs. Dissonance in the museum field is echoed throughout almost every sector, from the academy to the corporation. As in those fields, in every corner of the country, museum professionals are challenging old assumptions, conventional narratives, and customary practices.

The very names of new websites, virtual talking circles, and online communities suggest both the aspirations and antagonisms that now engulf museums: Death to Museums, Hyperallergic, MuseumHue, Facing Change Working Group, The Incluseum, Museums & Race, The Empathetic Museum, Museums Are Not Neutral, Museum Workers Speak, Museum as Site for Social Action, and so on. Many of these initiatives precede the pandemic and owe their voices to a prescient choir of pioneers, including such colleagues as La Tanya Autry and Mike Murawski (Museums Are Not Neutral), Adrianne Russell and Aleia Brown (Museums Respond to Ferguson), Richard Josey (Collective Journeys), Stephanie A. Johnson-Cunningham and Monica Montgomery (Museum Hue), June Ahn, Emma Turner-Trujillo, and Rose Cannon (Death to Museums), Rose Paquet, Aletheia Wittman, and Porchia Moore (The Incluseum), and numerous others.

Another indicator of upheaval: In just the past year, staff at some of our most prominent art museums—including the Guggenheim and New Museum in New York, the Philadelphia Museum of Art, and the Museum of Fine Arts in Boston—have voted to unionize, citing disparities in pay, abusive work cultures, and racial discrimination. Some museums have restructured themselves; some have created senior positions to promote diversity, equity, accessibility, and inclusion; some have lost established, prominent leaders to retirement or resignation.

Across the museum landscape, new voices are being raised, and their calls for transformation, internally and in society at large, can now be heard loudly and clearly. The editors and authors of this book are among the proponents of significant changes in the museum field. American museums have adapted and transformed repeatedly over the past century in response to social, political, and cultural change. Now, we believe, is the time to do so again. Although our past and even our present provide neither models nor solutions, what they do put before us are possibilities. It is the purpose of this book to envisage some of those possibilities and to suggest why and how they might be realized. The essential element, of course, is the will to change. We think that systemic change in museums can be energized by ideas that infuse and enrich our perspectives. And we think the time for that change is now.

We understand, of course, that no one idea, no single innovation, no particular model, can serve as a universal template. At a conservative estimate, there are more than 30,000 museums in the United States. Large and small, they are diverse and ubiquitous: Every state in the nation has hundreds of museums and even small communities can boast a local historical society and a historic house museum. We have museums dedicated to trolley cars and crayons, trout fishing and textile manufacture. Despite their radical diversity, museums generally share at least some values and practices, needs and challenges; suggestive ideas, then, can benefit museums of varied scales, stripes, and colors, wherever they may be located. It is our intention and hope that the ideas presented in this volume will resonate in many different museums and communities.

In its depth and range, this book constitutes an invitation to join in the growing, lively discourse about possible futures for museums in the United States. Our invitation extends not only to our professional colleagues but also to all those interested in cultural affairs and institutions—journalists and critics, artists and writers, museumgoers and general readers. Although museums are the topic at hand, similar disruptions have arisen in other organizations and in our everyday lives. Accordingly, the authors have eschewed technical terms, jargon, and obscure references in their essays, and they speak personally, in their own voices, to the ideas under consideration. By making this volume accessible—and, we hope, interesting—to many kinds of readers, we want to engage a broad audience in the surging conversation around what has long been a significant and valued type of institution in our society.

All the editors and authors are engaged, active practitioners in the museum field. In fact, the book is the product of a long and critical conversation that began in 2019 as a series of blogs by Yellis and Decter, that transformed, in partnership with Marsha Semmel, into several virtual convenings with more than thirty colleagues, and that led to a *Manifesto for Next Practice*, published by the Mid-Atlantic Association of Museums (MAAM) as its first-ever white paper. By early 2021, the three editors—all veterans of more than forty years of museum work—had drafted a prospectus for the book and were contracted by Rowman & Littlefield. Nine months of strenuous writing and editing have followed. In the end, more than fifty colleagues from all corners of the museum field joined in the composition of this book.

Because this volume is really a collection of reflections on contemporary America and its culture, we have taken pains to engage authors who are diverse in age, race, gender, expertise, and experience. Some are chief executives, others emerging museum professionals. About half of the authors are Black, Indigenous, or people of color (BIPOC), and a fair number identify as LBGTQ. Some have spent all or most of their professional lives in one institution; some have moved around; and some have worked in the field mostly as independent museum professionals consulting on a variety of projects. No one group of professionals, however diverse or broad-gauged, can hope to comprehensively represent a field, let alone a nation, but the contributors collectively are representative of both the museum sector and our multicultural society.

The book is structured to reflect many of the key issues that currently roil the museum world. Each chapter addresses one or more dimension of the museum journey, ranging from institutional purpose to the well-being of visitors to the metrics by which we measure success. For each chapter, we have invited multiple authors to share their perspectives and reflections. These are individual views, rather than institutional statements, grounded in personal and professional experience. Many authors reference the work of their home institutions, but their essays are intended to offer broad ideas rather than case studies. Readers will find plenty of granularity in these texts and lots of concrete instances; the authors are by and large a realistic lot, even as their thoughts and expectations are speculative and aspirational. In many chapters, readers will find a variety of lenses and topics, and because we are advocates for experimentation and next practice, we have made no effort to harmonize these diverse perspectives.

Although the authors address a multitude of issues and ideas, the gist of our collective concerns about the situation of contemporary museums can be summarized simply:

- Why should American museums change? What are the risks and costs of inaction?
- What might that change look like? What do we think museums must be able to do in the future?
- What will it take for museums to change? How can museums marshal the conviction and resources needed to change?

Why Must Museums Change?

Until recently, American museums, despite their remarkable variety and distinctiveness, have intended to promote one or more of three broad purposes:

- to produce new knowledge and encourage learning,
- to preserve and interpret cultural heritage and traditions, and
- to inspire wonder, awe, curiosity, and imagination.

Often, of course, these broad purposes were linked and embodied in a single institution.

But museums—like other forms of public institution—were established and maintained by society to serve yet another critical purpose: *to authenticate the social order*. They celebrated American entrepreneurship and economic success, the triumph of new technologies, the mastery of nature, and the historical progress of American life and culture. Validation of the American Way and of normative culture could be found in museums large and small, from the Museum of Modern Art's narrative of how abstraction triumphed in the United States to stories of pioneer pluck and provincial success in thousands of small historic sites and community museums. In one historic house museum after another, for example, one could encounter relics of early European settlement, demonstrations of "colonial" or traditional cooking, an array of items associated with prominent people, fancy furnishings, and stories of community adaptation and achievement, housed almost without exception in former homes of the rich and powerful. Questions like Who has been or is empowered? How did they win their power? and What did they do with their power? were generally unvoiced or evaded.

This began to change in the 1960s. A tremendous demographic wave coincided with the civil rights movement and opposition to the war in Vietnam to galvanize an American counterculture willing and ready to challenge the "Establishment" on a wide array of issues and ideas. Postmodernist theory and cultural studies probed the power structures and constructed meanings that undergirded conventional thinking. The New Social History, feminist, ethnic, and racial scholarship, and revisionist historians expanded the scope and depth of American historiography, creating a more inclusive and critical view of collective memory. Environmentalists called attention to the costs and consequences of the human conquest of nature. The efficacy of science and technology, even the longstanding idea of "progress," came under scrutiny.

By the 1980s and 1990s, the growing fissures in US society were manifested in an ongoing culture war over public education and collective imagination. In this struggle, America's museums were not exempt. Sporadically, and then more frequently, museums were embroiled in fierce and well-publicized cultural (and political) conflicts. Initially, museums became sites of contestation. Furors over exhibitions such as the photographs of Robert Mapplethorpe (Cincinnati Contemporary Arts Center, 1990), *The West as America* (National Museum of American Art, 1991), the Enola Gay project (National Air and Space Museum, 1995), and the *Sensation* show at the Brooklyn Museum of Art (1999) fueled the national debate over who gets to set the cultural agenda and define what is and what is not normative. As Timothy Luke puts it: "Art works, historical expositions, nature interpretations, and technological exhibits, as they are shown in museums, are products of the ongoing struggle by individuals and groups to establish what is real, to organize collective interests, and to gain command over what is regarded as having authority."[1]

The current crises have shown us what the world looks like when the facade of civility, tolerance, and good government are peeled away: unemployment, economic collapse, natural disasters, social protest, police violence, political division, and contention. The moral certainties have been dissolved. We are exiles from our former lives, from family and friends, from our work lives, and from our former recreations. Many of us feel like aliens in our own homes, our workplaces, and our places of faith. We have crossed over into uncharted territory; so, too, have our friends and neighbors, our workmates, and our fellow citizens.

A good part of our dislocation stems from a sudden, intense, inescapable reckoning with who we are as individuals, as communities, as a nation. In just a matter of months, Americans were forced to question the validity of some of our most cherished beliefs about the singularity of our national virtue, the character of our cultural authenticity, and the harmlessness of our mastery of nature. For a great many Americans—and a growing number of museums—these core myths have been exploded.

We need to be present for communities that are looking to museums for programs about diversity and understanding, expanded public menus, and greater civic engagement. Americans are now grappling with their history. Reconsidering exploitation, dispossession, and displacement as well as the unfulfilled potential of our democratic ideals will continue to bring pressure to bear on museums to engage issues like reconciliation and reparations, and to make clear the link between social and environmental justice. The potential begins to open for us to tell new stories in new ways, making the stories of previously invisible individuals an essential part of a reconsidered American narrative.

What Might Change Look Like?

In the face of unprecedented changes like these, efforts to return to the old normal are not only futile but fatuous. Museums were struggling for recognition and relevance before the pandemic and that struggle has only intensified in our disrupted present. Unless museums address the issues of the day, they will be less relevant than in the past. In a time when individuals, families, and communities across the country are trying to regain their footing in an uncertain time, irrelevance will, sooner rather than later, prove fatal to museums.

On the other hand, museums can respond in meaningful and timely ways to urgent social, cultural, and community questions, concerns, and challenges. The pandemic offers museums a unique opportunity to rethink and repurpose—above all, to refocus on earning the trust of our communities and the individuals that comprise them.

We don't need to overthink it: The way to find out what people need is to ask them. We also need to ask ourselves some fundamental questions: Why are our museums needed? What are our roles and who are they for? What can we mean to our communities, our regions, the world? How can our museums better listen to and communicate and co-create with our communities? By taking these questions seriously and addressing them transparently, we can begin to embody qualities at the heart of community building and position our museums as the vital centers and catalysts for meaning making and the positive social change our communities need.

At the outset, we will need to acknowledge that many of our current crises are bound up with one another. Climate change, extinction of species, immigration, demographic churn, ethical issues, pollution of the rivers, lakes, and oceans, and COVID-19 are inextricably tied to social injustice and inequity, racism, bigotry, colonialism, and divisive ideologies. We therefore need a global paradigm that embraces both nature and culture, science and society, environmental and social justice, open inquiry and democratic process and principles.

Our present reality finds us caught between tidy and messy. Tidy is more comfortable, but messy may be more productive. We need to be experimental; we need to take some calculated risks. The nation finds itself confronted with fundamental, even existential, challenges. We must question the systems and structures that obstruct greater equity and inclusion, transparency, and openness. We must rethink leadership and authority, giving greater priority to skills like openness, thoughtful listening, collaboration, and adaptability. We also need to open our decision-making by making space for more diverse participants, by amplifying the voices of emerging professionals, and by inviting our communities into the conversation.

We will need more porous structures that are open to diverse voices from all levels of staffing and from the community at large. We will need to develop new interdisciplinary, team processes. We will need to revalue public knowledge and multiple forms of expertise. We will need to tell new stories in new ways, making the experiences of previously invisible individuals an essential part of a reconsidered American narrative. And we will need to play a role as places of healing, focusing on the care, connection, and well-being of our staffs, volunteers, and audiences.

We must not go it alone. Instead, our museums need to work with other types of institutions within our communities, including other cultural, educational, and social service organizations, as well as to forge new alliances with museums across the country and around the globe. Sharing ideas and expertise will empower museums to try new things. Partnering will be a critical professional skill, an essential strategy in this networked age. Partnership is required to make a meaningful impact, to contribute to positive social change, and to make a difference, not only in the museum's bottom line but also in people's lives. Museums will therefore need to build a partnership mindset into their work and to create conditions for successful collaborations as part of the organizational chart, mission, vision, and infrastructure.

Creating an alternative paradigm for museums is no easy task. With more than thirty thousand museums in the United States alone, a single template is unlikely to apply to even most museums. Moreover, the field is sharply divided over what purpose and perspectives should prevail. In 2019, the International Council of Museums (ICOM) published a proposed new paradigm that viewed museums as "democratizing, inclusive and polyphonic spaces for critical dialogue about the pasts and the futures," that preserved and interpreted memories as well as objects, and that aimed "to contribute to human dignity and social justice, global equality, and planetary wellbeing." If we commit to rethinking and reinvention, this is what change might look like.

What Will It Take to Change?

Adapting to novelty is neither simple nor easy. Although people talk boldly about their readiness to change, we are all captives of our life experiences—and those experiences are familiar, customary, normal. Habits, as numerous studies report, are difficult if not impossible to break, especially in a time of great uncertainty. Added to the uncertainty of the present is the prospect of the unknown future. Thus, the overwhelming majority of institutional responses in the spring of 2020 was survival and return to the old normal (however dismal and unhappy that was).

Resistance to change slipped in wearing the mask of "resilience." Much has been said and written during the pandemic about the importance of resilience, "the capacity to recovery quickly from difficulties . . . and the ability of a substance or object to spring back into shape." Resilience may be apt and even essential when we consider individuals and their historical responses to tragedy and trauma as well as all our current struggles to "spring back into shape" after the disruptions of the past two years. Museums must and should help foster the resilience of those who work in and for them, and their programs and projects should help support the resilience of members of their surrounding communities.

But is resilience what is most needed by our museums now? Do we really want to spring back into former shapes? The events of the past months—from the uncertain, lingering, evolving presence of COVID-19 and its variants to the mandate for all museums to confront and address the ongoing impacts of our racist past and colonialist roots—require moving forward and not simply springing back. There are many problematic aspects to the current "shape" of many museums, and the recent disruptions compel us to embrace opportunities for necessary change.

We are in an acutely uncomfortable place to begin that work. Neither museums nor our society at large is set up to deal with unprecedented crises. We have no playbook, no tried-and-true strategies and not even a museum think tank to speculate on possible scenarios. We are, in short, at sea without a compass. But, as Andre Gide remarked, "One does not discover new lands without consenting to lose sight of the shore for a very long time."

We are reminded of the long, tortuous history of the modern environmental movement in the United States. For fifty years, anyone who could read had access to one study after another that warned of the disastrous effects of human impacts on climate and the even more consequential effects of impending climate changes. Today, amid drought and floods, wildfires and ocean warming, mass migration and extinction of species, we have reaped the whirlwind. And yet we as a nation and as a species have yet to embrace the changes needed to avert catastrophe. As biologist Edward O. Wilson puts it: "Too paralyzed with self-absorption to protect the rest of life, we continue to tear down the natural environment, our species' irreplaceable and most precious heritage."[2]

So what is to be done? The majority of US museums, zoos, gardens, historic sites, and arboreta will continue their struggle to return to the old normal. Smaller institutions, in particular, hardened to living with modest budgets and small circles of support, will hunker down to business as usual. Some large museums, notably the major science and technology centers, which earn a living at the gate, will struggle to regain their old revenues but are likely to stay the course. Large art and history museums will probably follow suit but with gestures sufficient to demonstrate their willingness to respond to the social and cultural movements of the day.

Likely, it is in the midsize museums that change is most likely to occur because they tend (but not always) to be relatively nimble, flexible, and open to the pressures and ideas of the moment. Some smaller community or culturally specific museums, which are closely connected to their constituents, may also be places with potential for fundamental change. They, together with a few visionary, experimental new projects, will probably lead the way, informed and inflected by the myriad of informal online groups who are advocating for museums to become more progressive, more activist, and more engaged.

The precondition for new initiatives is committed leadership. This may come in three distinct forms. Some boards, at least, are concerned about how to adapt to new realities. A recent survey of corporate boards reported that a substantial minority of those boards had embraced "at least one structural change, one process change, and one change to collaboration since the COVID-19 crisis began." For these boards, managing large-scale risks, revisiting their organization's purpose, encouraging innovation and growth, and staying current on technological trends were the keys to moving forward.

Museum executives and senior managers are another potential source of adaptation. Given a world of dramatic shifts and complex new challenges, for museums to move forward will require a new and different set of leadership skills. Museum leaders will need to exemplify the qualities of curiosity, humility, tolerating ambiguity, and probing the wider contexts and implications of current issues. They will need to understand the importance of responding to community needs and tapping into the wisdom of the crowd, whether that "crowd" be their own staffs or voices beyond the museum walls. As agents of change, leaders will need to be open and adaptable, inclusive and collaborative, decisive and transparent. They must encourage continuous reflection, while also being practical, linking aspirations to concrete actions.

Museum leaders who privilege listening, innovation, and experimentation will have to share authority with other members of the staff. Distributing authority and including a wide range of voices in decision-making will give younger and more junior members of the staff opportunities and agency in redirecting their institutions. Thanks to a proliferation of museum studies programs, the museum sector is now being populated by emerging museum professionals who are well-trained, thoughtful, and energetic. New hires trained as social workers and community organizers will also give the field a jolt. Museums are overdue for new ideas, and a new generation of young professionals are ready to accept the challenge and burden of leadership.

Perhaps the two most critical needs, if museums are to adapt and innovate, are a renewed sense of purpose and a compelling sense of urgency. We need to ask ourselves some fundamental questions: Why are our museums needed? What are our roles and who are they for? What can we mean to our communities, our regions, the world? Lacking a clear sense of purpose, we will not be able to advance. But we also need a deep sense of urgency. Unless we are prepared to act *now*, all our reflection and thoughtfulness and intentionality will go for naught. Urgency is the catalyst for change.

How change-ready *are* our museums? Why did it take a pandemic and social unrest to push us along? Why have we not been bolder and more skeptical of our structures and systems? We need—and we *know* we need—to better communicate our values and missions. Even so, despite many shared values and the impulse to do right, we sometimes find ourselves blocked by internal divisions over priorities, objectives, and values. We are frozen in these conversations even when there is goodwill on all sides because it is not altogether clear what doing right means in any given set of circumstances.

How can we find a way to signal to the public that we are doing meaningful work even as we reflect on what constitutes that work? Can we find ways to venture forward courageously, even with uncertainty, confident that the public has our back? Based on the essays in this volume and the exemplary initiatives of museums across the continent, we are encouraged to believe that American museums will continue to create public value and social capital and to contribute in meaningful ways to civic culture and individual fulfillment.

The challenge we face is to reimagine how to address our circumstances as we reimagine ourselves. Most important—and perhaps most difficult—we need to stop thinking about our museums as isolated institutions and, instead, to understand them as integral parts of the cultural sector and of our communities. If we are transparent, we will earn trust. If we are opaque, we will be seen as a lost cause with little redeeming social value. We need to recognize that building and maintaining trust is a long-term effort that requires sustained engagement and can be easily undermined by inconsistency in intent or action. Only by helping to make safe and comprehensible the places where people live and work and raise their families will we be valued by our communities and deserving of their trust.

Notes

1. Timothy W. Luke, *Museum Politics* (Minneapolis: University of Minnesota Press, 2002), xxiv.
2. Edward O. Wilson, *The Meaning of Human Existence* (New York: Liveright Publishing, 2014), 177.

~

PART I

CONFRONTING THE CRISIS

The twin crises of the pandemic and the racial reckoning affected virtually every museum in one form or another. Museums closed doors, implemented layoffs and furloughs, canceled exhibitions and programs, and faced reduced revenues and budget shortfalls. With the May murder of George Floyd, the long-simmering issues of systemic racism came to the fore and led to national demonstrations and calls for museums to examine their policies, programs, and positions on equity. The following months also saw an increased number of hate crimes against Asian Americans, given the purported links between the COVID virus and China. In fact, 2020 witnessed the largest number of recorded US hate crimes since 2008. In the wake of the national malaise, long-simmering museum worker dissatisfaction with their own status and their museums' stances on equity also reached a boiling point.

Although all our authors address ways in which museums have and could address the disruptions of 2020–2021, the reflections in this opening part introduce specific examples of how museum leaders have confronted them. Their stories provide a useful entry into the other perspectives articulated throughout the book.

Some contributors to this section, with years of experience in their respective museums, found that strategies, planning, and preparations that had been put in place before the pandemic served as sturdy foundations for significant pivots. Their museums' successful (although not cost-free) navigation through 2020 drew on practices rooted in earlier leadership and organizational decisions.

Kristin Leigh, for example, writes about how Explora's model of "transformative listening" and "turning outward" had positioned the museum as a trustworthy, dependable community partner—a recognized asset that had proven its ability to address community aspirations and needs. When COVID hit Albuquerque, the museum was invited to work with current partners—and cultivate new ones—to provide programs and services that served both its mission and the pressing priorities of its diverse and far-flung audiences.

In San Diego, Museum of Natural History director Judy Gradwohl had already worked with her board and staff to create a strategy "roadmap" that provided a "compass" for the museum's future while enabling year-to-year flexibility. They had reconsidered the role of the museum's physical building in its larger natural environment, diversified the financial model, stabilized operating expenses, distributed authority for budget planning, and established an Evolutionary Venture Fund (EVF) that supported the staff's "out-of-the-box" thinking, risk-taking, and experiments. Each of these strategic steps, in conjunction with a strengthening of the museum's already collaborative culture, served it in good stead during the unanticipated disruptions of 2020.

At the Los Angeles County Museum of Natural History, Su Oh, in her senior vice president role, had also retooled the museum's public experiences, and her team's efforts to broaden audiences had paid off handsomely. The innovation, experimentation, and risk-taking that had become her team's norms proved enormously valuable as the museum faced a slew of challenges brought on by COVID-19 and racial injustice within and beyond the museum walls. The crises called for leading with empathy and flexibility, empowering staff to create innovative virtual programming to keep audiences engaged. The younger, digital natives on staff became the idea generators and risk takers, with the crises unleashing their "vibrant creativity, depth of content knowledge, and enthusiastic engagement." Lower-level staff also took the lead on addressing inclusion and equity.

Leigh, Gradwohl, and Oh exemplify many established museum leaders who found people with previously unrecognized and untapped skills and ideas throughout their staffs. They supported and recognized these staff members for their nimble pivoting through the days of shutting down and reopening (and perhaps shutting down and reopening once more).

Finally, in chapter 4 Andrea Jones recognizes that 2020 created "a full-blown identity crisis for museums," with these organizations facing the same transition challenges as individuals, either getting stuck in the past; moving on without doing the necessary reflection and work required for real, lasting change; or using the transition to experiment with new models and forms.

She acknowledges the stresses and strains of living in uncertainty but argues that this need not result in paralysis. It can also fuel positive and courageous change. Jones invites museums to mourn what has been lost but then to "listen to the winds of change," consider, with intention, what may be possible, and experiment with new ideas—even new identities—that may provide the building blocks for successful reinvention.

The authors in this part have long recognized the "constancy" of change and the need for leaders, and organizations, to listen, learn, and adapt to fast-moving societal currents. They were buffeted by the extreme disruptions of 2020, but they benefited from the flexibility, adaptability, and experimentation they had incorporated into their individual and institutional mindsets. Despite the impossibility of predicting the future, each found ways to "seize the moment" and confront the looming crises, unleashing the talents of their staffs, solidifying connections to their communities, and inventing new roles and possibilities for their museums.

CHAPTER ONE

A Wake-Up Call

Kristin Leigh

Kristin Leigh is deputy director at Explora in Albuquerque, New Mexico. She began her career as a classroom teacher and joined the team opening Explora in 2001. Kristin received an Association of Science-Technology Centers' Roy E. Shafer Leading Edge Award for her work around authentic community listening and leadership of Explora's listen, welcome, and co-create community engagement approach.

Martin Luther King has remarked that "The ultimate measure of a man is not where he stands in moments of comfort and convenience, but where he stands at times of challenge and controversy." The "ultimate measure" of our museums has been tested in these challenging times. The past eighteen months exposed more clearly than ever the vast impacts of health inequities and systemic racism, with each morning's news bringing us story after horrifying story. At the same time, museums around the world were closing doors indefinitely due to pandemic-related public health orders. Extreme societal adversity forced us to take a raw, unfiltered glimpse into our organizational cultures. It helped us to see that those museums focused on turning outward, building trust, and increasing their relevance to their community, and whose organizational values and practices prioritized listening, purposeful partnerships, and deep community engagement, are more resilient and more essential to their communities.

The first step is to cultivate listening. Listening sounds simple, but it's also undervalued. Listening, really listening, can be transformative.

Transformative listening results in a museum taking an honest look at itself through the community's eyes, asking hard questions about the impact of its programs and services, and listening carefully for the answers. When we at Explora carried out a series of twenty-two community listening sessions, not one participant mentioned science when discussing the type of community in which they want to live. We had to reframe what this meant for our STEM-based organization.

We learned that our goals—inspiring inquiry and developing scientifically literate citizens—were not among the top community priorities. We had to understand that it may be a privilege for a family to even consider scientific literacy when worrying about ways to meet their children's most basic needs. Instead, many Albuquerque families cared deeply about their children being prepared for jobs that could end generational cycles of poverty. We heard story after story about opportunity gaps and inequitable educational and economic outcomes. We began to understand that Explora could contribute to systemic change in education and economic development.

STEM could lead to inspirational discovery and scientifically literate citizens, but of more relevance was the fact that STEM jobs are some of the highest paying in New Mexico. The more we heard parents talk about their aspirations for their children, the more we realized the power of STEM for achieving their hopes and dreams. Accordingly, we reframed our message and chose strategic partners and allies to place our STEM education efforts in a workforce development context. With that repositioning, our programs and exhibits became much more meaningful for families. We had found the sweet spot where our mission and core values intersected with our community's aspirations.

Transformative listening confirmed our museum's role as an honest broker, an essential player in a larger ecosystem that acknowledges the value of public knowledge and local wisdom, collectively addresses community aspirations, and overcomes the barriers to achieving them. Transformative listening was essential to remaining abreast of changing community rhythms, the ebb and flow of the generally accepted public narrative—whether one of hope or despair—that can indicate the community's readiness for change. Understanding this "public knowledge" joined STEM-related content and effective learning pedagogies as core staff competencies.

Listening also builds the trust necessary to create effective partnerships essential to fulfilling community aspirations. No single organization can address all pressing needs. Creating change is difficult; it takes time, and it takes systemic, collective effort. Trust paves the way for co-creation with community members and other area organizations and increases the likelihood that we are spending time and resources on projects of real significance and greater impact.

Partnerships proved essential during the pandemic, both for the communities we serve and for the sustainability of the museum itself. In partnership with the school district, Explora had planned to provide thirty-six family science events, but we couldn't bring anyone inside the building due to pandemic-related closures. Instead, we developed a menu of options for schools, teachers, and families and a school year that included Explora educators providing televised science lessons in both English and Spanish on the local PBS station; home delivery of science kits with trays of enchiladas; online teacher professional development and Maker-in-Residence programs; and gather-your-own-materials virtual family science events. By March 2021, more than sixty-nine hundred people from sixty-seven schools had participated in the Explora/Albuquerque Public Schools Title I partnership.

Effective museum-community partnerships work best when both parties have invested time and resources to nurture and grow the relationship. Successful partnerships must be based on shared goals, authentic listening, relationships of trust, and co-creation that involves give and take, along with fair compensation for all the partners and community members involved in the work. Partnerships are hard, however; developing them takes practice. Some cocreation projects go well, and others do not. It takes experience to look ahead, anticipate some missteps, and know how to course-correct. Authentic partnerships can grow and evolve over time, continuing to add value and make a difference.

Last year, even with a menu of new online programs, it became clear that families in New Mexico were struggling as they attempted to support their children's at-home learning. At the midpoint of the past school year, more than twenty-two thousand enrolled students in our state were listed as "chronically absent," having missed more than 20 percent of instructional time, and almost six thousand students were completely unaccounted for. Because of our community-based organizational culture and deep relationships across the learning ecosystem, many of Explora's civic, cultural, and educational partners asked us to double-down to support families learning from home. We worked closely with the public schools to expand virtual programming and support remote learning.

Virtual learning works, however, only for families with broadband access. One-on-one phone conversations with partners at the Office of Diné Youth and Navajo Transitional Energy Company addressed the question of how to provide similar support for families in the Navajo Nation without broadband access. Based in an area deeply affected by COVID-19, these partners explained that local regional newspapers remained the critical source of information for families; they suggested Explora use ad space in the papers to share family science activities. They also provided translation of the activities into Diné. We managed to remain relevant and useful as we addressed basic community needs. Having to learn how to do this work for the first time amid the many challenges of the past year would have been incredibly difficult. Our long-held practice of co-creating with partners was, therefore, critically important during the pandemic and will remain vital in the future.

In museum partnerships, as the organization turns outward, internal shifts are also required. A commitment to a partnership ethos affects a museum's organizational structure and dictates necessary staff skills and mindsets. A museum might start with a new position created solely to focus on authentic community engagement and partnership building; as museums get better at incorporating transformative listening and co-creation efforts, it becomes important for each staff member to take a learner's stance and embrace a humble curiosity.

It is also important to find staff who demonstrate an abundance mindset, rather than one of scarcity. When working in true partnerships, our museums must be generous with time and resources. A grant we may have hoped to use entirely for our museum, for example, must be shared with our partners. Any credits must also be shared. To embed this within the organizational culture, these values must be held and lived throughout all levels of staff and on the board. At Explora, we have used storytelling as one way of helping staff and board members understand the power of transformative listening and authentic partnerships. We regularly share the stories of new doors that have opened because of this work.

An effective partnership practice can ensure that museums are invited to the table when community issues and challenges are being considered; the more actively the museum participates in these conversations, the more critical we can be to the civic ecosystem. Effective partnering is essential to demonstrating our public value and garnering the community buy-in that can grow and sustain a thriving museum. Our partners and community members can help ensure our museums have needed resources. They can help our museums come back from pandemic-related closures and financial challenges.

What began in 2020 and continues today has been a wake-up call, catalyzing long-overdue work around racial justice, health inequity, and opportunity gaps. This must be a wake-up call for museums as well. It's time to go all in. It's time to understand the barriers and listen to the aspirations in your community, aligning them to your organization's mission and vision, and framing your work through this lens. Only then will museums be seen as highly relevant contributors to community change, during emergencies like the ones we're facing now and throughout future highs and lows. It's time to do more.

CHAPTER TWO

Making Lemonade

Learning from the Pandemic

Judy Gradwohl

Judy Gradwohl is president and CEO of the San Diego Natural History Museum. Trained as a scientist, she spent thirty-five years in various capacities at the Smithsonian Institution before returning to her native state of California. Known for her innovative practices, she has published extensively in scientific, popular, and museum publications.

Back in the disbelief phase of the pandemic when we were still wiping down our groceries, I would lightheartedly introduce online programs by saying "This is not the job I signed up for." In fact, it was. Steering through a crisis is any leader's job, and this past year was when leadership counted the most. Although it will be years before we can truly assess the value of our actions and decisions, the pandemic and related societal crises forced a reassessment of museum values and activities. It was a time of rapid change and learning, and it wasn't all bad. Much of what we learned about our museum culture, as well as how to expand beyond our walls, will serve us well in the future.

This is not meant to minimize the loss, fear, and sadness for museum staff and organizations themselves. Uncertainty about the extent and severity of the pandemic cast a pall over home and work life. At the San Diego Natural History Museum, adversity made us a stronger and more resilient museum. In a sense, it accelerated an organizational evolution that was already underway.

Several ongoing initiatives and practices unintentionally—yet fortuitously—helped us prepare for the pandemic, both before I arrived in 2016, and during my subsequent four years as president and CEO. We developed a Strategy Roadmap that provided a strong compass for our museum's future but purposefully stopped short of specifying annual goals in advance. The roadmap, therefore, remained valid even with the building closed. We had been planning for our 150th anniversary in 2024 and working to stabilize our operating budget by controlling costs and building our endowment. We moved away from the boom-and-bust economy of blockbuster traveling exhibitions and focused instead on in-house exhibitions and energy savings.

As we adjusted our planning and our budget forecasts, we cultivated distributed authority for budget planning and monitoring spending. We were already actively fostering a culture that valued innovation and experimentation and aimed for greater risk tolerance. I inherited talented and convivial staff who had developed strong relationships across the museum. This camaraderie built up goodwill and emphasized that whatever happened we were in it together. Additionally, we have long had a diversified financial model, with significant earned revenue from consulting work by paleontologists and biologists, that decreased our dependence on admissions revenue for survival.

We were closed to the public for thirteen months. Less than a week after the March 2020 shutdown we assembled a remote version of the museum, with people working out of more than one hundred homes across San Diego County. With fewer people on site to monitor climate in collections areas, we converted to remote devices that will serve us with accurate, twenty-four-hour monitoring long past the pandemic. Everyone had to develop better communication skills, and the systems we used to keep in touch with our colleagues, our board, and our community will also have lasting benefits. We all had to improvise, learn new skills, and stretch. We strengthened our methods for learning from other museums and nonprofits through virtual meetings and more regular email information exchange. We also learned the extent of our community support when a local philanthropist stepped up with a challenge grant that was matched by more than four hundred gifts.

It hasn't been all unicorns and roses. It was difficult to stay engaged with a dispersed staff and even harder to keep up with our volunteers. Many staff struggled to balance caregiving responsibilities and work. There were equipment and connectivity issues that made already tiresome Zoom and Teams calls even more challenging. Despite weekly updates, ongoing staff meetings, and online social meetups, nerves were frayed, and some felt disengaged or disenfranchised. And even though our building was closed we had to respond to maintenance emergencies. Given California occupational health and safety regulations, the museum reopened to the public long before back-of-house staff returned, creating an awkward period with some staff entirely on site and others still calling in to virtual meetings.

Previous experience working in a museum closed for a two-year-long renovation taught me that closure and the subsequent reopening can be tremendous opportunities for rapid change. Policies that seem impossible to implement during normal operations become easy, and strong traditions fade. About six weeks into the pandemic, I produced a manifesto to urge staff and board to reassess our model and to set goals for our museum once we recovered. The manifesto called for diversifying our public-facing operations into a hybrid model of programming that would be offered on site, online, and in nature itself. It suggested principles for decision-making and challenged everyone to focus on what we could accomplish with—or without—a building. We saw immediate success with online engagement and virtual, self-guided activities that encouraged people to get into nature.

We tried to focus on online programming that could not be accomplished in our building. Programs entirely in Spanish, and with simultaneous translation, expanded our audiences and helped us fulfill the bi-national part of our mission. We booked speakers from as far away as Australia and hosted participants from across the globe. Our educational programs featured museum careers and took students into our collections and into the field with our scientists. Our social media focused on scientific discovery, seasonally appropriate hikes, and the nature around us, instead of promoting visitation.

Downtime during the pandemic allowed us to focus on planning for exhibitions, completing projects identified in the 2019 building master plan, and tuning up operations like retail and food and beverage service. We designed an e-commerce program and cleaned out our storage building and our offices. We planned two new outdoor initiatives: native gardens that will surround our building and a community science program that studies and celebrates urban wildlife in San Diego's canyons. Funds designated for building improvements were used to install a new accessible entrance ramp compliant with the Americans with Disabilities Act, convert office space into a new exhibition gallery, and install new chillers to bring our prehistoric heating, ventilation, and air conditioning system into the twenty-first century.

With the pandemic far from over, it is too early to confidently point to permanent changes triggered by the crisis and related societal issues. However, some of our new ventures and the lessons we learned will likely persist and guide our future thinking. For us that means retaining some online educational programming, a continued focus on outdoor activities and engagement, flexible workspaces, and modified public visiting hours. It also means greater emphasis on cooperation and information sharing with other organizations, continuing new modes of communication, and questioning our assumptions and habits.

The pandemic reframed the building from being a venue for special exhibitions to being one of our many tools for serving our mission of scientific
inquiry, education, and stewardship of nature. It pushed us toward being
more outward facing—from expecting interactions to be centered on visits
to actively reaching out via digital media and working with local communities. The closure validated our prior work to define a strategic compass for
the organization and to foster a culture of experimentation, innovation, and
risk-taking. Our strong organizational culture helped us retain a semblance of
unity through our dispersed existence. Finally, our diversified income stream
and the incredible community of philanthropists provided budget stability
until the Federal Paycheck Protection Program loans became available.

Although it was neither smooth nor easy, and we're still living with uncertainty, adversity strengthened the organization. The challenge is how we can
build on this period of rapid learning and intentionally build our new model.
The only way to fail is to continue with pre-pandemic business as usual or
return to the same museum we closed in March 2020.

If the recent past has taught us anything, it is to expect the unexpected.
Before the pandemic, there was the Great Recession of 2007–2009, as well
as fires, floods, cyberattacks, and other disasters that have stricken museums.
If museums are going to aim for future sustainability, we need to pay greater
attention to the lessons we learned during the pandemic. They range from issues as broad as generalized strategic planning to specific and concrete needs,
like moving from desktops to laptops for greater workplace agility.

Museums will need more utility players on our teams and fewer specialists,
so we are ready to adapt to changing conditions. Along those lines we should
be cross-training and investing in skill-building for our staff. We need to reexamine our operating models and address lack of financial sustainability and
overdependence on admissions. We need to diversify our staff, our thinking,
and be more open to experimentation. We need to constantly question our
assumptions and habits to keep our operations and programming finely tuned
and maximally effective.

As a scientist in a nearly 150-year-old natural history museum, I can't help
but make an evolutionary analogy. If museums want to be ready to withstand
societal, political, and environmental change, we need to be less rigid and
directed in our stances, ready to foster new ideas and directions. Unpredictable disruptions and change will continue, and we can't anticipate every possibility, but we can try to be more sustainable, agile, and adaptable. Building
on what we learned during the pandemic is a great first step.

CHAPTER THREE

Beyond Command and Control

Inclusive Leadership in a Crisis

Su Oh

Su Oh is the senior vice president of education, exhibitions, and community engagement at the Natural History Museums of Los Angeles County (NHMLAC), which includes the La Brea Tar Pits. She employs diversity, equity, accessibility, and inclusiveness principles and community engagement practice to design transformative, content-rich experiences that promote lifelong science and cultural learning.

The year 2020 was a historic one, with a worldwide pandemic, the George Floyd murder followed by national protests demanding racial justice, the rise of anti-Asian hate crimes, the end of the Trump era, and the election of the first African American and first Asian American Vice President. This un-precedented time of national trauma and dramatic change has been a test of our collective humanity. What have we learned about leadership, and which of these lessons do we need to continue into the future?

One definition of a leader is a person who has commanding authority or influence. But, in a year like 2020, how does "commanding authority" work in a time of so much fear, anxiety, and pain? This command-and-control definition of leadership was flipped on its head as turbulent waves of change, pushing from the inside and out, crashed into our family of museums. Our colleagues challenged us with #changethemuseum and #deathtomuseums alongside the rise of cancel culture. We came face to face with the reality that "Museums Are Not Neutral" and that we are all accountable for our actions within and outside our museums. This is especially true for those of us in leadership positions.

I had been recently appointed as the Senior Vice President of Education, Exhibitions and Community Engagement, with a large department responsible for public-facing engagement in all its various forms from pre-K to adult. Our signature experiences included hands-on exhibitions, in-person interpretation, and activities through visitor-focused programs. We were at the height of our engagement practice, building audiences at large volume, and celebrating success.

When COVID-19 hit California and our doors closed on March 13, 2020, our museum engagement practice had to change quickly. The word of the day was "pivot." But pivot was not sufficient. I had to make progress in a challenging, dynamic, unknown landscape that constantly shifted beneath me. The responsibility was immense, the challenge formidable, and the situation called on every skill set I had, along with strong doses of empathy.

Our executive team had to come together with a laser-like focus to address the museum's financial needs as well as the urgent mandate to address racial justice and social change within our institution. The future of our institution and the related fallout of losing revenue, visitors, and stagnating growth was at risk. We needed to keep our museum's mission and public service at the heart of our activities. As always, all was in service to the public, our schools and teachers, and as the months progressed, the new network of visitors outside our walls. Each decision would affect everything: Our field, our communities, our institution, our departments, our jobs, and mostly importantly, our staff.

How can you be strategic when the last pandemic occurred in 1918, providing scant precedent for effective action? How do you work through racial injustice when Los Angeles' experience of civil unrest and burning city blocks triggered by the Rodney King verdict in 1992 happened before some of our youngest staff were even born? How do we address issues like anti-Black, anti-Asian, and anti-Indigenous racism when our nation was in conflict to acknowledge our own history of systemic racism and exclusion?

What did we learn during those months? How have those lessons changed our leadership practices even as we reopen our doors? We understood that the leader cannot do it alone but must harness the collective intelligence and resources of the entire institution and its staff. The leader needs to let go of the desire to "control" the situation. Leaders need to work with a fearlessness in the face of anxiety about an unknown future, where there are many paths to take, and all have some inherent risk of not having been tested nor have data to prove their possibility.

Instead, the leader must model and foster the cross-departmental collaboration necessary for innovating in uncertain times. The leader must transparently communicate as much as possible as they and their staff move through the uncharted terrain together. The leader must clearly share the sacrifices that all staff make. During COVID, that meant that our team needed to work together to ensure that the burdens of our new situation were acknowledged, recognized, and shared by all.

During the pandemic, as we all worked from home, we recognized that this imposed major stress on many of us. Our personal lives blended into our work lives. Parents with children at home because of school closures juggled childcare, home teaching, working full-time, and managing staff online. We all shifted to digital platforms for operating both internally and externally, and Zoom became our prevalent communication platform. This shift had the unexpected benefit of liberating heretofore unrecognized and underused staff skills. Our staff led us in exploiting the possibilities of the digital, and we began to see the emergence of talent that was not to be denied.

Our millennial digital natives—the public programmers and museum educators—shared our programs, activities, and educational practices online. They were the idea generators, the risk takers, and they grabbed the opportunity to try something new and different to share our stories. In this new space, we saw—and unleashed—their vibrant creativity, depth of content knowledge, and enthusiastic engagement. They became visible in full view and in ways that resonated beyond what was evident in their previous work on the museum floor. We created virtual dinosaur tours in Armenian, Korean, Spanish, Chinese, and Tagalog. Curators shared their collections virtually and connected them to pop culture, art, and science in the United States and around the world. The live animal staff came from "behind the scenes" and began creating videos to share how they were caring for and playing with the animals. They emerged as our best ambassadors with increasing counts on YouTube and "likes" on social media. Thanks to popular demand, these programs often recurred.

We also developed companion online exhibitions for the physical exhibitions that were sitting, unseen and unvisited, in the dark museum halls. The rise of user experience design, with its process design teams that focused on creating meaningful encounters for participants, contributed to our development of online interactive maps and increased video and social media production. This required intense cross-departmental collaboration as we shifted the website from a marketing tool principally used to drive museum attendance to a content-rich platform. As a closed museum, we began to come to terms with declining revenue from no attendance, membership loss as our public also made difficult financial choices, and donors who were reassessing their allocations.

Despite these realities, we benefited enormously from setting our staff free. They guided the way for what we could do in our programs and services and kept the museum visible and valuable to our audiences. At the same time, this same empowered staff vocally questioned the status quo of our internal culture and the depth and authenticity of our work related to diversity, equity, access, and inclusion (DEAI).

Leadership needed, therefore, to confront, and address, the conditions within the museum, specifically around DEAI. We needed to contend with—and act on—the staff's impatience with past inactions. We needed to acknowledge that progress in this area was too slow and that change needed to happen faster. The sense of urgency was real, and staff were holding up a mirror that leadership had to face. Self-organized affinity groups assembled, and our president invested in our staff to bring forward a cross-departmental team to make recommendations for our DEAI statement and action plan.

This team began forging a path where the executives would need to learn from them, with staff assuming leadership roles in this ongoing process. This shifted the established hierarchy, and we are still engaged in what needs to be a long, ongoing, and intentional process of understanding and addressing the complexities and nuances of inclusion and equity. We need to continue to lead with humility, empathy, and understanding. More changes are due.

Before the pandemic, we considered our department a "learning community." As we moved through the pandemic, we became an antiracist learning organization. When the landscape changes, the definition of success changes, and the possibilities of who succeeds shifts as well. New voices and different empowered leaders emerge and are recognized.

What worked was not command and control, it was opening up, listening, and walking in partnership with my empowered staff. I knew to trust that our united vision to keep ourselves together and save the museum we felt passionate about was worth all the challenging effort.

As I write this, our museum has reopened, vaccinations are being widely distributed in Los Angeles County, and we are gradually seeing joyous visitors coming back to our exhibition spaces. We can read each other's smiles behind the masks. We will never forget what we have accomplished in this past year, and we will carry these lessons forward.

The leadership insights gained during the pandemic will endure as we go forward. I have only grown stronger as a leader through the will and support of our spirited staff and shepherding the rise of their superpowers. We were resilient warriors together, and we're not going back.

CHAPTER FOUR

Getting Lost on Purpose

Andrea Jones

Andrea Jones is associate director of education for Smithsonian's Anacostia Community Museum. She has more than twenty years of experience as a change agent and education strategist. She was formerly an independent consultant operating under the name Peak Experience Lab. Recently, she has authored a popular blog post titled Empathetic Audience Engagement during the Apocalypse.

~

How many psychiatrists does it take to screw in a light bulb? One, but the bulb has to really *want* to change.
Joke remix for 2020:
How many pandemics does it take to get museums to be empathetic and responsive to audience needs? One, but they have to want to change.

The year 2020 was not just a challenging time. It created a full-blown identity crisis for museums. Museums had to answer some important, game-changing question: Who are we without visitors? Who are we in a moment of racial reckoning? Who are we in a crisis?

Although the year brought profound loss and emotional turmoil, many of us who had been pushing for change for years, or even decades, also saw this as an opening. As community organizer Aja Taylor said, "This could be the very apocalypse we've been waiting for."

Would our elitist, academic institutions look past self-preservation and reach out to people in their time of need? Could this finally be the time to address our white-dominated power structure and terrible wages?

Sadly, we saw too many museums experience the same pitfalls that individual humans do during big life transitions—either getting stuck in the past or moving on without doing the work. Think of the young person who has trouble accepting the responsibilities of adulthood. Or the partner who hops into the next relationship a few days after the break up. These are people who are not ready for inner change. They are not moving purposefully and healthily through the transformation that life is requiring of them. A museum friend of mine said, "I never thought I'd see world events this massive simultaneously change everything and nothing about museums."

The missing ingredient is *intention*. In any transition into a new identity, there is a period of experimentation mixed with uneasiness. It feels like getting lost. This is normal. To do it right is to do it on purpose. Listen in the stillness. There is so much possibility! It's this middle part—between the person we used to be and the person we will be next—that has been ignored by many museums.

I get it. It's uncomfortable to live in limbo. How do you plan ahead? How do you keep your organization afloat? But grieving old definitions and embracing this murky middle is the most important part of a healthy transition. William Bridges, writing in *Transition: Making Sense of Life's Changes*, calls this stage "The Neutral Zone," an experimental in-between time. It's both scary and exhilarating but often not even acknowledged or talked about in American culture. In this country, we value what is next much more than the process required to get there healthily.

In the Neutral Zone, people set out to find what is "essential" about their identities by tinkering and iterating. In the context of museums, the Neutral Zone could be used to reevaluate all that came before—exhibits, programs, mission, internal culture—and ask: What do we want to carry with us into the next chapter? What do we want to leave behind? It's literally all on the table. Then embark on a period of trying on new selves.

Old Salem Museum and Gardens began feeding local families in Winston-Salem by repurposing education gardens and a historic bakery operation to serve present-day needs. Is that a museum's job? What is a museum, anyway? Old Salem staff, led by Frank Vagnone, began experimenting with identity in a purposeful way and helped its community in the process.

My own museum, Smithsonian's Anacostia Community Museum, transformed a traveling history exhibition meant for indoors into eight separate outdoor displays encircling two square blocks in an underserved neighborhood. But this meant exploring new ways of thinking about impact—beyond counting visitors or evaluating learning goals. All those traditional metrics went out the window. The impact really needed to be measured in the quality of relationships that were built and the ability to gain positive visibility for a community that was consistently in the news for its deficits. Can a Smithsonian exhibit affect people's perception of a neighborhood? This project de-prioritized the goal of visitor learning in a way that I had never considered before.

When slow ticket sales forced the closure of the Louisiana Children's Museum, it loaned out its building to create make-shift classrooms for a local school. The A + D Design Museum in Los Angeles picked up stakes and abandoned its building altogether . Does a museum exist if it's not in a physical space? Why not find out, rather than lay off dozens of staffers?

A white-run nonprofit called Yale Union in Portland, Oregon, that was in the business of exhibiting contemporary art, repatriated its land and building to the Native Arts and Cultures Foundation. The pandemic offered the staff space for reflecting on what they called their "unearned privilege of property ownership." In the name of restorative justice, Yale Union will literally dissolve its nonprofit. This bold move would not be possible without purposefully creating a safe environment for vulnerability and soul searching.

As these examples show, necessity can be the mother of invention—but only if you are ready to leave the old ways behind. And many museums were not. There were mass layoffs that prioritized objects over people. There were perhaps hundreds of virtual tours and programs that merely repackaged the same old content for online audiences. White, privileged executive leadership held tight to their power. And in response, a scathing new online conference called Death to Museums was christened by a younger generation. A sign of the times: a CNN article asked, "Should museums be abolished?" Yes, that's how serious it is.

Doing the same programs, but in a mask, will not save our field. Hiring that one Black diversity director will not do the trick. Museums that did not put in the work, that did not become vulnerable, and that did not wrestle with identity-rocking questions, during a time that screamed at us to change, are dragging us all down.

One thing about the Neutral Zone, as Bridges explains, is that if you ignore it, it will eventually catch up with you. There we are in the new house or the new job only to discover we have not given up old ties or old rhythms. Unhappiness, resentment, and anger sets in beneath the surface—festering like a sore.

The events of the last year and a half have pushed us beyond a threshold. We cannot go back. As life slowly returns to normal (pandemically speaking), we will notice that many museums have unfinished transitions. But it's never too late to start being intentional about reflection.

Author and activist Adrienne Maree Brown advocates ditching the traditional culture of strategic planning in favor of a culture of strategic intentions. Looking at every operational part of an organization, she suggests asking "How can we bring our intentions to life through every aspect of our work?" That intention could be to make space for the organization's metaphorical field to lay fallow—to enter the Neutral Zone. Or it could be that reflection time has resulted in a new identity that needs enacting.

Build something new together. But build it not as a knee-jerk reaction to circumstances. Take the time to grieve the loss of what used to work. Listen to the winds of change and get lost on purpose. Then, create a new identity for the organization from a deep well of intention.

Further Reading

William Bridges, *Transitions: Making Sense of Life's Changes* (Boston: Da Capo Press, 2004).

Adrienne Maree Brown, *Emergent Strategy: Shaping Change, Changing Worlds* (Chico, CA: AK Press, 2017).

"Tools and Approached for Transforming Museum Experience," by Cooper Hewitt's Interaction Lab.

"Empathetic Audience Engagement During the Apocalypse," by Andres Jones (peak experiencelab.com).

"The Power of Intention: Reinventing the Prayer Wheel," an exhibition by the Rubin Museum (rubinmuseum.org).

PART II

~

THE TURN TO DIGITAL

With COVID shutdowns, virtual platforms became the learning, information, meeting, and communications sites of choice for most of the world's
populations. Museums, like every other form of culture and education,
turned to digital for managing their operations and delivering programs and
services.

The era of participatory culture arrived decades ago, yet many museums
have lagged in developing and updating their digital infrastructures and
creating programs and experiences that effectively use to its full advantage
technology's ability to create, share, and connect new knowledge. For many
museums, despite the overwhelming numbers of people turning to digital
sources for learning, information, and social connections, digital interactivity, and community co-creation have been afterthoughts. Too often, museums have resorted to replicating in-person experiences or back-of-house
information in their virtual spaces, thus, creating museum websites jammed
with online collections lists, digital exhibition catalogs and curricula, and
videos of speakers and panel presentations.

Yet some museums have long taken creative advantage of technology to
augment their missions and engage more audiences, both on- and off-site,
with tech-connected makerspaces, augmented reality experiences, gaming,
citizen science species identification and environmental watchdog efforts,
citizen historian transcription projects, and distance learning programs for
school and lifelong learning audiences. Planet Word, a museum in Washington, DC, several years in the making, is but one example of a relatively new

museum, in this case focused on words, language, and reading, that relies on interactive (often voice-activated) digital techniques to create the preponderance of its immersive learning experiences.

Recent data show the attraction (and greater participation) of ethnically and racially diverse audiences in digital cultural offerings. Citing the "bigger tent" of digital experiences, *Centering the Picture: The Role of Race & Ethnicity in Cultural Engagement* (December 2020), noted, "Crucially, in many art-forms or content-areas, that 'digital only' subset is much more diverse than recent in-person attenders, with significantly higher proportions of Blacks/African Americans and Hispanics/Latinx Americans." Digital may yet be perceived as more welcoming and inclusive to those very publics that museums have yearned to reach.[1]

As the contributors to this part note, museums must come to grips with the particularities of living in a virtual world—where access to information is immediate and ubiquitous, where digital media invite, often require, interactivity and participation, and where social relations and individual expression are digitally mediated.

Robin White Owen describes ways in which the pandemic propelled most museums into digital space. In their efforts to maintain a presence and retain the loyalty of their supporters, they tried virtual conferences, exhibition tours, talks with curators, performances, and fundraising events. White Owen argues that the future of museums must be social, collaborative, and virtual—and that going digital does not lessen the need for the human presence. "Museums can (and must) remain hybrids, providing onsite, off-site and virtual experiences that serve both global and local audiences . . . using digital resources to be more inclusive, transparent, and interactive, and thus more impactful."

Lath Carlson's chapter addresses the question of what will make museums' turn to digital stand out in an ocean of compelling, innovative, free, and even addictive digital offerings. How can museums' power to create meaningful and welcoming social experiences translate compellingly to the digital domain? To date, he notes, few museums have been able to adopt the formulas that make digital programs successfully programmatically and monetarily. Carlson cites several successful museum examples along a spectrum of digital formats. He also contends that museums can learn powerful, interactive, storytelling techniques from other media, some translated from reality television, that can enhance their success in the virtual realm.

In his parable about an imaginary encounter with a time traveler, Michael Peter Edson argues that, with the urgent crises posed by climate change, mass displacement and migration—a world of "ceaseless uncertainty and accelerating change"—primarily analog responses don't suffice. Museums need to activate the trust they have amassed to "embrace their civic responsibilities" and address, with imagination and courage, the daunting challenges we face. Edson contends that although museums can't do it alone, they haven't come close to leveraging all of the tools at their disposal to fulfill their potential role in a digitally connected world. He challenges them to create "a new paradigm of practice—faster, open, more social"—that can better help museums deliver, at scale, on their claims of making a positive difference in our society.

Clearly, bold new visions, new paradigms, and new skill sets, such as media and digital literacy, are essential elements of the museum toolkit if our institutions are to thrive in the virtual world. The museum's digital infrastructure must be supported, maintained, and nurtured with the same care and attention as its physical site and collections. Most important, in a world where algorithms can, and are, contributing to the spread of misinformation, disinformation, and political and cultural polarization, museums cannot afford to sit on the sidelines. If they care about accurate and inclusive historical narratives, democratic principles, scientific evidence, and environmental justice, if they want to make a positive, scalable impact in people's lives, museums need be right there on the digital playing field.

Note

1. *Centering the Picture: The Role of Race & Ethnicity in Cultural Engagement* (December 2020). The survey distills the results of a national survey, "Culture and Community in a Time of Crisis," that was a collaboration between LaPlaca Cohen and Slover Linett, conducted in early months of pandemic. https://sloverlinett.com /insights/centering-the-picture-the-role-of-race-ethnicity-in-cultural-engagement/

CHAPTER FIVE

The Virtuous Circle

From Local to Global and Back Again

Robin White Owen

Robin White Owen is a co-founder and principal of MediaCombo where she's been leading teams to develop award-winning mixed reality experiences as well as web applications, videos, and audio tours for museums, visitor centers, and government agencies since 2004. She is a frequent speaker at industry conferences on immersive experiences.

They say, "Necessity is the mother of invention." The pandemic created conditions that drove museums to invent myriad new ways to stay connected to their audiences. In that process, many discovered their untapped potential to play a much broader role in their local communities and to expand their relationships around the world through digital technology.

In the first few weeks of COVID's spread across the globe, Indian writer Arundhati Roy suggested that the pandemic could be a portal to a new vision for the future. Now that we've crossed that threshold and begun to socialize and work together again in physical spaces, we're seeing the world from a very different perspective than before.

What did museums devise during COVID that can also signal future directions and possibilities?

- They found new channels to connect with and bring joy to audiences in virtual space on meeting platforms, including Zoom, Hopin, and Second Life, and on social media like TikTok, Instagram, and Animal Crossing.

- They added novel content to their websites, creating games, musical performances, children's art workshops, science classes, exhibition tours, film screenings, even cocktails with curators, as ways to serve people's learning, creative expression, and social connection needs globally and locally.
- Many looked for and found new ways to support their local communities. They went out into neighborhoods to deliver art supplies to families and mounted outdoor exhibitions. They created new partnerships with local groups to host food distribution, register voters, or offer outdoor yoga classes. Some even cleared the hurdles of working with city agencies to set up vaccination sites in their lobbies and galleries.

Museums have shared their collections, their buildings and grounds, their digital resources, and their staffs to alleviate suffering, relieve pandemic-induced stress, and help people feel informed, cared for, and connected.

We know some museums had been doing these things before the pandemic; now, the genie can't (and won't) be put back into the bottle. Museums can (and must) remain hybrids, providing onsite, off-site, and virtual experiences that serve both global and local audiences. They can build on what they've learned and accomplished during recent months and continue to design their programming to be relevant beyond their core traditional audiences, using digital resources to be more inclusive, transparent, and interactive, and thus, more impactful.

Embedding Digital Experiences in Local Communities

The pandemic brought into sharper focus the role that museums could play locally. To quote Lonnie Bunch, III, Secretary of the Smithsonian Institution, museums need to "be at the center of their communities."

What might this look like? It could be maintaining an active and ongoing virtual presence on community websites and social media pages. It could be museum stalls at street and county fairs. Libraries, nonprofit agencies, artisans, and government agencies routinely participate in these informal, no-pressure, grazing opportunities to meet, greet, and exchange information. What a great place to be present!

Conversation starters and content could be available on iPads or tablets loaded with preexisting games, current exhibition information, or social media sites. QR codes strategically placed for people to scan on their own phones would help them connect to a museum's website, Instagram, or TikTok account, with the possibility to access content later. Using tablets preloaded with content means Wi-Fi wouldn't be a necessity. Visitors could use 4G or 5G on their phones.

Museums that want to create deep ties to local communities will continue to seek out partnerships with neighborhood associations, climate and social justice organizations, Rotary Clubs, and others, to listen, learn, and establish trust. This is how they become, as Lori Fogarty, Director and CEO of the Oakland Museum of California, puts it, "part of an ecology and landscape with others, other . . . organizations that are looking to do the same collective action."

Digital channels can usefully facilitate a two-way flow of information, from the community to the museum and from the museum out into the community, creating a new context and relationship for both. Neighborhoods and communities have their own histories, artists, hopes, needs, and dreams. By listening to community members, museums can find ways to respectfully recognize the significance of these stories, individuals, and objects and incorporate them into their programming.

The Peale Center for History and Architecture's program, Baltimore Stories, represents one model to consider (https://www.thepealecenter.org /bherebmore/). Focused on collecting and sharing stories of residents, this museum's mission is "to ensure the whole story of the City is told, and, by amplifying its communities' voices, to help people everywhere see Baltimore in a new light."

Although museums have traditionally seen their role as custodians of the past, today's digital technology is helping them capture snapshot stories and long-form oral histories of the present. Equally important is working with residents to ensure that museum resources are available to nurture their hopes and visions for the future. The community councils established by the Oakland Museum provide a useful framework for such meaningful and ongoing reciprocal relationships.

Connecting the Dots—From Local to Global

COVID helped us see how important digital technologies are for keeping us connected. Virtual interactions were often our only social life. But beyond providing social connections, digital can also seamlessly illuminate the connections between local issues and global concerns and connect audiences near and far.

A successful, though pre-COVID, example of this idea was the exhibition at the Carnegie Museum of Natural History in Pittsburgh, Pennsylvania, *We Are Nature: Living in the Anthropocene*. The show linked the local community to the global issue of climate change, exhibiting homeowners' bills to repair flooded basements due to overflowing rivers as an instance of how climate change and environmental degradation affected Pittsburgh citizens' everyday lives. The project offered recommendations about how people could do specific things for both local and national impact. A virtual tour extended the life of the exhibition indefinitely, while also taking the message far and wide. Such tours are an improvement over catalogues to document an exhibition are much less expensive to produce, and have a much broader reach and, thus, potential impact.

The Future Is Collaboration

It's expensive to maintain the production and distribution of digital content, and many museums are strategizing how to succeed with hybrid programming now that their doors have reopened. In addition to creating content for onsite visitors, museums must also develop those virtual experiences that their digital audiences have come to expect. How can digital technology help them usefully serve their local and their far-flung communities in a cost-effective way?

One solution is collaborating with international, national, or local museums to share the costs of creating and disseminating digital resources. In addition to lowering costs for each collaborating entity, the resulting projects are likely to have larger audiences and wider impact.

One recent example is Vaccines and Us: Cultural Organizations for Community Health (https://www.si.edu/vaccinesandus). Founded in 2021 by ten organizations and three independent museum professionals in collaboration with the Smithsonian, its purpose is to develop a coordinated, national approach to vaccine education and access. In addition to featuring the latest scientific information about COVID, the multilingual site promotes current exhibitions, mobile apps, and educational resources at participating museums. This is a model for ways that museums can leverage the web to connect global issues with their local resources and effective community action.

The Future Is Social and Virtual

COVID pushed museums to create more branded virtual events. Although people can once again share the social pleasures of attending exhibitions and programs, the convenience of virtual experiences ensures their staying power. Indeed, for many, including those with special needs, virtual experiences have often been the only ones accessible to them.

Another technology, social virtual reality (VR), will make it easier than ever for museums to provide authentic digital experiences to meet the social needs of visitors, wherever they might be. In social VR, people wearing VR headsets can be "together" no matter where they are geographically. VR offers users such a strong sense of "presence" that the virtual space becomes more real than physical space. People sharing that virtual space feel like they're standing next to each other conversing, listening, or playing.

The sense of "really being there" is enhanced by spatial audio, which mimics the way visitors hear things in real life. People can design avatars to represent themselves visually, and the avatar assumes their voice, so the virtual avatar and physical person are authentically one and the same. Although the VR headset experience is more immersive, the social interactions can also occur in desktop versions.

Platforms like AltspaceVR, Engage, Mozilla Hubs, Rec Room, and Wonder Room have already hosted all kinds of experiences, from meditation groups to corporate meetings, from nightclubs to high school science classes, from Alcoholics Anonymous to Educators in VR conferences—even weddings! So, why not museums?

In the near future, museums will be building virtual galleries, virtual buildings, or imaginary spaces for cultural exchange, local/global meetups, exhibitions, school groups, public programs, tours, international conferences, and other purposes.

VR represents a paradigm shift, much like the world wide web and mobile technology, and it will require a lot of learning and planning for museums to take advantage of its possibilities. Museums adopted earlier digital tools to meet people where they were spending time, and they will adopt VR for the same reason. Some of the sites mentioned are free to use and explore. There are also museums, like the Museum of Other Realities and the Better World Museum, that are strictly virtual, and this trend too will continue.

Now that we've stepped through the portal that Arundhati Roy described, it's clear that museums can have deeper, more meaningful, and mutually beneficial relationships with their local communities as well as develop lasting relationships with new audiences no matter where they're located. They can connect the people right outside their doors to those around the world. They can harness the power of these new digital tools to help realize their visions for the future.

CHAPTER SIX

Expanding Museums
into Digital Spaces

Lath Carlson

Lath Carlson is the director of the Museum of the Future in Dubai. He is a museum visionary, a change agent who excels at channeling constituent need into sustainable action, and a passionate communicator able to build committed coalitions.

Lately, the notion of what a museum is has become strained. Shut down during the early months of the pandemic, traditional museums pivoted to social media and online collections. Commercial operators have taken public domain art and turned it into large-scale projection experiences, such as the multiple versions of the Van Gogh immersive experiences (https://www.ny times.com/2021/03/07/arts/design/van-gogh-immersive-experiences.html/). Instagrammers have fashioned museums of ice cream and color (https://color factory.co/). We have even seen the rise of online-only museums as diverse as the Museum of Black Joy and the Femicom museum (http://www.femicom .org/) of "femme" electronics and games.

How Has the Rise of Digital Experiences Changed
Our Understanding of What a Museum Can Be?

A museum can be defined as a place that uses objects to tell stories that might be true. Let's use this working definition to interrogate this current expansion of the institution and what we might learn from the spectrum of museums, from the physical to the purely digital.

For most museums, "place" means a physical location where humans go, a destination where social intercourse and interaction with objects occurs. It's in this social dimension of the museum visit that value is created for communities. Without it, a museum is just a warehouse. Yet in the past (and, in many cases, even today), a sense of belonging or social connection within a museum was not accessible for all. Even worse, the stories most museums told were exclusive rather than inclusive. Inevitably, this led to museum visitation being skewed in countries like the United States to largely white, middle-, and upper-class urban visitors.

For museums to fulfill a more inclusive social role, not only do we need more diverse storytelling but also more accessible places. Digital spaces can potentially afford opportunities for expansion in both these dimensions.

Can a purely digital place still function as a museum? I think it can, if it truly fosters a conversation with users around the stories being told. I think this is true for both online museums as well as experiences, like the Van Gogh productions, which use purely digital content—either as projections or reproductions.

Virtual Museums

The COVID-19 pandemic has forced much discourse into online spaces, and the museum world is no exception. At their best, online museums foster exploration, commentary, and learning. Users will often share links to these sites on social media, leave comments on the pages or on the museum's social media accounts, and use the sites as a jumping-off point to learn more about different topics. And, thanks to no admission charges and ease of access, museum websites can see more of this type of engagement than traditional museums. The nearly global access they provide (excepting countries that actively block online content), along with no-cost, low-barrier entry, makes them good forums for addressing subjects that have been excluded from traditional museums.

The Museum of Black Joy, for example, bills itself as "a borderless refuge for the observation, cultivation, celebration and preservation of Black joy" (https://www.museumofblackjoy.com/). This free access can also present a challenge because without entry fees how might these museums be maintained for the long term? Without established institutional histories and typical governance structures, how might these museums access public or private funding? Often these online museums are passion projects of individuals, and this may make it hard to maintain them for the long term. Even those that are offshoots of other institutions may not find lasting support.

Museums and Other Content Creators

If we look at popular contemporary "content creators," we can see opportunities for creating more sustainable online museum models, as well as better engaging users in blended online/onsite museums. From Instagram and TikTok to YouTube and podcasts, creators that thrive understand they are creating a community with their followers. They cultivate that community by engaging in two-way dialogues in their "comments" sections, sharing "members-only" accessible videos, and hosting in-person meetups. They also post across a wide range of platforms in ways that maximize exposure and revenue generation.

They actively engage with other creators and frequently collaborate with them, increasing their audiences. Finally, they make producing their content financially sustainable by selling advertising, seeking sponsorships, and cultivating paying patrons through platforms like Partreon (www.patreon.com). Oddly, these are all standard practices for many traditional museums, yet this has rarely carried over into the digital environment.

I once met with a producer of reality TV shows, which can be seen as a precursor to online content creators. He outlined the points that make for a successful show. What captivates and sustains viewers, he argued, are distinct personalities, the drama surrounding a deadline or crisis, and the perception of total behind-the-scenes access.

Successful online content creators nail these points: Their programs are personality driven, often named after a person or couple and feature a project or journey that's being tackled or undertaken. Most content revolves around travel, events, or a challenging project. The inherent drama often provides classic "clickbait" headlines for these shows. Finally, across multiple platforms, audiences have unprecedented access to content creators' lives. In fact, much of our mainstream news is now founded on these principles, with newscasters becoming more important than the news they report and the headlines ever more dramatic.

This formula may be hard for museums to replicate. Most often, museums are telling other people's stories, not their own. And if they are telling stories of the past, which most museums do, there is unlikely to be the drama of an unknown outcome. Finally, museums have traditionally been quite protective of what they do behind the scenes. It's worth considering which of these limitations might be worth trying to change, and not just to gain traction online but also to move away from past exclusivity.

Installation-Based Digital Museum Experiences

Installation-based digital museum experiences include the Van Gogh projection shows, Banksy reproduction exhibits, and original digital art installations such as those from TeamLab and Refik Anadol. These are proving to be popular with the public, with TeamLab Borderless at the MORI Building in Tokyo now the world's most visited single-artist museum, taking the title from the Van Gogh Museum in Amsterdam.

Like the best online museums, these experiences are tailored to a world where much of the interaction is on social media. They consciously design their offerings to be visually rich, dramatic, multisensory, and less didactic than what traditional museums produce. They also carefully maintain their online presence and actively engage users there. Like the best online content creators, they also seem to have been able to make themselves commercially successful through earned revenue and sponsorship.

"Traditional" Museums Achieving Digital Success

Many museums that closed for extended periods during the global COVID-19 pandemic became more committed to online digital spaces as well, yet few have found lasting and sustainable success there. Museums that have succeeded with their digital offerings are often not the biggest institutions, nor those with the best marketing agencies. Examples include the success of the Twitter account for the Museum of English Rural Life (MERL) (158K followers), Cocktails with a Curator from the Frick Collection on YouTube (32K subscribers), The Brain Scoop from the Field Museum (591K subscribers), and the Sacramento History Museum on TikTok (1.8 M followers). All share some of the attributes of successful digital content creators and reality TV shows.

Each of these museums focuses on charismatic individuals: from Adam Koszary at the MERL, to Emily Graslie at the Field Museum and Howard Hatch in Sacramento. Each of these personalities is telling interesting stories and engaging directly with their audiences. Each institution also provides behind-the-scenes access: Adam mined the collections of the Museum of English Rural Life for meme-worthy visual content. Cocktails with a Curator brought the curators out of the back rooms, along with the artworks they are passionate about. The Brain Scoop went deep into the research conducted by the museum (and sometimes deep in animal guts). And, finally, Howard shows us a master at work in a craft most have lost all experience with as he operates manual printing presses.

Hybrid Experiences

Aside from the purely digital museums and museums making effective use of digital platforms, there are a small number of museums trying to create unique hybrid experiences. Typically, these center on creating bespoke (customized for the client) apps that are meant to be extensions of the physical museum experience, sometimes with novel interface devices as well.

The point of this hybrid approach is to create an experience that transcends the boundaries of both commercial digital platforms and the physical museum space. The best known of these may be two projects led by Seb Chan: *The Pen* at the Cooper Hewitt National Design Museum and *The Lens* at the Australian Center for the Moving Image. Both projects use a personal interface device to activate exhibition components and create or collect personally meaningful artifacts from the in-person museum visit. Users can then access this content via a web- or app-based interface after their visit.

These projects drew in part from multiple iterations of the Tech Tag and SmartMuseum platform implemented at the Tech Museum of Innovation in San Jose (now The Tech Interactive). That platform allowed users to customize aspects of their user experience, such as the language the exhibits used, as well as to collect user-generated content for later viewing. Other museums are experimenting with more passive interaction, such as the use of Real Time Locations Services at the Hyde Park Barracks at the Sydney Living Museums and now at the Museum of the Future in Dubai. These systems can make content available to visitors based on their location in the museum and other personal attributes.

Conclusion

The long-term success of all these projects is likely to rest on the same principles that underlie the other digital efforts I've described. They need to tell compelling stories, leverage the community-building aspects of digital platforms, and be commercially sustainable.

Whether they are fully digital museums, museums using digital platforms, or novel hybrid approaches, the increase in use of digital platforms is expanding the definition of museums. This is leading to broader access and more diverse storytelling, yet challenges in sustaining these efforts also exist. The success of other digital content creators may provide a model for addressing some of these challenges if museums can adapt them to their unique circumstances. If they can, this holds potential as a vibrant and sustainable aspect of museums that may help them reach more broadly distributed and diverse audiences with unique forms of storytelling.

CHAPTER SEVEN

I Went to a Bar for Time Travelers

Michael Peter Edson

Michael Peter Edson is a strategist, consultant, and thought leader at the forefront of digital transformation in the cultural sector. Michael was the Smithsonian Institution's Director of Web and New Media Strategy, and co-founder of the Museum for the United Nations, an emerging institution designed to catalyze global change.

I went to a bar for time travelers, one cold, rainy night, to drown my sorrows and see what I could learn.

"I'm dejected," I told a patron as we waited for our drinks at the bar. "Climate change. Racism. Fascism. Neoliberalism. Conspiracy theories and fake news. At the museum where I work, we say we care about truth and the future—societal good—but the world is changing quickly, and when the chips are down, we hardly do anything at all."

"A museum?" she said, with a sympathetic smile. "In the 2020s?"

Yes, I nodded, surprised by her insight as we took our drinks and found a place at the bar.

"I feel like museums, in my time, claim all this power and privilege in society," I told her. "We supposedly study the past and elevate the mind and spirit to shape a better future—'A well-educated citizenry being crucial to the proper function of democracy,' and all that. That's at the heart of our social contract."

"I see," she said.

"People trust us. Some do, or at least that's what we hear. But have we used that trust to make society better? Maybe in small ways, but I don't see it working at scale, or quickly enough, by far," I confided, as I gulped my beer.

"Compared to the challenges we're up against," I said, as I took another drink, "like the climate emergency and social justice, which work at a scale and speed we're not accustomed to, our ambitions in the museum sector are infuriatingly cautious, narrow, and small. Nero fiddling as Rome burns, if we're lucky enough to have a fiddle at all. Most museums are barely even online in any meaningful way." She gave me a thoughtful look as she slowly swirled her drink in her hand. "What was the big problem?" she asked. "Weren't there billions of people on the internet with smartphones and the World Wide Web? Hungry for knowledge and insight? Hungry for a better world?"

Yes, there were. I told her I had thought the internet would usher in a new paradigm of museum practice. Faster, relevant, and connected. Outward looking and focused on the people in our communities, rather than inward looking and focused on our own reputation and control. "Open, social, peer-to-peer, and read-write—a commons, just like the Web," as we used to say.

I described how excited we were when we started to share our work online for everyone to see and use. And how we were even more excited when they started to share *their* work online for us and each other as well. We were amazed by how much they knew and what they could do. How much more they learned from each other. How enthusiastic and grateful they were, and how much they cared.

Here, finally, were the tools we had always wanted, always yearned for: a giant web of knowledge, faster, more inclusive, and more democratic than the best exhibition and research project ever could be. It seemed a paradise had come true!

"But what happened?" She asked, looking at me with an understanding smile, as if she already knew the answer.

Technology is useful only if the people in charge want what it offers, I thought, as a wave of memories flooded my mind—folk wisdom from thirty years in museums and IT.

When you're a hammer everything looks like a nail.
You can't fix a cultural problem with a technical solution.
You can lead a horse to water . . .
Lipstick on a pig.
Pushing rope.

I told her that I remembered working at the Smithsonian the morning of 9/11, when the airplanes crashed into the World Trade Center in New York, a field in Pennsylvania, and the Pentagon, across the river from DC. We were launching a new website that morning, and we couldn't figure out why the internet and phones were down, why there was smoke drifting across the National Mall. I didn't understand what had happened until I made my way home that night and sat in bed with my wife and infant daughter, watching the news on TV.

In the months and years that followed 9/11, I often looked out my office window, across the Washington skyline. To my left was the National Archives. To my right was the Library of Congress. And in front of me was the Smithsonian Institution, the world's largest museum and research complex with six thousand employees, a $1.2 billion budget, and a mission dedicated to the increase and diffusion of knowledge.

How would these three august institutions help us understand what had happened to us as a nation? What would they do to help us chart our way forward in this complex and dangerous world?

"Not much, it turns out," I solemnly said.

As I stared into my beer, I couldn't think of a single thing that any of these institutions, or even museums in general, had done to help Americans think clearer thoughts or make better decisions after 9/11. It wasn't a museum's job, or so we thought. Just hunker down, entertain the guests, and don't rock the boat. So we lost our minds and went to war for twenty years without even an exhibition catalog as a souvenir.

"A generation lost," she said.

"What worries me the most," I said to her, coming down off the rush of memories, "is if we couldn't do it for 9/11, a dramatic act of deadly violence that commanded the attention of the entire nation for years, what impact could museums hope to have in a future that is faster and more difficult than the world we know today?"

A world of three degrees of global warming. Mass displacement and migration. Sea level rise. Ocean acidification. Artificial intelligence. Nanotech and materials science. Bioengineering—not just new branches on the tree of life, as Richard Dawkins has said, but new trees entirely, made by our own hands. In that world, the digital revolution is just a harbinger—a prerequisite for revolutions yet to come. Ceaseless uncertainty and accelerating change.

It was quiet between us then, each lost in thought as conversations and laughter swirled around us and the rain and wind whipped the windows outside.

"How does it turn out?" I finally asked her. "Do we save the world?"

"Yes," she told me quietly, after a long moment's pause. "The future is so bright now—sustainable, joyous, and just."

She told me of an end to injustice and war. The defeat of fascism and bigotry. The remaking of the world's economies. The celebration of a new vision for humanity and a new relationship with the natural world.

"But how did we do it?" I stammered. "What did we do to make this dream come true?" She didn't know.

We asked everyone in the bar. They all knew that the world was saved by a great global effort, a new enlightenment rising from civic engagement, dialogue, and action at a scale and speed that had never been seen before. The internet was essential in this culture, too—as was the energy and outrage of young people and the young at heart. But nobody knew about museum institutions or what they had done.

Had museums been among the heroes of this story? Had they been awakened by the crisis to embrace their civic responsibilities? Had they created a new paradigm of practice—faster, more open, more social—inspired to play their part in a digitally connected world? Had museums used *all* the tools available to them to help us think clearer thoughts and make better decisions about the future? Did they help us to become better citizens, a better people, in an uncertain world?

Or had museums mattered not at all?

I felt dizzy as I said my goodbyes and walked into the damp night air. We know the future can be beautiful, but how to make it so?

It's hard to say for sure. But, as I think of the time travelers I met that night and the decades I've spent working with technology in museums, I'm pretty sure of this: The museum sector's ideas about technology are a reflection of our soul; our ambivalence about technology is an ambivalence about our mission, relevance, and impact in society; and once we work that part out the decisions about which technologies are important, which to use, and how and when to use them will become abundantly clear.

Until then, the answers won't be found in virtual reality, augmented reality, artificial intelligence, and virtual exhibitions. The future we want will only come true if we have the imagination and courage to rethink old assumptions, lift our vision, and make the world anew.

PART III

~

THE TURN TO COMMUNITY

It is now more than a century since John Cotton Dana penned perhaps the most famous line in American museum history, contending that a museum "is good only insofar as it is of use." And more than a generation has passed since Stephen E. Weil argued that American museums needed to shift "From being *about* something to being *for* somebody." But who did these reform-minded advocates have in mind? The people of the local community in which the museum is embedded. More recently, Bryan Stevenson, creator of the Legacy Museum and the Peace and Justice Memorial in Montgomery, Alabama, argues for four critical dimensions for social change: proximity ("walking in another's shoes"), changing the narrative, conveying hope, and being comfortable in discomfort.

When museums closed their facilities en masse, relatively few seized the opportunity to make themselves directly useful to their neighbors in need. Some did respond with programs, services, spaces, and collaborations that contributed not only to their own benefit but to the health, well-being, and needs of their communities. They took their offerings virtual, created outdoor pop-up experiences, supported food banks, voter registration, meditative outdoor yoga, after-school learning programs, and other directly useful resources.

The five authors represented in this section have demonstrated experience in successful community engagement. They have walked in their communities' shoes. They have been willing to change the narrative. They have remained hopeful and humble, and they expected, and welcomed, discomfort.

They recognize the critical importance of consultation, collaboration, and co-creation with communities. They appreciate, respect, and incorporate public knowledge and communal expertise, which often serve to complement, correct, or counterpoint traditional scholarship.

They've employed ingenuity and openness to change, combined with an expanded sense of moral and social responsibility, to develop new formats for engaging youth, families, and neighborhoods and providing them with meaningful learning experiences. Further, some have discovered that the turn to digital, when done with sensitivity and purpose, can make a museum accessible to wider and more distant communities of interest.

These authors recognize that being "of" community requires looking inside the museum and thinking hard about how (or whether) the museum provides a welcoming invitation to all, from the staff it hires to the programs it offers and the stories it tells. Working with and of community means ensuring that the museum is a place of meaning, memory, and authentic engagement. The axiom "progress proceeds at the rate of trust" is especially true when museums embark on community work; issues of unearned authority, unequal power, misguided assumptions and stereotypes, and superficial or one-off events and programs are likely to result in suspicion and alienation. As a colleague once remarked, too many museums mistakenly believe that the three Fs, "fun, food, and festivals," are the key to successful community engagement, especially with racially or culturally specific groups. Too often their efforts stop there, resulting in a fourth "F" for failure.

In chapter 8, Armando Orduña delves into the principles of authentic community engagement and the processes of learning, trust-building, and continuous communication that this requires. He notes that each community is unique and warns against defaulting to stereotyped assumptions that are instantly recognized—and rejected—by the community.

Darryl Williams emphasizes the need for museums to adapt to ever-changing stores of knowledge and discovery. Just as science relies on experimentation to move forward, museums, as they seek to make a difference within their communities, must be attuned to new paradigms and approaches, especially as they seek to make a difference with ever more diverse publics. Williams advocates designing with audiences, moving from "sharing power" to "empowering" communities. More specifically, he employs the concept of "science capital" to help develop robust science identities in historically marginalized communities. Emphasizing access and inclusion, in turn, necessitates that museums, especially science museums, confront uncomfortable truths about omissions and obfuscations in their own past practice, including elitist, racist, and sexist constructs.

As the director of a historic farmhouse museum in the Bronx, Meredith Sorin Horsford has also had to upend past interpretation, tell new stories, uncover unknown histories, and create new relationships with surrounding communities. This has included revisiting everything from the museum's mission to its relationships with local businesses, developing new online programming that has extended the museum's community beyond its geographic neighborhood, and leveraging the outdoor areas around the museum.

Horsford estimates that in the process of making the museum a vibrant community center she created close to one hundred community partnerships. LaNesha DeBardelaben and Nafisa Isa also stress the essential role of partnerships if museums seek to move from "nice to necessary." DeBardelaben touts the enhanced outcomes for all participating entities in local, regional, and national collaborations. "Museums can no longer be islands of isolation," she states. "They must become integral parts of the civic ecosystem of their communities." Thoughtful collaborations are not only the "right" thing to do; DeBardelaben believes that robust relationships can yield financial prosperity as well.

Moving from her experience as a community organizer to the Smithsonian Institution's Asian Pacific American Center (APAC), Isa advises museums to adopt community-centered design, working closely with community members as co-creators. Museums need to understand community issues "from the perspectives of people living those challenges." In the wake of COVID-19 and the rise in hate crimes, Isa counsels museums to prioritize partnerships that combine content and care, addressing the health and well-being of the publics to be served, including museum staff.

Although all acknowledge that much remains to be done, these authors, representing diverse disciplines, foci, and platforms, provide useful, hopeful guideposts to ways in which museums' turn to community can, with intention and reshaped policies and practice, truly contribute to positive social change.

CHAPTER EIGHT

Beyond the Handshake

Effective Steps in Community Engagement

Armando Orduña

Armando Orduña, EdD, managing director—programs and partnerships for Latinos for Education, works within the intersectionality of STEAM access for immigrant-origin families and STEAM learning in language acquisition. He served as Director of Outreach Programs for Children's Museum Houston where he led the export of multilingual family learning throughout Houston.

Prior to the pandemic I led outreach programs for a children's museum in a metropolitan city in Texas. As an institution we had made the decision in the mid-late 1990s that our outreach programs would be engineered for immigrant-origin families, low-income families, multilingual families, and families who face the barriers of distance and time in integrating the museum into their lives. The pace was fast; we experienced much growth in funded as well as fee-for-service programs. We received much recognition from our industry peers as we reaped rewards of a strategic shift that moved the museum beyond its appeal as an attraction site and redefined its identity to engage new audiences from nearby communities. We reimagined where and how we would go to meet these communities, and we shaped exhibits and programming to meet their evolving needs. We achieved much success, and these communities became the primary audiences for our exhibits and programming.

My experience in community engagement leads me to view the recent, pandemically inspired turn to digital with caution. Successful and authentic

57

community engagement only grows in importance as our population becomes more diverse. Such engagement requires a nuanced and sensitive approach, one that recognizes the limitations of a primarily digital focus. Some communities employ digital media only rarely; they prefer to socialize, work, play and learn in person. Even when these communities are social media savvy, they may use a specific subset of platforms and apps and ignore many or even most opportunities for online connection. Despite the disruptions of the pandemic, I remain committed to the importance of authentic, face-to-face, engagement. Here are some principles I believe essential for museums for museums following that path.

To know one community is not to know another. Neighborhoods, like individuals, have character. To understand the composition and adaptive customs of a Vietnamese community in Seattle is not the same as understanding another Vietnamese community in Gulf Coastal Louisiana. There are countless adaptive measures taken by immigrant populations as well as their American-born descendants that are geo-culturally specific to the region in which they live. The advantages of language fluency or familiarity with general cultural practices may expedite an introductory period between museum and community but cannot exempt museums from the time and effort needed to gain a firm grasp of the specific community they want to engage.

Representation expedites relationship building. Recruit staff from the communities you want to engage. I am an American-born, bilingual Latino, the son of a Mexican immigrant by my father and a sixth-generation Tejano by my mother. My cultural background, from some of the communities our museum had hoped to work alongside, enabled me to use my cultural fluency, along with my language skills, to move the initial courtship with these communities along at a faster clip. Museums should make a conscientious effort to hire and assemble outreach teams with the critical cultural context needed to facilitate meaningful exchanges with community stakeholders. Otherwise, as Ralph Ellison reminds us, "When they approach me they see only my surroundings, themselves, or figments of their imagination—indeed, everything and anything except me." This cultural representation can be vital to establishing an effective communication infrastructure. It expedites building community confidence by changing community perspectives from "them" to "us."

Communities within the same locale may have different needs, interests, and expectations. There needs to be a logical match between community needs and museum resources. Resources need to be allocated to determine which communities will welcome specific types of programming. Neighborhood needs assessments became useful tools to understand significant neighborhood differences. Only after these assessments can authentic dialogues and engagement begin. For example, we could develop a community-embedded out-of-school-time program designed for children from low-income backgrounds that could fit across many areas in the city. However, only after conducting needs assessments at the neighborhood level could we decide on the age-appropriate audiences, transportation infrastructure, and required parental and school support to facilitate a strong and successful program.

Getting to know and understand a community requires intense effort and deep engagement. Even before beginning community conversations, we pulled demographic data from local sources to understand community composition, such as ethnic make-up, economic status, immigration rates, and formal education levels. In this way we gained a preliminary understanding of data that facilitated meaningful conversations with community leaders. It is vital to participate in that community. Through attendance at civic meetings (city council, school district, and neighborhood meetings), we learned about current community concerns. We identified the trusted "gatekeepers," such as city council members, social service organizations, apartment managers, and school principals who facilitated entry into the greater community at large and endorse the museum's efforts. Active listening became another vital tool in our getting-acquainted efforts.

When executed with clear intention and transparency, community engagement still takes time. A common obstacle can be demonstrating a sincere desire and effort to prospective constituents with whom you are seeking to establish a continuous presence that is integrated within the fabric of their community. Museums can face high walls of mistrust particularly when engaging with marginalized populations that have been ignored by local government services or have felt exploited by nonprofits receiving funds to come in to "fix" their communities, leaving the work unfinished when funding diverts elsewhere. Authentic relationships need to be established among museum staff, individual agency representatives, and community members as they invest the time and effort to understand a community from the inside.

Engaging community stakeholders requires experiencing their communities. I believe authenticity is still fixed in shared, live interactions. Especially at the start of relationship building, virtual engagement shows its limitations. There are progressive, and simultaneous, measures to take in the immersion of the communities which museums hope to impact. Engaging community stakeholders requires *experiencing* their communities. It is at the start of the relationship building where I have observed the limits of virtual engagement. Mobile devices are certainly becoming more common even among the most under-resourced populations in this country. Yet if a museum wishes for its messages to stand out from the noise of ceaseless bombarding of information, its first contact must be authentic. A connection is formed between people through shared experiences that echoes much stronger and longer than through passive viewing of virtual content. It is this negotiation of living in two worlds (a digital and a *live* world) that necessitates diverse ways for museums to participate in the lives of their partner patrons. In response to signals from community leaders, we participated in health fairs, block parties, church bazaars, and cultural festivals. These events became optimal opportunities to personally engage community members in their "home" contexts. They also serve as low-stakes opportunities to introduce more museum personnel to the new communities they are currently courting.

Partnership is a hallmark of effective community engagement. Museums should seek collaborative partnerships with governmental agencies, schools, and social service nonprofits in ways that align their missions with the goals of other organizations. Partnerships can amplify success and create the collective impact required by many funders and supporters. Be clear about how your mission and goals complement or magnify those of agencies already embedded in the desired communities. Strategic partnerships with neighborhood agencies can prove instrumental in bolstering communication feedback loops with communities. Sit on advisory committees alongside the people with whom you wish to partner. Invite community members to sit on your museum advisory committees. Once communication loops are established, implement regular review of incoming communication from partners. It is an easy mistake to establish channels of communication (i.e., social media channels) preferred by new constituents without assigning museum personnel to regularly review and respond via those channels.

Customize communication methods to fit the community. With communication systems having grown more varied in recent years, there is a genuine temptation to use all communication means at one's disposal. Rather than expending massive efforts to communicate with a specific community using every means of communication in our toolbox, we assigned team members holding key community relationships to specify which communication methods were the most impactful from their engagement with community stakeholders. For example, through our engagement we found that many younger, immigrant parents were more likely to use internationally favored social media platforms such as WhatsApp or opt-in to receive mass text messaging through mobile devices rather than sign up for email list servs, traditional mail notices, community postings, or in-person interactions at physical gatherings.

The disruption of work practices caused by the pandemic are deep and numerous. Museums have made impressive strides in their digital offerings. Nevertheless, we are experiencing a deep yearning for returning to each other and to our many social and cultural rituals, gatherings, and events. For museums to fulfill their potential as relevant, meaningful institutions that make a difference in the lives of our diverse community members, we must take the time to cultivate the many steps necessary for effective engagement, including background research and relationship building, authentically participating in the practices and preferences of the desired community, creating continuous and responsive communication models that privilege museum listening more than talking, and hiring staff representatives of our communities. In this way our cultural institutions will morph into their new identity (or perhaps fall back into an old one) as community forums for cooperative learning, where patrons view themselves as integral parts in the advancement of the missions aimed at enriching their own lives.

CHAPTER NINE

Notions of Permanence, Visions of Change

Darryl Williams

Darryl Williams, PhD, senior vice president of science and education at the Franklin Institute, is known for his contributions over the past decade as a leader across the enterprise of STEM education research, evaluation, and program development in both formal and informal settings.

Success is simple—do what's right, the right way, at the right time.

—Arnold Glasow

Notions of permanence have been a paradigm long followed by science museums and other cultural institutions, applied with variations governed by their nature, purposes, and settings, and directed by their architectural spaces and intended experiences. Although this is a widely accepted way of conceiving museums, it doesn't necessarily make for the best fit with museums devoted to science.

In fact, it seems counterintuitive. In practice, science is a dynamic process built from the premise of curiosity, exploration, and discovery. In its relentless pursuit of truth, science constantly evolves as we learn more about the world around us and apply that knowledge to gain more insights and expand our understanding. If science is neither framed nor practiced from a perspective of permanence, why has the expectation for permanence suffused the design and execution of spaces, exhibits, and experiences throughout the science museum landscape?

The disconnect between the idea of permanence and the ever-changing realities of science can be seen via the latest buzz in the realm of particle physics. Scientists around the world believe they are on the verge of confirming the discovery of particles that could challenge the accepted understanding of fundamental particles and forces that comprise the standard particle physics model. If the new particles prove dispositive it will be a serious game changer that could alter not only physics but aspects of science more generally.

There are some lessons here. First, accepting that some things that we hold dear are capable of being reimagined and, second, that science is intentionally about experimentation, which sheds light on and brings new possibilities. This openness to experimentation and reimagination should be the same approach science museums emulate as they navigate the pandemic and embark on new ways of thinking and being. Science museums should take this moment to be bold and unafraid to push the envelope in how they create and share compelling, entertaining stories about science. These stories can and should provide inclusive experiences for diverse audiences and confirm the relevancy and value of science in everyday life. And although my experience is rooted in science and science museums, I think that the dynamic nature of science, with scholarship and research opening our eyes to new paradigms and evidence, occurs in other disciplines, including history, anthropology, and the arts.

Given this, we share the opportunity to paint a new canvas that fosters curiosity, experimentation, and exploration for all audiences. For science museums, in particular, this means new paradigms for authentic, personal experiences that explore the processes and practice of science through the lens of the communities they serve. The recent disruptions we have faced make it possible to intentionally rethink and redesign with audience input and experience as our focal point; we can also be more purposeful in serving as key partners for building and supporting science identities, particularly for historically marginalized and under-resourced communities.

In recent years, I have become aware of a concept called "science capital" that might be a key in building and supporting science identities and belonging, specifically for historically marginalized and under-resourced communities. Coined and researched by Professor Louise Archer and team at University College London, the concept shows how individuals can cultivate and sustain ways of being in the world with science as an integral part of their lives. Science capital examines the points of intersection that connect one's knowledge, beliefs, social networks, and access to resources with ongoing pursuit of and persistence in science-related activities and career pathways. Because of this, science capital provides a model for how to think about the work science museums currently do to engage various audiences. As museums rebuild and forge new paths for the future, this concept also expands their capacity to design content and deliver experiences with substantive and measurable impact.

The science capital model also aligns well with broader conversations about diversity, equity, access, and inclusion (DEAI) in and across the cultural sector. I would like to believe there is an opportunity to resituate DEAI in this context by using the tools provided by Archer's work to change the conversation, so that we place less emphasis on diversity and more on equity, access, and inclusion. Based on decades of research and practice, diversity, without these three factors, amounts to descriptive statistics. This leads institutions to check a box and tells them little about "how" and "why" their efforts are or are not working. So, what would happen if science museums and other cultural institutions change focus and emphasize equity, access, and inclusion instead? I postulate that a new approach that intentionally leads with equity, access, and inclusion will ultimately result in the diversity that our institutions seek. However, for this to manifest, we will have to become comfortable being uncomfortable tackling some of the challenging histories that are embedded in our practices.

For example, the high place science holds in society comes with the complexities and nuances of elitism, along with a host of other historically challenging constructs (e.g., racism, sexism, etc.). These have plagued science and resulted in barriers to entry in the continuum of formal education and science-related careers for many marginalized communities. It should come as no surprise that many science museums have been stuck in a sociocultural quagmire, seeing as they have deep roots in the same paradigm that discriminates against many communities.

The disruptive convergence of COVID-19 and the longstanding pandemic of social and racial injustices has created a unique moment for a stark pause and pivot to allow for transparency, honesty, and (my favorite word) intentionality about changing these structures. I would be remiss if I did not acknowledge the significant resources that have been cultivated and put to good use in support of science museums that build connections and engage marginalized communities through targeted programming. Now more than ever, science museums have the chance to truly shake things up and get down to root cause to effectively lead a sociocultural course correction. For it is quite possible that science museums are poised to serve as key influencers and activators in what could be a sociocultural revolution for the field of science entirely.

The opportunities are in front of us, if only we are brave enough to accept the charge to change. Experimentation and reimagination are crucial principles to embrace now. We cannot let the window of opportunity slip away before we put them into practice. Science museums remain uniquely positioned to respond to recent disruptions—in part because science provides some affordances due to its dynamic nature and the continuous emergence of new scientific knowledge and technologies. As such, it is likely that there will always be compelling science stories to share and hands-on, immersive experiences to create.

However, competition for the public's time and attention is becoming increasingly strong due to the demands for themed entertainment across the board. These kinds of experiences have done well understanding the needs and expectations of diverse audiences. They are becoming more sensitive and responsive to accessibility and inclusivity as core tenets of their business models. As a result, audience engagement in these attractions is growing because of the increased perception of relevancy, which leads to perceived value for time and money. From this vantage point, it would behoove science museums, as well as the culture sector more generally, to reevaluate their models and rebuild operational frameworks anchored in equity, access, and inclusion if just to keep pace.

After all, there are big ideas science museums should explore:

- Embrace in their programs and practices the core dynamic nature of science while showing courage, imagination, curiosity, and readiness to experiment, explore, and discover new possibilities.
- Focus on the relevancy of science in everyday life, creating new and authentic experiences and redesigning with—not just for—our audiences.
- Move away from a "bean-counting" focus on diversity and instead focus on equity, access, and inclusion to engage our audiences more effectively, particularly those in marginalized and under-resourced communities.
- Position ourselves to share power with communities rather than defaulting to "empower" communities because empowerment places the authority in our hands. Our goal should be to broaden participation and move toward reciprocity. This means dealing with elitism head on.

Finally, let's embrace the ideas of science capital as an approach that can enhance the connections between social networks, the practice of science, and individuals from a variety of backgrounds and communities. These considerations are important for our relevance and missions. They are also important for the bottom line because audiences/potential customers are making their own choices about how they spend their limited time and money. Given these circumstances, it would behoove science museums to revisit their models and rebuild operational frameworks anchored in equity, access, and inclusion. At the end of the day, these decisions to transform should not be driven solely by dollars and cents, but should come because they are simply the right things to do. And because they are the right things to do, they will yield success as well.

CHAPTER TEN

Slaves Lived Here
[*Esclavos Vivieron Aqui*]

Meredith Sorin Horsford

Meredith Sorin Horsford, executive director, Dyckman Farmhouse Museum, is a museum and nonprofit leader. Her work focuses on creative and inclusive programming and interpretation, highlighting underrepresented narratives with a community-focused perspective. She has served as a grant reviewer for numerous funders and as a lecturer on the future of the museum field.

History museums and historic sites are by far the most numerous category of museums in the United States. They are among our most trusted sources of ideas and information and beloved by many. But they can also embody a great deal of misinformation, shaped by racism, prejudice, and gender bias, but, particularly the desire to ignore unpleasant stories about the American past, fearing that they might somehow taint the national narrative and that visitors would find them off-putting. We Americans tend to say we are interested in American history, but we don't like to look at that history too closely. But far from corrupting the national narrative, adopting a "warts and all" history makes historical figures all the more human and the national story one that represents continuous questioning and movement toward greater inclusion. Moreover, the broad American narrative reflects the nature of a multicultural democracy.

However, historic houses and history museums have long been complicit in colonialism, exploitation, and other inequities by ignoring their own histories, the ways that they obtained their collections, and the way they have constructed limited narratives. It is no longer enough to focus solely on the museum's original narrative of the wealthy white landowners or on the material objects that decorate the house, ignoring the rest of the story and giving visitors partial information, which in many cases constitutes misinformation. We know that deep research and an examination of collections objects in new ways can reveal the stories of enslaved people, indentured servants, women, and others whose history has not traditionally been a part of the record. Museums will never have every piece of historical information that they would like, but prioritizing this research and reshaping museum narratives by looking at the history through a variety of lenses brings new insights.

The public history profession has, for some time, urged an expansion of our historical narratives. But beyond just telling these stories we must find ways to integrate our communities into the decision-making, the art making, and the overall structure of our museums. Museums need to change who they are both from the top down and from the bottom up. Boards and board structure must represent multiple aspects of their constituents and not simply those who have the money to be generous donors. And adding one or two token members of color is insufficient if changes are not being made throughout the institution.

This requires rethinking everything from the museum's mission to its caterers, the companies the museum does business with, and the diversity of the staff. Shopping in local businesses, using caterers from different community groups for museum events, and purchasing museum supplies locally all signal to the community that the museum genuinely cares about serving its constituents. Museums can learn a great deal about welcoming visitors from the hospitality industry and from the for-profit sector that depends on its customers for its success. Staff and board members should engage in hospitality training and anti-bias training; they also need to find ways to immerse themselves in the neighborhoods in which their museums are located.

This also requires reimaginings of our past exhibition and interpretive strategies. Many historic sites were founded in a time when visitors were content to peek into never changing period rooms. Recreating authentic period spaces—carpets, drapery, furniture, paint colors—can be quite dramatic in the right setting but are extremely expensive and can also provide little "bang for the buck" in terms of encouraging visitors to make repeat visits and helping them to understand abstract ideas. These rooms are primarily exhibitions of the decorative arts that you visited once on a fourth-grade field trip and never went back to again. As historic sites have sought to discuss such things as gender roles, slavery, Indigenous history, social interactions and relationships, etiquette, and even politics in these domestic spaces, the inclusion of theater, flat screens, holograms, iPads, and other contemporary devices paired with a small number of authentic objects can provide the catalyst for the visitors' imaginations and questions.

Modern audiences, particularly younger audiences, expect and learn through technology, and these forms can animate historic spaces and provide insight into aspects of the story that are absent. Sites can also animate their rooms by using the spaces as stage sets for small theatrical presentations or by asking artists to respond to the room with contemporary installations. The Newark Museum's raucous dining room reinterpreted by artist Yinka Shonibare is an excellent example of an artist-rendered space.

The pandemic provided my site, the Dyckman Farmhouse Museum, with the opportunity to expand our audiences in new ways. Located in Upper Manhattan, the Dutch Colonial historic site is a small clapboard and stone structure up an uneven set of stone steps that is currently hard to access for those with physical disabilities. Thus, online programming made us more accessible to many in our immediate neighborhood as well as those across the country and even in the Netherlands. For a long time, the house was not welcoming, and some local residents did not even know that it was a museum or that the site was open to the public.

Yet, the major transformation from an insular and boring historic site to an essential, community-focused institution began years before the recent recognition that museums needed to change. I say this because COVID-19 and the murder of George Floyd accelerated but did not initiate these changes. They are a part of our institutional DNA.

How did a Dutch Colonial site make itself relevant to a neighborhood that is 70 percent Latinx with 37 percent of our children living below the poverty level—a twenty-first-century neighborhood that also includes a wide variety of young families with children, and a Jewish community? By focusing on the various needs and interests of our neighbors and looking for the intersections between their lives and what we have to offer, we are making ourselves a vital resource.

We made the commitment to consider the stories of historical people in concert with the needs of contemporary communities, rather than simply considering the objects and preservation of the structure. We seized the opportunity to recruit new leaders and partners to work with us in realizing our new mission. And, through audience feedback, we figured out how to be more welcoming to our neighbors and potential new audiences. We began, as every museum can, with simple changes—removing room barriers that prevented visitors from entering period rooms, installing lighting that allowed visitors to see the museum clearly, creating bilingual labels, training staff to welcome everyone no matter what language they spoke. We also eliminated our entrance fees to remove that barrier to accessibility and connected with community organizations to make sure that our neighbors knew they were welcome.

We experimented with and evaluated dozens of different public programs and created close to one hundred community partnerships. Our visitation increased nearly 70 percent, and we increased our social media following by 400 percent. The park in which the building sits provided much needed green space for the neighborhood and a wonderful space for a summer science camp for children. Because many of the children could not afford to bring lunch, we provided a healthy Dominican meal with a nutritious fruit smoothie each day.

One of the most important things that we uncovered in our research were names. How empowering it was to our community to be able to talk about Francis Cudjoe, Hannah, Gilbert Horton, Harey, and Will and to start to share with visitors what we discovered about their lives and their work. The interpretive story is now much richer. In connection with this research project, we also created several new community–facing programs that speak to the topic of enslavement and the Black experience but only after conducting community conversations to engage our neighbors in the work that we were planning and gathering their feedback.

We asked local artists to respond to the house and exhibit their artwork throughout the museum and created a lecture series that focuses on the topic of race in America. Artist Reggie Black's, *No Records* installation projected the words "Slaves Lived Here" in English and Spanish on the side of the museum, a dramatic installation that could be viewed from the street during the heart of the COVID-19 pandemic. These changes showed our neighbors what we value as an institution and made it clear that we will not shy away from talking about uncomfortable parts of history. This is no longer just a place for only one aspect of New York's story but the story of many people interacting with one another to survive and to build a nation.

Other historic sites in New York have begun to reflect the vibrancy and diversity of the city. At Sylvester Manor Educational Farm on Shelter Island, the focus of the site is telling the story of *all* the inhabitants of the land, including the original Indigenous people who lived there, the enslaved Africans that worked the land, and the European settler family. They use this holistic approach to the site's history to engage visitors today in conversations about food, art, and inventiveness. The Alice Austen House Museum on Staten Island highlights the life and photography of that nineteenth- and twentieth-century female photographer and is now a nationally recognized site of LGBTQ history. Through permanent and changing exhibitions, the museum uses Austen's pioneering work and contemporary pieces to lift marginalized voices and highlight female and LGBTQ artists.

All these histories enrich our understanding of our shared past, create a dialogue with contemporary audiences, and help to foster a better understanding of where we have been as a nation and how we can move forward together. We need a reckoning that will enable us to face past mistakes head-on as well as to find ways to use history to understand current problems and perhaps how to begin solving them. We need more than hollow words like the oft repeated—"We stand with George Floyd's family." What is your institution prepared to do?

∽

CHAPTER ELEVEN

We Are Each Other's Harvest

Prospering through Partnerships

LaNesha DeBardelaben

LaNesha DeBardelaben, president and CEO of the Northwest African American Museum, specializes in organizational leadership and management, institutional programming, and strategic engagement. She has global experience with museums and libraries and is currently national president of the Association of African American Museums Board of Directors.

∽

Over the past year, the closing of physical museum spaces due to the COVID-19 pandemic challenged museums to reimagine our institutions and consider novel ways of operating. We had to find unique ways to convene community, hold critical conversations about justice and equity during social protests, and invest in the healing of our communities.

For our survival and sustainability, museums pivoted from tradition to innovation, and the future looks promising. Our museums are no longer limited entirely by geographic boundaries. Digital capabilities discovered over the past year enabled us to reach viewers anywhere in the world as seamlessly as we could reach audiences down the block.

The questions now are Where do we go from here? What practices will keep museums vibrant and vital institutions far into the future? What skills and approaches do museum practitioners now need to master in this new post-COVID reality? What will require more energy and attention as we move beyond the current horizon?

When museums are clear on their purpose with an eye toward the unfolding future, partnerships become a key answer to these fundamental questions. Although the future is unpredictable, it is not entirely uncertain: We know for sure that partnerships, alliances, and networks will play an increasingly essential role for museums to thrive. The world is becoming more connected and networked. Museums can no longer be islands of isolation. They must become integral parts of the civic ecosystem of their communities. Certainly, a recent incentive for museum collaborations has been changes in funders' priorities that favor collaborative efforts. Many funders believe that collective action multiplies programmatic impact, and they have distributed funds accordingly. A more important incentive, however, is that partnerships benefit the communities we serve.

Community voices will be vital in future museum planning and decision-making for all museums. Many of our Black museums have long reflected the voices of our community members. Now, to effect changes that our communities desire and deserve, all museums need to consider more meaningful, inclusive, and innovative collaborations. The universal truths found in such African proverbs as "If you want to go fast, go alone. If you want to go far, go together" will continue to define the promise of partnerships for museums. We are, indeed, stronger, more impactful, and more sustainable working in collaboration with those around us, near and far.

As we approach the other side of the pandemic-inspired shift, museums need to make a radical commitment to partnerships. Even before COVID-19, museums had tremendous influence in society. Black museums, in particular, have long been essential gathering places for communities. Post-COVID, museums will hold even greater potential as spaces to help communities reflect, reframe, and reset, individually and collectively. Museums can work together with other organizations to support communities and societies as they transition, heal, and recover.

Partnerships can bring new prosperity to museums, and this goes beyond their potential financial benefits. Cultivating a shared vision of impact with other organizations can yield rich relationships, expand networks of goodwill, and build community and individual well-being. Museums can leverage their resources to be at the center of this critical work and stand to gain from the resulting benefits.

Museum partnerships empower—and demand—us to invest in people, from connecting staff members across institutions to engaging diverse audiences normally not within our reach. To succeed, partnerships require the soft skills of open-mindedness, inclusivity, and agility as well as hard skills of technology innovation and project management. Museums will need to hire versatile individuals with a broad range of expertise and interests as well as invest in professional development that will sharpen the interpersonal communication skills of all staff.

Creative partnerships enable museums to operate beyond traditional practices. In the midst of the pandemic, during the racial reckoning of 2020 and early 2021, Seattle's Northwest African American Museum (NAAM) partnered with talented vocalists from a retired local choir to create a new inspirational choir called the African American Cultural Ensemble. The ensemble performs heart-stirring inspirational music rooted in African American history and inspires audiences to face these times with resolve and determination.

Although this initiative was a far cry from the expected work of museums, current times require museums to be bold in building alliances with a variety of sectors and unlikely networks. Partnering with local homeless shelters, professional sports teams, affordable housing complexes, civil rights organizations, prisons and correctional facilities, nursing homes, and other non-museum-centric spaces can lead to inspirational, long-lasting outcomes for the publics served by those organizations. The participation of museums in these kinds of diverse partnerships sends a strong signal that heritage, arts, science, and culture matter to all our community members. Through the bold and purposeful presence of museums, these partnerships demonstrate that museums contribute to the civic, educational, and cultural health of communities beyond our four walls.

When the pandemic temporarily closed the doors of museums and halted earned revenues, this cleared the way for museums to build new kinds of partnerships built on resource-sharing and keeping museums relevant and engaged despite staff furloughs. At the onset of the pandemic, for instance, Seattle's NAAM created the Black Education, History, and Heritage Alliance (BEHHA). Bringing together six distinct local Black-centric organizations, BEHHA exists to foster the collaboration of collective resources with a shared commitment to advancing knowledge that honors the rich lives, legacies, and stories of African Americans.

All six organizations collectively set the direction and goals of BEHHA. In its first year, BEHHA helped to diversify the Seattle public schools' teaching pool by supporting the Academy of Rising Educators, an initiative to diversity the teaching pipeline with Black, Indigenous, and people of color teachers. BEHHA is currently developing an online Black history course. This is work that goes further than the scope of one organization. Although each is a long-standing, respected institution, if we would have gone it alone, the project's scale and reach would have been diminished. By working together, we demonstrated Black unity in addressing this important educational goal. When we pursue our vision together, we make greater impact.

NAAM also helped to establish a national network called the Blk Freedom Collective, a partnership among African American museums from coast to coast that now produces an annual virtual educational production about Juneteenth. The program was initially envisioned when all our museums abruptly closed in early 2020 due to the pandemic. We needed to pivot to virtual programming. The urgency escalated after George Floyd's televised murder and the subsequent global uprisings for a racial reckoning.

During the first year of the collective, six museums joined forces to produce the national virtual production attracting more than ninety thousand viewers. We repeated the partnership in 2021 by expanding the number of partners and reached more than 130,000 viewers. We will do so again in 2022 with an eye on increasing impact. Our goal is to interpret the meaning of major historical events like Juneteenth for future generations. By harnessing the power of our collaboration to preserve and disseminate the stories and traditions of our shared culture, the Blk Freedom Collective is hoping to inspire others to rise above the challenges they face and enlist in the fight for justice and equity.

These post-COVID times necessitate robust, attentive partnerships. When our museum ecosystem is inclusive, collaborative, and networked, we increase our impact and our relevance. And when we do so, our sector can become more essential, our society can become more equitable, our communities can become healthier, lives can be changed, and minds can be opened. We grow stronger together. As Gwendolyn Brooks reminds us, "We are each other's harvest: we are each other's business: we are each other's magnitude and bond."

CHAPTER TWELVE

Communities over Collections

Three Principles for Partnership

Nafisa Isa

Nafisa Isa is a designer, advocate, and community educator, and is currently program manager at the Smithsonian Asian Pacific American Center. She has been building intentionally inclusive spaces and designing community learning initiatives for most of her life. Outside of work, Nafisa was featured in *Time* Magazine's Women Across America series in 2018 for her leadership efforts in creating soulful third spaces for Muslim American women.

I never thought I would work in museums.

From the outside, it seemed like museums were places led by white, wealthy academics, where I—an immigrant, Muslim community educator from a working-class background—could have neither a voice nor a role. Still, I took a chance on a job application at the Smithsonian's Asian Pacific American Center (APAC) some six years ago. When I was asked in my first interview what I could offer the center, it began to dawn on me that my experiences in fostering community conversations about race and social justice were not only relevant but necessary for this field. And good news: I got the job! In the years since, the museum world continues to reckon with systemic racism, entrenched hierarchies, and waning social relevance. But at the same time, through APAC's work and elsewhere, I have also seen that we can still be integral to building a healthier society.

Community partnerships are among the most powerful keys to unlock this potential. Putting communities right at the center of our program planning, particularly the grassroots organizations and community members historically excluded from the museum world, is essential to efforts to address our field's failure to support transformative social changes. What are the right ways to go about this? Our team at APAC has achieved success with three basic partnership principles: pursuing community-centered design; prioritizing care; and seeing staff themselves as community members. These principles, which I discuss in detail, remain central to our work and, I would argue, could be widely adopted by museums of all shapes and sizes.

Museums, like other nonprofit organizations with social goals, must ask themselves: What are our values? Who do we listen to? How do we choose to engage? How can we collaborate across areas of expertise? Eighteen months into the COVID-19 pandemic's disproportionate impact on Black, Indigenous and People of Color (BIPOC) communities, a year after the 2020 Black Lives Matter uprisings, and several years into an era of heightened xenophobia, museums face an urgent need to prioritize communities over collections and to live the values of inclusion, equity, and relevance. Partnerships following the three following principles can be powerful ways to achieve these goals.

Community-Centered Design

The first partnership principle, community-centered design, highlights the importance of process as much as, if not more than, content. My introduction to a community-centered design approach took place after the 2014 uprisings in response to police brutality. Black Lives Matter, the most successful nonhierarchical social and political movement of my lifetime, spurred conversations at all levels of society about inclusion, equity, and justice. In 2014, I had the privilege of organizing and facilitating community dialogues focused on racial justice at Busboys and Poets, a restaurant, bookstore, and community gathering place in Washington, DC. As an organizer and non-Black POC, I made mistakes. I made assumptions about what topics might be important. I took up too much space with my own thoughts, when I should have been listening to Black educators, organizers, and community members.

The experience of organizing, making mistakes, and humbling myself before the knowledge and experience of Black organizers led me to question the norm of deferring to experts in ivory towers or even the idea of expertise at all. I achieved more success designing and organizing *with* the community rather than *for* them. Local activists, parents, youth poets, and service workers emerged as the most appropriate experts to inspire and inform our collective efforts to grapple with race, identity, and bias.

The experience was instructive for my future work in museums, particularly APAC's Culture Lab pop-up exhibition model. Culture Labs are designed to provide a space for our partner activists, artists, educators, and community organizations to co-create opportunities for hands-on engagement with a chosen theme. As our Culture Lab Manifesto states: "We developed Culture Labs to bring [people] together in creative and ambitious ways—and to show that anyone can make a 'museum without walls' by curating collaborative, participatory, and socially responsible spaces where people can come as their true selves."

As a personal link to the power of this approach, I still vividly recall the moment in the first Culture Lab when artist Tracy Keza asked my mother to be a part of her "Hijabs and Hoodies" portrait initiative. The collection of portraits aimed to question the American dress code and explore the intersection between anti-Blackness and Islamophobia. When my mother shyly agreed to be photographed, Tracy approached her with care and not just as a subject but as a partner in the creation of art, deferring to her vision and preference for how and where she would be photographed. In a time when Islamophobic and xenophobic rhetoric had reached its peak in media and politics, I saw myself reflected through my mother's portrait and her excitement about being part of—not just a subject of—a socially responsive art installation, all thanks to Tracy and the community-centered environment of the Culture Lab.

In this, among other moments, my previous sense of being unseen and unheard in museums was no longer true. But moments like this can only occur if the people involved in designing and organizing programs and projects practice humility, seek out diverse co-creators, and truly try to understand the historical and social contexts of the challenge at hand from the perspectives of people living those challenges.

Prioritizing Care

After 2014, especially when working with communities of color, it was necessary to consider historical traumas, grief, resilience, and healing. Presently, the dual pandemics of COVID and systemic injustice continue to call for prioritizing empathy, reflection, and listening in a completely new way, with greater urgency to promote healing and care. Museums should embrace the opportunity to be "partners in caring" with other community organizations.

One inspirational community-centered partnership during the height of the COVID pandemic was the Smithsonian Institution's Anacostia Community Museum's (ACM) collaboration with Feed the Fridge DC, a local nonprofit that places refrigerators in the DC metro area and pays local restaurants to fill them with fresh food daily. The organization began as a response to the pandemic and continues to address widespread food insecurity.

Food for the People: Eating and Activism in Greater Washington, an exhibition focused on food justice issues in the Washington DC area, made visible the local people—from farm workers to restaurant workers—in food-related occupations. The partnership enabled ACM to install a fully stocked refrigerator in a publicly accessible space, regularly replenished with free, high-quality meals for local community members to take at any time, no questions asked. The exhibition provided a thoughtful and thorough context for local food justice issues, including stories of the people at the heart of those issues. Through the partnership with Feed the Fridge DC, the museum participated in an act of care, directly addressing community hunger and supporting the local small business economy.

Museums can also show care by acknowledging, responding to, and combating various forms of social trauma and violence. At APAC, one of our main partners during 2020 was Act to Change, an Asian American Pacific Islander (AAPI) antibullying organization. As we planned the #KindnessHeals art campaign, we centered the experiences, creativity, and needs of youth during the dual pandemics. Although the APAC staff contributed skills in creating educational content, the Act to Change planning team brought their expertise in trauma-informed care. We co-created a three-page, downloadable activity with the personal protective equipment mask as a blank canvas for design and other activities that asked young people to reflect on their hopes for the future and the importance of their support networks. This partnership proved prescient as anti-Asian hate crimes proliferated during the year. Although the #KindnessHeals campaign was meant to start and end around specific dates, the content created through the partnership has remained a resource for families and educators.

Staff as Members of the Community

Finally, our museums need to remember that our staff are themselves members of our community. How often do we take the time to engage directly with and listen to our frontline and support staff about their needs and priorities and what interests them about the role of the museum, their employer, in their community? There is knowledge, wisdom, and community in the staff. The trust and empathy that museums seek to build externally must start from within. By turning to staff as community members, we can ensure that we all can better serve our communities and succeed in our work. Taking this on more intentionally will involve patience, flexibility, sustained effort, and a fundamental rethinking of the value of our people.

At APAC we were all grateful to continue working in 2020 but intentionally slowed down—with support from our director—to allow time for reflection and reorientation to our new realities. I also heard of museums beginning to acknowledge frontline staff as the essential workers who were risking their lives to ensure the operational continuity of our spaces. These are only a few examples, but I hope to see more instances of this principle in practice throughout the field.

Museum leadership needs to manifest compassion and understanding of the stressors that each of us has in managing our own lives, as well as the emotional, physical, and intellectual labor we are doing in our sphere of responsibility. A dual pandemic is no time for business as usual. The push for greater diversity, equity, inclusion, and access in our organizations demands a culture shift, and how museums leverage and support the valuable resource present in their staff will determine how the field fares in the future. And the priority of caring for staff must not be relinquished in post-COVID times either. We will be better and healthier for the care that we demonstrate internally as well as externally.

Conclusion

In stressful and divisive times, these three principles can and should guide museum-community partnerships. As we seek to create compelling experiences for our audiences, the best ideas may well arise from collaboration with community organizers, educators, and artists—as well as those who show up to keep our organizations running daily.

When I accepted that first museum job offer, I hoped that community would still be at the center of my professional life. I'm so grateful to have seen and heard countless anecdotes about the joy, excitement, and social connection that can arise when people and community are treated as partners in work within museums. As Grace Lee Boggs reminds us in *The Next American Revolution* (2011), "We have entered the epoch of responsibilities, which requires new, more socially-minded human beings and new, more participatory and place-based concepts of citizenship and democracy." The question we must ask is whether we can continue being ambitious, caring, and thoughtful in our partnerships moving forward for the sake of our communities, our field, and society.

For Further Reading

For an introduction to Design Thinking: https://designthinking.ideo.com/

Community-Centered Design: Evolving the Mission of the Creative Industry, https://www.epicpeople.org/community-centered-design-evolving-the-mission-of-the-creative-industry/

Equity-Centered Community Design, Creative Reaction Lab, https://www.creativereactionlab.com/our-approach

Culture Lab Manifesto and Playbook, Smithsonian Asian Pacific American Center, https://smithsonianapa.org/culturelab/

PART IV

~

THE TURN TO EQUITY

When the plague of COVID-19 hit the United States at the very moment the Black Lives Matter protests intensified, Americans of differing political outlooks found themselves grappling with the great tragedies of our national errors, failings, and crimes. As the nation was again called to a reckoning with its racist and colonialist past, American museums issued calls for racial equity and justice. The national uproar, however, brought with it renewed demands for museums to acknowledge their own historical complicity in colonialism, racism, and inequity and to abandon the traditional claim of "museum neutrality." Aroused minority groups challenged the biases and distortions embedded in museums and were soon joined by museum professionals and cultural critics attentive to the currents of contemporary social activism.

Demands for a reckoning across the museum field only intensified when the pandemic forced the closing of virtually all American museums, leaving thousands of staff unemployed or involuntarily furloughed. Protests erupted against inequitable salaries and opportunities for advancement, abusive working conditions, and the performative gestures of many museums. Demands for systemic structural change proliferated, in some cases leading to resignations and retirements by established museum leaders, lay and professional, and, in several instances, to the formation of unions at major museums.

A chorus of voices could be heard calling for change in American museums. In response, museums began to publicly declare their adherence to diversity, equity, accessibility, and inclusion (DEAI), both in their own institutional cultures and in society at large. But, as a September 2020 survey reported, only a few museums responded with comprehensive action as well as words.[1] Some museums announced the appointment of DEAI officers, others expanded the diversity of voices in decision-making, and still others developed programs explicitly targeted toward previously underserved and unengaged audiences. As the survey noted, however, even museums reporting that DEAI is an organizational priority had not taken "strategic, consistent action at an organizational level foundational enough to support and achieve enduring equity and inclusion."

None of these responses is sufficient, according to Kayleigh Bryant-Greenwell and Janeen Bryant. "Our structures and hierarchies, our processes and procedures, and our lived values . . . continue to embody oppressive norms and behaviors, exclusive and elitist practices, and systemic, structural barriers to equity." What is needed, they argue, "is sustained, systemic change in our internal values, structures and practices. The first, essential step is an honest interrogation of museum practices, behaviors, norms, and history." Instead of incompetent, failed leadership, American museums need to become community-centered collaborators. Revisioning our museums, they suggest, is the key to future resilience and relevance.

Brandie Macdonald also takes up the theme of revisioning in her comments about the need for decolonization across the museum field. "Decolonial work is a multifaceted process," she writes, "that calls for critical reflection, accountability, truth-telling, transparency, policy and practices reform, repatriation, restitution, and the integration of BIPOC peoples at all levels of decision-making." Only when museum leaders give this work priority and resources will museums be able to change their structures and their ecology, Macdonald argues, and because colonial systems and colonial harm remain active forces in our lives today, we need to commit to an ongoing, continuous process of rebuilding trust with Indigenous peoples.

Many other biases persist in our museum cultures. Izetta Autumn Mobley points to one of the most ubiquitous, but also most ignored: ableism, or discrimination and prejudice against people whose minds or bodies are perceived as falling out of the range of normal or acceptable. As Mobley argues, "Over a lifetime, congenital disability, accidents, illness, or aging impact how we move through the world and what accommodations we need to function as full members of society. Disability is far from outside the norm. Disability and disabled people *are* the norm." Museums must, therefore, acknowledge their biases and accept their responsibility to welcome, serve, and represent people with disabilities, within our museums and in our communities.

Racism, colonialism, and ableism are but three among a constellation of unacknowledged prejudices that distort our institutional cultures and our core narratives. Internal and external challenges persist, and many American museums are only beginning to confront their dark histories, engage in difficult conversations, reform their institutional cultures, and actively participate in public discourse about enlarging the circle of moral responsibility.

We can, however, see signs of change even as museums across the country grapple with the complexities of turning to equity. Museums will need to address pressing issues of repatriation, reparations, and deaccessioning. They will need to acknowledge and remedy their own patterns of bias. They will need to redefine roles and generate more equitable avenues of advancement. They will need to create more porous structures that are open to diverse voices from all levels of staffing and from the community at large. And they will need to prepare an emotional looking-after for the well-being of their volunteers and staff.

Note

1. Cultural Competence Learning Institute, *National Landscape Study: DEAI Practices in Museums*, (2020), https://higherlogicdownload.s3.amazonaws.com/ASTC/a6c0 f3de-e0b1-4198-8ab7-01cee4a55b00/UploadedImages/CCLI_National_Landscape _Study-DEAI_Practices_in_Museums_2020.pdf. Accessed October 10, 2021.

Further Reading

For an introduction to Design Thinking: https://designthinking.ideo.com/
Community-Centered Design: Evolving the Mission of the Creative Industry, https://www.epicpeople.org/community-centered-design-evolving-the-mission-of-the-creative-industry/
Equity-Centered Community Design," Creative Reaction Lab, https://www.creativereactionlab.com/our-approach
Culture Lab Manifesto and Playbook, Smithsonian Asian Pacific American Center, https://smithsonianapa.org/culturelab/

CHAPTER THIRTEEN

Speaking Truth to Power Begins Internally

Confronting White Supremacy in Museums

Kayleigh Bryant-Greenwell and Janeen Bryant

Kayleigh Bryant-Greenwell, community engagement specialist at Smithsonian American Art Museum, is a GLAM strategist with over a decade of experience in audience engagement, programming, and cultural leadership. She contributes to Museum as Site for Social Action and Empathetic Museum cultural movements. She is a sought-after contributing writer and speaker nationally and abroad.

Janeen Bryant, a core member of the Empathetic Museum, is an inter-sectional educator, organizer, and community engagement consultant. She is active within multiple industry-wide initiatives including Museums & Race and Mass Action. Janeen Bryant is the founder of Facilitate Movement, a consulting firm that helps cultural institutions authentically connect to their staff and the larger community.

Given a global public health crisis, nationwide financial instability, and ongoing racial inequity, today's museums are operating in challenging circumstances. All these issues complicate our work in museums, and together they compound our struggle to improve our structures and our practice. However, these external forces are not the only challenge facing museums today. It is forces internal to museums that pose a significant threat to our future.

The history of museums is one marked by plunder, theft, colonialism, and cultural hierarchy. Museums have been guilty of oppression and exploitation, ranging from how museums have acquired their collections to the cultural rankings they've assigned in interpretation. Although many of these behaviors are emblematic of the past, museum practices continue to do harm, from refusing to acknowledge problematic truths to actively dismissing new forms of inclusive and equitable interpretation. The results are the same: The status quo remains.

How we operate, our structures and hierarchies, our processes and procedures, and our lived values present the core issues defining twenty-first-century museums. These continue to embody oppressive norms and behaviors, exclusive and elitist practices, and systemic, structural barriers to equity. To confront the lethargy that threatens twenty-first-century museum life, institutions must tackle the colonialism, racism, and inequities that continue to thrive within our walls. As Angela Davis has written, "[D]ifferent frameworks, perhaps restorative justice frameworks, need to be invoked in order to begin to imagine a society that is secure." The same goes for our museums.

As external pressures to respond to social-racial inequities and state-sanctioned violence have grown, many museums have engaged in performative empathy and launched diversity, equity, accessibility, and inclusion (DEAI) initiatives. However, performative empathy generally masks institutional resistance and stasis behind a cover of public-facing, often temporary, social media posts or website statements proclaiming diversity, inclusion, and equity as necessary institutional postures, while seldom changing the organizational infrastructure that supports continued inequity.

One of the most obvious examples was June 2, 2020, "Blackout Day" on social media, when hundreds of organizations posted a single black square on Instagram, tagging the Black Lives Matter movement, as a "sign" of solidarity. What did this performance do? The real answer is that it did little. It did not prevent organizations from conducting mass layoffs of largely Black, Indigenous, and people of color (BIPOC) workers across the field. It did not spur a hiring frenzy of new BIPOC workers to the field. It did not provide tangible community support to BIPOC neighborhoods. It did not reallocate funds from traditional programs toward radical justice and liberative reimagining. It did not instill a commitment to social justice in the strategic plan. The list goes on.

What performative empathy attempted to do was to market to BIPOC audiences the message that the museum wants their attention but isn't willing to earn it by making any meaningful changes. Museums have yet to learn that you can't have your white supremacy and your BIPOC participation, too.

DEAI, too, has so far failed to create pathways toward racial equity. In a DEAI approach, museums ultimately sprinkle in color throughout their white-centered work.

Radical interrogation of institutional histories, white supremacist culture, and white centeredness generally does not happen in DEAI. In fact, DEAI centers whiteness. In DEAI, the museum's perspective remains white-focused and seeks simply to *add* other perspectives without shifting the central white perspective.

Black audiences and museum staff have widely dismissed symbolic and inauthentic expressions of solidarity, from posting a black square on social media to statements lacking actions and accountability. Some BIPOC leaders, such as curator Kelli Morgan and educator Andrea Montiel de Shuman, have resigned their positions in protest of harmful practices and structures.

What we need is sustained, systemic change in our internal values, structures, and practices. The first, essential step is an honest interrogation of museum practices, behaviors, norms, and history. Museums are unequivocally racist. From racist collections practices, racist displays, racist hiring, and racist internships to racist audience priorities and racist engagement programs, museums continue to demonstrate their inherent racism.

Much of the problem lies in museum leaders who have resisted countering racist and white supremacist narratives at the board and policy level. Their leadership competencies apparently extend only to budget shortfalls and exploiting artists, rather than to the self-interrogation and change work required to address working conditions, pay equity, resource allocation, fair representation, intentional stakeholder engagement, and assessing impact through transparent metrics.

This stranglehold of widespread leadership incompetence masks true calls for justice and the necessary noticing, naming, and empowering of those who are most vulnerable. As one executive director in a DC museum noted, he didn't want to be "too inclusive, enabling a Frankenstein monster" of staff and stakeholder input. The staff at this institution feared reprisal from the C-suite for pointing out that their furloughed colleagues might rightfully resent the institution. The development director at this same museum, who has been on payroll for the entirety of the pandemic, questioned why any furloughed employee would be upset, remarking, "Surely, they understand we have financial constraints!"

This lack of leadership and vision stifle the organization's work. Museums are limited by their failure to understand community harm done in their efforts to repair damage without real interrogation of what hurts. As a field, following examples from inadequate leaders, we replicate harm, waste money, and expend hours of staff time only to reinforce supremacist concepts that are normed as "best practice."

Instead of relying exclusively on traditional, great-man leadership, our museums need competent, diverse perspectives in every dimension of our work. We need to view all members of the museum staff and community as genuinely and intimately connected and, therefore, necessarily represented, recognized, and valued in relationships. In layman's terms, we are all inherently valuable parts of a larger society; when we engage each other with care and empathy, we support our system, institution, and interpersonal engagement for optimal experiences.

When museums, libraries, and other cultural spaces see themselves as outside of the "community," they cast themselves as irrelevant. The 2020 pandemic and resulting social distancing and safety protocols forced many institutions to redefine their relationship with their audiences and to better understand their public value. Tying the museum's value to its physical location rather than as a reciprocal and trusted community resource will force many institutions to shut their doors forever. The lesson: Reciprocal, community-driven value creates sustainable relevance.

This means practicing cultural shifts that rely on community-informed processes at every level of institutional leadership. Generally, museums rely on a model of "community engagement" in which the museum sets the terms of discourse. Community engagement is almost always framed as outreach— bringing the unengaged Other into our unchanged, oppressive spaces.

Instead, we need to view community relationships as a core function of the museum's culture and to treat community engagement as an inherent, essential practice in rebuilding the museum from the inside out. Most internal cultures are defined by privileged, powerful leadership, hierarchies, and siloed department structures. Instead, we should give greater priority to centering the voices and experiences of the most marginalized and underrepresented members of our communities. What happens to internal culture when it is defined by community relationships? When communities are centered in museum practice, this leads to actual inclusion.

Pursuing diversity and equity initiatives lead us into empathetic practice. Our personal and professional journeys are intimately and inextricably tangled, requiring us to daily pursue deeper relationships with each other and reflective activities for ourselves. As Brené Brown notes, "In order to understand someone's experiences, you must be willing to believe them as they see it and not how you imagine their experiences to be." Empathy as an organizational framework is not the destination, but it is a key step toward institutional maturity.

In recent months, we have seen several radical revisionings of what museums can be and how they can operate if they are really dedicated to equity and inclusion. At the *individual* level, leadership means inquiry and curiosity about a future that has yet to be actualized. Dr. Porchia Moore exemplifies these qualities in supporting museum professional development. She employs deep listening, community awareness, and joy as pedagogical frameworks for cultural leadership.

At the *institutional* level, museums must be willing to challenge the status quo and engage in generative conflict, as exemplified by the Baltimore Museum of Art's commitment to correcting the traditional art historical canon and revising its acquisition practices and exhibition norms. And, at the *community* level, museums need to reexamine all their operational practices, including contracting and purchases. In Minneapolis, two museums canceled their use of the Minneapolis police department as their contracted security providers until additional training protocols were put in place to protect community members of color.

Still, challenges remain. Every outreach program based on an "Us/Them" design is racist. Every collection object belonging to an historically harmed community is maintained in racism. Every initiative or policy created outside of collective decision-making is racist. Every program that attempts to maintain neutrality is racist.

Museums need to shift from a reactive to a proactive mode. Internal work requires new models, dismantling existing structures, and sponsoring work shaped by racial equity. Internal work is reflected in the ways museums position themselves and the community.

Internal work is ongoing. It does not have an expiration date. It does not end once external work begins. Internal work is iterative. It is a priority. It is essential to the museum's existence. This is a moment of crisis. Museums do not have another decade to stall, flounder, and defer. It's time to do the work.

For Further Reading

Gretchen Jennings, et al., "The Empathetic Museum: A New Institutional Identity," *Curator: The Museum Journal* 62 No.4 (October 2019): 505–526.

CHAPTER FOURTEEN

What Keeps Me Awake at Night

A *Letter on Decolonization*

Brandie Macdonald

Brandie Macdonald (she/her; Chickasaw/Choctaw) is senior director of Decolonizing Initiatives at Museum of Us and a PhD fellow at UC San Diego. Her work and publications focus on transformative systemic change within museums driven by anticolonial and decolonial theory in practice to redress colonial harm domestically and internationally.

Dear Friend: I am constantly asked, "What keeps you up at night?" The short answer: decolonization and museums. My mind is in a constant swirl of reflection—questioning practice and policies, holding space for my concerns around colonial co-opting of the decolonial movement, searching for patterns, and trying to understand how shared definitions play a role in linking the linear mind to the nonlinear process. These thoughts show up in my dreams, my research, panel discussions, and conversations around the dining room table (yes, I am a huge hit at dinner parties). It is on my mind as I sit here writing to you, and I find that my thoughts are organized by a series of questions that I ask myself and that others ask of me. My hope is that this letter may support you and your decolonial journey in some way and extend reciprocal feelings of solidarity and relief to comfort both our minds.

Decolonization is a complex movement that addresses the colonial patterns systemically embedded within our organizational structure, language, policies, culture, and practices. Decolonial work is a multifaceted process that calls for critical reflection, accountability, truth-telling, transparency, policy and practices reform, repatriation, restitution, and the integration of Black, Indigenous, and people of color (BIPOC) peoples at all levels of decision-making. Furthermore, I believe we see decolonial change happen in the field when museums, and their leadership, make it a priority—a priority that holds the same value and legitimacy as the other institutional goals and is integrated into the budgeting process. Throughout this letter, I use the words "decolonial," "decolonizing," and "decolonization" interchangeably in an effort to unpack this complex, nuanced, and global topic.

I begin this conversation with you by uplifting my ancestors by way of an introduction. I am a citizen of the Chickasaw Nation with Choctaw and Scottish ancestry. I am an able-bodied, cis-gendered, queer, Indigenous woman, who is phenotypically light skinned—which affords me various privileges and can make me more palatable to the colonial gaze due to the prevalence of white supremacy.

It is also important for me to recognize and honor the Indigenous land from which I write to you—the unceded ancestral homeland and territory of the Kumeyaay Nation. Furthermore, we are all on Indigenous lands, and Indigenous peoples globally are stewards who have maintained their connection to these lands since time immemorial. It is because of global Indigenous and non-Indigenous peoples' sacrifices, their emotional and physical labor, and their expressions of radical love that I am here today.

What Is This Decolonization Movement We See Manifesting in Museums Today?

My answer is one that is fluid, malleable, and nonlinear. Globally, the decolonial movement is a powerful current that changes the ecology of museums, holds inherently colonial museums accountable, and pushes for change structurally and culturally. Decolonization is not a finite deliverable that is achieved at the end of a fiscal year or grant cycle. Decolonization is a process, a process that is arduous and that changes based on the wants and needs of each community harmed by colonialism and each organization's colonial legacy. Decolonization is an ethos that requires our institutions to redress the colonial harm perpetrated against BIPOC.

We must remember that colonial systems and colonial harm are not just something of the past; they are active forces existing in our lives and industry today. We also need to acknowledge that museums (and by way of extension, the museum's staff and researchers) are not the experts on the lives, culture, and traditions of Indigenous peoples. Indigenous peoples are the experts on their own histories, traditions, and culture. Consultations are important, and representation is an essential starting point. However, this is not enough, and it certainly does not make your organization decolonized. Decolonizing is an intentional paradigm shift, one that works to change the colonial nature of a museum's systems and culture. And, honestly, all of this is long overdue.

Are We Decolonizing or Indigenizing?

My answer to this question is: It depends. From where I sit in the world, Indigenizing is focused on the integration and centering of Indigenous language, practices, stewardship, ethos, history, and culture. Indigenizing, for me, is the practice of curating the space for, with, and by Indigenous peoples. When grappling with which word applies, we need to sit in a space of reflection around the context of our work and our collective goal. Is the entirety of the work focused on Indigenous peoples and are we actively collaborating with Indigenous peoples? Are we simultaneously redressing colonial harm by being accountable for the organization's (and society's) colonial legacy, disrupting the colonial voice, and actively changing the colonial paradigm in which we operate? If I find that I am answering "yes" to the former question and "no" to the latter question, then I lean into the answer that we most likely are Indigenizing.

This is not to say that Indigenizing is not also an important aspect in, and entry point for, decolonial work. Because it is, especially due to the many ways in which museums violently impact(ed) and profit(ed) off Indigenous people's bodies, cultural resources, land, and knowledge, Indigenous peoples must not be left out of our decolonial work. But working with and referencing Indigenous peoples is only part of decolonial work. When engaging in decolonial work, we must also redress how our museum's colonial legacy continues to harm BIPOC (both locally and globally).

What I see happening in the field lately is that a lot of decolonization work falls under the umbrella of being Indigenizing. I say this not to delegitimize anyone's current or future work in the field: Both Indigenizing and decolonizing are fundamental, important practices. I recognize that the dividing line between Indigenizing and decolonizing can feel blurry. Decolonial work is fluid; it is not a static model. In a field that holds on to so many binaries, it can be challenging to live without a clean-cut answer. I would encourage us to lean into this discomfort, to pause and reflect on our place in it all, and not let the need for absolutes inhibit the work that needs to be done.

Can an Inherently Colonial Institution Be Decolonized?

I grapple with this question frequently; it is a conundrum. The museum field was birthed from colonization. Museums are intentionally and unintentionally beneficiaries and perpetrators of the colonial project, and they are slow to change because they are institutions that hold power, privilege, cultural resources, and ancestors from around the world. Shifting from the colonial to the decolonial isn't something that occurs overnight. Undoing colonialism, and redressing harm takes time; (re)building trust takes time, patience, and accountability through action. We are beginning to see museums nationally and globally make a commitment to this process by way of dedicated staff, budget support, and repatriation due to both legal mandate and social mobilization. This growth gives me hope and excitement for the future.

However, I would be remiss if I was not transparent with you about the apprehension I feel when museums claim that they are the experts and the leaders in decolonization. Many times, we see these assertions of expertise coupled with self-congratulatory statements designed to justify their existence and legitimize their right to power and authority. White supremacy and colonialism are systemic within our field. Even when our museums commit to a decolonial future and employ decolonial thought, colonialism and white supremacy will continue to find ways to manifest within our transformed systems (e.g., in meeting structures, human resources, language, consultants hired, exhibition and preservation, governance, etc.).

Do I know the answer to this question—not yet. I invite you to reflect on these questions that also keep me up at night: Is it ethical for an inherently colonial institution to claim expertise? Is this a replication of colonial practice and BIPOC erasure, yet another iteration of how our field perpetuates colonial harm? And how can we share our successes and challenges and build a decolonial movement in the field, while also being cautious in making grand statements and claiming ownership of the movement?

Is Decolonization a Collective Endeavor?

It is easy to become overwhelmed by the enormity of how deeply embedded colonization is in our lives and in society at large. Colonialism impacts populations differently, and this impact is constantly changing due to intergenerational shifts and social pressures. Decolonial practices need to be adaptive to the ever-changing wants and needs of the communities that are constantly navigating in addressing the different manifestations of colonialism.

I have mentioned that decolonization is a process, one that is fluid and nonlinear. When I think about the transformative effect of decolonization, I think about it in relationship to water. Water is malleable. Water adapts to its surroundings and meets the needs of its environment. Over time, water can change the entire ecology of a place. Water carves valleys, moves mountains, and brings back life. Water connects us to our ancestors and to future generations. Even single drops of water that consistently hit the surface will eventually break through rock, create an opening, and grow into a passage. Like water, one person working toward decolonizing in the field can make a difference, can create a passageway for present and future generations. Similarly, when we work collectively, we move mountains and change the ecology of the museum field. We are water and together we can affect transformative decolonial change.

In Conclusion

Decolonizing practices call for more than being performative in our public programs by setting decolonization as this year's theme for the upcoming webinar series or annual conference. Instead, my request to the field, my relatives and colleagues, and my call to action for museum leaders, is to make both decolonizing and Indigenizing our collective priorities. Let us be accountable to our place in the world and recognize that for many of us the path to authentically achieving our goal is to integrate Indigenizing and decolonizing practices into our strategic plans, our organizational and departmental missions, our fiscal year budgets, and our professional values. What are our excuses for not making a commitment to this work?

Colonial thought is systemic and is still the norm within Euro-American society. I firmly believe that a decolonial future will take deep and ongoing critical reflection, both individually and collectively. It is important for us to honor the actionable pause that creates space to breathe, to ask questions, and to acknowledge that we do not yet know the answers. For myself, I try to look at the relationship between the microscale work and macroscale work and to recognize that in much of our decolonial work the micro is what makes the macro possible. I also encourage us to keep our egos in check and realize that this work is not about us individually, and yet, we must be accountable for our own mistakes. We may all misstep along the way, but it is essential we take action to ensure that the harm and violence of colonialism are not continually perpetuated and replicated.

CHAPTER FIFTEEN

Museums, Disability, and "Uncertain Afters"

Izetta Autumn Mobley

Izetta Autumn Mobley, PhD, is a scholar, facilitator, and museum educator. Her academic work focuses on public history, material and visual culture, gender, race, medicine, and disability. She is the Director of Interpretation, Collections, and Education at the Reginald F. Lewis Museum of African American History and Culture.

The pandemic and social protest have made museums acutely aware of their own biases. Many of us are now deeply familiar with systems of inequity and oppression. Many more now understand that racism, sexism, transphobia, and homophobia are structural. Ableism—discrimination and prejudice against people whose minds or bodies are perceived as falling out of the range of normal or acceptable—however, is a less well-recognized bias. But ableism affects the lives of many Americans, indeed, the lives of almost everyone.

In the United States today approximately sixty million people live with a disability, representing one of the largest—and often unacknowledged—minoritized groups in the United States. As author and disability activist Alice Wong explains, "Disabled people have always existed, whether the word *disability* is used or not. To me, disability is not a monolith, nor is it a clear-cut binary of disabled and nondisabled. Disability is mutable and ever-evolving." Change and difference, in one's body or mind, are conditions of living. Over a lifetime, congenital disability, accidents, illness, or aging impact how we move through the world and what accommodations we need to function as full members of society. Disability is far from outside of the norm. Disability and disabled people *are* the norm.

And the number of disabled people is growing rapidly. Today, right now, over six hundred thousand people have died from COVID-19 in the United States, and more than four million worldwide (both estimated to be gross undercounts). Several studies have noted that at least one in three of those who contract COVID-19 have long-lasting effects, now known as long-haul COVID. Symptoms include continued fatigue, respiratory distress, and cognitive difficulties (brain fog). If one in three of the over 100 million people who contracted COVID in the United States now has long-lasting disability, how are our museums going to respond? How can we build an equitable museum landscape?

More than a decade ago, I served as the docent council chair at the Smithsonian National Museum of African Art. The Smithsonian's docent program attracts brilliant, energetic, and engaged volunteers, whose average age often hovers between sixty and seventy. The docents regularly participate in peer-to-peer learning workshops known among docents as an in-service. But there was a problem. Docents had voiced a bevy of complaints about the in-services, specifically issues related to physical and sensory access.

In an effort to make these programs more accessible and effective, I suggested we set out chairs in the gallery so that participants could see more clearly, take notes during the program, and avoid fatigue caused by standing throughout the workshop. As we began to plan our logistics, I explained that we would need to set up chairs in advance of the program. I wasn't prepared for the battle that ensued and the passionate opinions expressed—not over the role of colonialism in determining African art's presence in American museums, but rather over the message that chairs might convey. I was baffled.

We'd conducted a survey in which docent corps members said they were struggling to stand during our time in the gallery. Folding chairs seemed an easy, simple answer. Yet the Docent Council was against the idea of chairs. Most tellingly, the most frequently voiced objection was one grounded in ableism: that if docents couldn't stand in the gallery during an in-service, then perhaps they shouldn't be giving tours in the first place.

I came to realize this resistance reflected ableist beliefs and more specifically, internalized ableism. Ableism is primarily directed at the disabled; but, it also occurs when a group is labeled as less physically or mentally robust. For instance a corps of incredibly capable and brilliant docents—many of them over sixty and adjusting to new demands and needs from their own bodies—replicates society's ideas about which bodies and minds matter. Having internalized ideas about youth being healthier and stronger, or those who can stand being more worthy, docents couldn't see past their own able-ism to provide the accessibility that would benefit us all.

I wouldn't give up, however. I resorted to setting up more than forty chairs myself, in advance of the session. An interesting thing happened. The very people who had most vociferously complained that there was no need for chairs were some of the first to avail themselves of seats. Those who found they needed to sit after thirty minutes of standing were able to walk over and pull a chair off of the cart. Because the chairs were pre-set, we didn't lose time getting settled and arranged at each object. We no longer lost time as people jockeyed to see the object. And chairs weren't the only accessibility features I'd incorporated. I also made sure every docent had a paper copy of all the objects we would see, so that no one would have to strain to see the artwork. We recorded the presentation so that people could return to get information they missed or had forgotten. The result was an intentional docent learning experience with accessibility built in, and because accessibility was built in, the entire experience was improved.

While disability may be the norm, in the United States at least, we don't all carry the same vulnerabilities around disability. Race, gender, and socio-economic status often impact one's experience with and relationship to disability. Historic redlining policies in cities like Baltimore, Maryland, for instance, often forced low-income people of color, particularly Black Americans, into substandard housing that in turn increased the likelihood of exposure to dangerous and disabling toxins like lead. Nearly 20 percent of students in the District of Columbia have a disability according to the IDEA state profile; DC's percentage of disabled students is nearly six points above the national average of 14 percent.

In February 2019, I spent a crowded afternoon at the National Gallery of Art viewing "Gordon Parks: The New Tide, Early Work 1940–1950." Tucked into a corner of the room was a June 1942 photograph of a young boy standing in the doorway of his Seaton Place southeast home. The young boy's back is to us as he faces the street, leaning slightly to his left as he braces himself on wooden crutches. The caption explained that the young boy lost his right leg when a streetcar hit him while he was playing in his neighborhood.

As a scholar who studies the intersection of race and disability, I was struck by the power of this image. I spent time looking slowly and carefully at it, wondering why I'd never seen it before. As I turned, looking for a perch from which to continue to contemplate the image, I realized there was nowhere to sit in the gallery. If that young boy, now a man in his eighties, came to see his image at the National Gallery, and wanted to linger and think about that moment, where would he have taken a moment to sit and reflect? Was the only place for a Black disabled child in the museum on the wall as a display?

Ableism, like racism, heterosexism, homophobia, and gender bias is structural. Ableism is a core feature of other structural oppressions, all of which can trace their roots back to valuations of bodies, as in, which bodies and thus people, matter, when, where, and why. Because ableism is structural, our responses to it must be both intersectional and structural. That means thinking systemically about where and how we consider and apply equitable practices—especially regarding disability, and most especially in the wake of COVID-19, the largest disabling event in the twenty-first century. That means building structures to respond ethically and equitably to the needs of museum visitors, communities, staff, and stakeholders.

How do we build more equitable structures? Here are some questions museums wishing to address ableism and think critically about disability should consider:

- What are the assumptions we make about our visitors and their disabilities?
- What level of accessibility is present in our built environment, our programming, and our approach? What aspects of access equity are missing? How did we miss them?
- Are we ADA compliant and do we understand the difference between ADA compliance and true access equity?
- What if museums had public health experts on staff? What if there was a psychologist or social worker available through the museum?
- How might a policy of access equity improve the experience for *all* stakeholders in our institution?

Ableism not only impacts our visitors and communities but also reflects the urgent need to drive forward in our work for equity, both inside and outside our institutions. We currently exist in what scholar Keguro Macharia calls an "uncertain after." What comes after a global pandemic that is likely the largest disabling event in US history? What comes after months of protest for racial justice? What comes after an attack on the Capitol? What comes more than thirty years after the passage of the Americans with Disabilities Act?

We live in deeply uncertain times. But what is not uncertain is our need to create and implement structures of equity within our museums. From attending to the accessibility of our built environments to considering how our programming centers accessibility, disability justice, and equity will not happen magically. We must plan for it. Someone must arrive to set up the chairs. How will we build an equitable museum landscape? Not in a meta-phorical way, but in a way that allows Gordon Parks's young boy to have a seat and that invites and challenges the docents to reconsider who belongs in museums and who literally has a right to take a seat at the table.

Uncertain afters may be daunting. They may be a reality of our twenty-first century museum landscape. There is power, however, in planning for and building access equity into our work. There is power in the ability to imagine an otherwise where disability justice and equity are centered in our intersectional anti-bias work in museums. There is power in being willing to do the work of putting out more chairs so that more people can journey with us.

PART V

~

RETHINKING STEWARDSHIP

For more than 200 years, collections have been a defining feature of museums as a class of institution. While some museums do not collect, most do—and these collections are generally deemed to be a resource, the soil and seed stock from which ideas and projects could germinate. Collections were, therefore, generally deemed to be preserved in perpetuity as a public trust and imbued with special—one might say "sacred"—status and significance. But in recent years, growing numbers of museums see collections as a burden and stewardship as a term whose meaning is contested.

Press and media attention has tended to focus on controversies around acquisition (how museums have come to hold different collection items) and deaccessioning (how museums discard or sell objects from their collections). But while these important and vexing issues were being debated, larger, deeper, and more profoundly troubling questions about collections stewardship were being raised. How do collections reflect museums' tangled histories of racism, misogyny, and colonialism? What, exactly, are the utility of canons and the authority of academic expertise? How should museum collections represent their communities and especially people of color, women, LGBTQ persons, the poor, and the powerless? Meanwhile, born-digital collections and the digitizing of physical collections raise additional challenges to conventional ideas of stewardship.

These are not trivial matters. Collections-related questions reflect the large social, cultural, and political concerns of the moment; they also encompass many of the challenges of internal transformation, especially diversity, equity, access, and inclusion (DEAI). And, as complicated as each particular concern or question is on its own, they are deeply entangled with one another, making the project of rethinking stewardship intensely demanding and urgent.

Moving forward is no easy task. As Sven Haakanson points out, museums and other repositories that hold the material culture and histories of Indigenous and other marginalized communities frequently do not understand the meanings and significance of their holdings; in some cases, they do not even know the names by which things are called in communal contexts. This failure of understanding, coupled with ever-changing usages, make museum nomenclature and documentation suspect, impede access by researchers and community members, and render invisible evidence of new and suppressed narratives.

Compromised knowledge also raises questions about the canon and about the authority of experts. Traditional canons, while useful for organizing disparate collections, are really one form of overarching narrative. And to the degree that canons, like other narratives, are partial, skewed, and blinkered, they need to be—and are now being—interrogated. The stewards of those canonical narratives—curators and collections managers—are under pressure to reflect on the limits of their expertise; they are also being asked to step out of their silos and to engage in new forms of transdisciplinary discourse and knowledge production.

At a minimum, as Haakanson suggests, this means taking community knowledge into consideration in framing exhibitions, curricula, and programs. As he notes, museums need to empower Indigenous peoples in "setting the agenda for historical and collections research, and giving them a voice in how their stories are shared with others." Haakanson also argues that both museums and communities can benefit from thoughtful collaboration. If museums accept the challenge of collaboration, they have a chance to become "places of recontextualization, learning, growth, and healing."

In her essay, Mariah Berlanga-Shevchuk takes up the theme of re-visioning collections. The future of collections stewardship, she suggests, is "one in which our collections are active, people-centered, and collaborative." Lazy, unused collections, she writes, are a drain on the museum; trimming collections can actually help to build up museums. Moreover, "deaccessioning is a chance to work collaboratively and practice transparency around decision-making," which in turn creates opportunities to invite communities into the process and will help to produce collections—and new narratives—that are more reflective of the community the museum seeks to serve.

Museums today face growing pressure to decolonize their collections. Looking at how collections came into the possession of museums can be a fraught enterprise, since in many instances, objects of material culture—as well as territory and sacred spaces—were wrested from Indigenous peoples (and from Jewish victims of Nazism) by forced sale, fraud, and outright theft. Other significant objects were simply looted as spoils of conquest and war. Making things right entails dealing with the unsettling prospects of repatriation and reparations, as well as radical deaccessioning.

These are not the only critical issues that arise in considering collections. Scott Carter questions the very term "collections" as it is applied to zoos and related institutions that are responsible for the care of living creatures. In fact, he argues, zoos need to expand their purpose and moral responsibility to embrace the well-being of the non-human, but sentient, animals in their care. As Carter puts it, "We need to understand what animals in zoos need to thrive, how they experience their environment, how they respond to handling and other interactions . . . [and to] structure the visitor experience so that we are enhancing the well-being of both humans and nonhumans."

Collections principles and practices as we have known them for over a century are subject—like all other aspects of museum operations—to radical challenge and continuous change. Museums build significant collections of materials and objects to be able to tell the stories they are charged to tell. But the stories museums tell are in flux. Discrepancies and gaps in collections are coming more clearly into view. And the ways collections are deployed to connect museums with users and communities are changing. In coming years, we can expect that museums will see their stewardship role less as owning and preserving "stuff" and more as centers of moral responsibility, charged with custody of personal and communal stories.

CHAPTER SIXTEEN

Caretakers of Our Histories
Sven Haakanson

Sven Haakanson is an anthropologist at the University of Washington who engages with Indigenous communities in cultural revitalization using material reconstruction as a form of scholarship and teaching. In 2007, he was named a MacArthur Fellow as the "driving force behind the revitalization of indigenous language."

Museums are repositories of our collective humanity that actively reflect histories of our past treatment of each other, the world, and our heritages. Because of what they hold in their collections, many museums control, either knowingly or unknowingly, the histories of Indigenous peoples.

Indigenous peoples have only recently begun to see museums as repositories of their histories, with the power to amplify the traditional values, knowledges, and practices that were erased during times of cultural and colonial genocide. As a tribal member I have seen my culture "owned" by museums across the world, and this situation sparks complex emotions and societal implications. In my view, it is time to transform museums from being "owners of objects" to being "caretakers of our histories."

At present, Indigenous communities seek to better understand histories entangled with conflicts, survival, awareness, reawakening, and change. Many Indigenous communities have not yet fully realized how powerful suppression and exploitation have been and still are for their community members. This historical trauma is now starting to be understood and discussed beyond just Indigenous communities, and for many community members the emotions that are evoked can be overwhelming. However, even with this ongoing legacy of trauma, the resilience of Indigenous communities has given them the strength to survive and start to thrive.

Museums can play an important role in helping support Indigenous communities on their journey toward greater understanding and self-awareness. But museum staff who engage with Indigenous communities need to be knowledgeable about these tangled, contentious colonial histories. Staff need to understand how challenging it can be for Indigenous individuals to encounter their cultural heritage, and, for some, seeing and touching their material culture for the first time. It is important for staff to be prepared for encountering multiple levels of emotional, spiritual, intellectual, and cultural response from Indigenous individuals and communities.

An important first step for museums practicing ethical stewardship is for them to acknowledge their own colonial and racist histories and to train their staffs about systemic racism and historical trauma. They should not avoid the difficult or painful histories because this only leads to ongoing misunderstandings about what really happened in the past. By actively collaborating with communities, museums can change what they share with their visitors.

Starting in 2017 my colleague, Holly Barker, and I were given an opportunity to create an entirely new exhibition for our cultural space. We took this opportunity to actively engage and collaborate with our communities. Throughout this experience we realized that we needed to tell our visitors how we hold ourselves accountable. When the newly built Burke Museum (Washington State Museum) opened its doors to the public in 2019, one of the first signs our visitors encounter in the "Culture Is Living" exhibit is the following statement:

THE BURKE ACKNOWLEDGES

THE VIOLENT LEGACIES OF COLONIALISM

Museums reflect a history of colonialism, a form of cultural dominance, that alienates and misrepresents many communities. Collecting practices often disconnect cultural belongings and art from their people and homes. We recognize that museums often undervalue the involvement of communities by imposing their own authority when deciding how to collect, care for and interpret cultural property. We acknowledge that colonialism continues to exist, and we strive to identify and stop the cycle of objectifying, exotifying and discriminating against communities and cultures.

Haakanson and Barker, Curators of the New Burke "Culture Is Living" Gallery

The process of creating this statement was not only challenging and lengthy, but cathartic and collaborative, allowing our staff to get on board with a new vision for our practices. This took us over a year of active collaboration to draft up with the communities. Items of Indigenous culture may have been taken, stolen, found, gifted, purchased, gathered, or commissioned and then donated or sold to a museum—and to openly state this, changes how a museum treats, understands, and shares this knowledge with communities.

Even in the post-NAGPRA[1] era—when museums were required by law to inventory and share with federally recognized US tribes what human remains, burial materials, and sacred and religious items were housed in their collections—many museums still don't have a clear inventory of what is in their collections locally or from other regions of the world. Ancestral peoples imbued each object with historical and cultural knowledge, and it is no small task to untangle and decipher the intangible cultural knowledge that is embodied within them. Even when museums invest time and energy in studying their Indigenous collections, these materials are frequently misunderstood, misinterpreted, and miscatalogued, and much of this information is neither readily accessible nor verifiable.

My research with collections over the past twenty years has centered on dealing with mislabeled pieces. An example is the large open boats from the Arctic, which were labeled as "umiaq" in every museum I visited up until recently. What I learned from elders is that the name and design of open boats to the south of Nome, Alaska, are called "angyaaq" and not "umiaq." These two types of vessels are similar only because they are framed boats wrapped in skins; however, they are different in their design. A umiak is made for icy waters, whereas an angyaaq is designed for open waters.

This mislabeling has made it seem that the southern angyaaq had disappeared entirely from material history and made it hard for the Sugpiat/Alutiiq communities to find their traditional angyaat (plural in Alutiiq) in collections. This is just one example of mislabeled cultural pieces that has resulted in the effective erasure of Supgiat culture, as reflected by museums, the "owners" and "namers" of the cultural pieces.

My own community had no living knowledge of having large open boats but were able to take a model angyaaq from the Burke Museum's collection and reverse-engineer it to make two full-sized functioning angyaat. As we learned about the unique construction of these seagoing vessels, we shared this knowledge with the museum, changing their understanding of Sugpiat material culture. We also changed the way our Sugpiat youth and community saw our history—not as being limited to the past but as a living and thriving culture. Learning about the angyaaq and bringing this knowledge back into a living context has strengthened the resilience of our communities as we recover and learn about what was once lost.

Caretaking needs to be proactive and collaborative, which requires museums to rethink their relationships with Indigenous peoples. Museums need to acknowledge Indigenous peoples as living communities with living cultures. All too frequently, museums refer to Indigenous peoples only in the past tense or even as extinct. Signage should refer to Indigenous people in the present tense, not only internally but also in exhibitions, public programs, and publications.

Museums should take responsibility for inviting Indigenous communities in, empowering Indigenous peoples to help set the agenda for historical and collections research, and giving them a voice in how their stories are shared with others. Many Indigenous communities want to share their history and culture with museums and other repositories and with the general public. But this need not be a one-way street. Both museums and communities can benefit from thoughtful collaboration.

Reframing museums as caretakers of Indigenous histories and narratives means that museums are obligated to establish and maintain long-term relationships with Indigenous communities. These relationships must go beyond occasional consultations and embrace ongoing collaborations, in which museums hold themselves accountable and get consent from the communities to share their knowledge. In fact, museums will need to support community projects that go beyond the museum walls and engage collaboratively with communities on their terms. These four points—consultation, collaboration, accountability, and consent—are critical steps that a museum can take toward shifting the power dynamics within its own walls.

Acting on these principles will alter the museum's social, ethical, moral, and cultural practices relative to Indigenous peoples and cultures. What is important to understand is that the same learned and inculcated behavior continues to be repeated in our communities and expressed in our museums. Learning about historical trauma is emotionally exhausting, yet it is important to know and understand. Once museums learn about this history, they cannot ignore it nor pretend it is not an issue, especially when this history continues to impact the lives of Indigenous communities.

We are only just starting to open the festering wound of colonialism across our country. To start healing, it is important to use the knowledge that is embodied within collections to show and share the deep cultural knowledge, rich culture, and history our ancestors had prior to colonialism and even now, so that our Indigenous communities can shift from being victims to being active participants in their own futures. Knowing one's cultural heritage and history empowers individuals to create and make their own paths, paths that are not reliant on outsiders telling them who they are or what they can do. By assisting communities in recontextualizing their cultural objects, we are shifting power from museums to the culture bearer as it rightfully should be.

This stewardship compact applies to other populations as well—Africans and African Americans, Latinx, and Asians and Asian Americans—who, like Indigenous peoples, confront systemic racism, erasure, and collective trauma. Even Euro-Americans have histories of ethnic, religious, and racial discrimination. By engaging in collaboration with Indigenous communities, museums are also preparing themselves to address the contested histories and problematic stereotypes of multiple American communities.

We have arrived at an inflection point within our society today. As a nation, we are expanding our awareness of the full diversity of cultural histories; individuals are starting to face and understand at a deeper level the systemic practices of racism and the historical traumas still unfolding today. The consequences of our national policies and the realities of how Indigenous collections came to exist in our museums are now slowly being unraveled and revealed. As we make visible our complex, entangled histories, museums have the power to shift their roles to becoming caretakers of our histories, places of recontextualization, learning, growth, and healing.

Note

1. Native American Graves Protection and Repatriation Act (NAGPRA), Pub. L. 101-601, 25 U.S.C. 3001 et seq., 104 Stat. 304,3, is a United States federal law enacted on November 16, 1990.

CHAPTER SEVENTEEN

The Collective Collection

Active, People-Centered, and Collaborative

Mariah Berlanga-Shevchuk

Mariah Berlanga-Shevchuk is the cultural resources manager at Five Oaks Museum in Washington County, Oregon, where she cares for the museum's archive, object collection, and research library. She also co-manages the guest curator program, which decentralizes the museum's authority in favor of community members to ensure their stories are told equitably and authentically.

> *No volveremos a la normalidad porque la normalidad era el problema.*
> [We won't go back to normal because normal was the problem.]
>
> —Antigovernment protest projection in Santiago, Chile,
> November 2019

Humans collect things. Whether it's seashells, shoes, baseball cards, or books, we like to surround ourselves with the things that remind us of who we are and where we find meaning. But humans also hoard, which has created quite a predicament for museum collections today, especially history museums. We claim that we're collecting, stewarding, or preserving history in the form of physical objects for the public good, but how do permanent collection objects serve the public good if they're relegated to dusty back shelves and boxes, rarely seen and never used? Although some of the objects we collect are rare or exceptional and worth preserving in perpetuity, more often than not, what we've collected does little for the museum holding it or for its audiences. It's evident that we need to change how, why, and what we collect.

The year 2020 forced the entire world to take a critical look at systemic inequality, and museums were not spared in this reckoning. Hyper-consumption, scarcity mindsets, exploitation, and rugged individualism—societal features rooted in white supremacy, colonialism, and capitalism—have made our museums, like all our public institutions, sick. The responses to overlapping racial justice, public health, and climate crises have sent the message loud and clear: The status quo cannot, and will not, stand. If collections are central to the existence of museums (arguably, gathering and interpreting material culture is how museums came to be) then they too should be subject to radical reimagining. So how can we, as collections stewards, respond to the current moment and chart a brave new path forward?

I believe the future of museum collections—and museums themselves—is one in which our collections are active, people-centered, and collaborative. If we want to be the trusted, relevant, social institutions we claim to be, then we must course correct *now*. After all, what are museums (and their collections) without the communities they exist to serve? In my experience, this course correction is challenging but necessary to our survival as an industry.

When I say "active" museum collections, I am referring to the definition set forth in *Active Collections*, edited by Elizabeth Wood, Rainey Tisdale, and Trevor Jones. An active collection is one that *actively* supports its museum's mission through effective use. It is capable of telling many stories and is as much a member of the team as anyone on staff. Most museum professionals know of storage rooms that are overflowing with objects—some 95 to 99 percent of which will never be displayed, handled, or researched. Museums, as nonprofits, need to recognize the drain that lazy, unused collections create on already strained budgets and staff, to say nothing of the environmental costs required for their responsible care.

To ensure our collections are worth the resources it takes to maintain them *and* that they're in service of the greater good, I believe that most, if not all, collections will need to be trimmed down. It is high time museums and their boards address the taboo of deaccessioning. Let's lean into the fact that trimming down can paradoxically build us up as an organization. A commitment to thoughtful, intentional, and transparent deaccessioning allows us to take better care of the objects we wish to preserve in perpetuity and prevents wasting time and labor pseudo-caring for items we know we'll never use. *Active Collections'* proposals for how to give deaccessioned objects another life are based on the well-being of the museum itself and lay to rest fears about the collection becoming a source of financial gain.

Besides the obvious benefits of saving staff time and money, deaccessioning presents a huge opportunity for community involvement. Many museums have a history of exploiting marginalized communities. That exploitation has manifested physically in collections that are harmful to the very communities that museums now wish to engage. Sometimes these collections' contents are racist, violent, and discriminatory; when displayed, these materials are often interpreted through a single voice that only perpetuates feelings of exclusion. These types of collections rarely resonate with visitors beyond a select, privileged few. After the racial reckoning of the Black Lives Matter movement and other responses to police brutality, land theft, and anti-immigration cruelty, many museums rushed to put out hollow statements attempting to make Black, Indigenous, Asian, Latinx, and other people of color feel safe and welcome, despite decades of policies and procedures that indicated otherwise. Although moving toward antiracist and decolonized museum practices is a long-term and ongoing institutional, financial, and individual commitment, collections management is one avenue where we can take immediate action.

As in all arenas of museum work, deaccessioning is a chance to work collaboratively and practice transparency around decision-making. Museum collections in which the museum's community see themselves reflected and represented are the future we need to work toward. This is only possible if our communities are invited into the process and feel that they are stakeholders with a say in how the collection is developed and maintained.

Welcoming community into the collections mix can take shape in many ways. I've had experience with community engagement in collections through advisory committees, guest curator programs, and community collecting initiatives. As Associate Curator at LA Plaza de Cultura y Artes (a Mexican American history museum) from 2018 to 2020, I developed the museum's first exhibition about the Afro-Latinx experience in Los Angeles. LA Plaza is a noncollecting institution, so all exhibition objects must be borrowed from local repositories and individuals. In assembling the exhibition, titled *afroLAtinidad: mi casa, my city*, I quickly realized how little of this community's history had been formally collected by any cultural institution. My advisory committee (composed entirely of Afro-Latinx and Black scholars, activists, and creatives) and I hosted a series of community collecting initiatives based on a model from the Smithsonian National Museum of American History, one of our partners for the project.

The project took an unexpected turn when Afro-Latinx community members, who had agreed to lend their items to our exhibition, were offered the opportunity to donate those items to the Smithsonian to help the national museum tell a fuller story about Afrolatinidad on the West Coast. To my surprise, not a single lender took advantage of this opportunity. Perhaps it should not have been unexpected because it had taken our team many days of listening and explaining before anyone agreed to lend their objects to us. Our community members were concerned that if they loaned us their personal belongings (even temporarily) they might never get them back. This was a huge lesson in the level of mistrust many communities of color feel toward museums.

In instituting the guest curator program at Five Oaks Museum, through which all major exhibitions are created, I encountered similar feelings of mistrust from the communities we wanted to engage. Prior to January 2020, Five Oaks Museum was known as the Washington County Museum, founded early in the twentieth century to tell the stories of European-American settlers in this part of Oregon. Because the museum's aim was largely to preserve and glorify histories that were overwhelmingly violent toward marginalized communities, the collection reflected those histories, with few items that celebrated communities of color. By becoming Five Oaks Museum, we made a commitment to do our best to repair harm and rebuild trust in the communities who had been previously mistreated by our museum.

We realized that the only way to move forward was to give our community members the power to tell their own stories. We invited guest curators to help identify the glaring gaps in our collections—despite our archive, research library, and artifact holdings totaling nearly one hundred thousand items. The gaps reflected decades of privileging a dominant white narrative. There were and continue to be many missing voices and stories. Our collection was criticized not just for what it contained but also for what it didn't. These critiques have been integral to rethinking our museum's role in the community. Working with our guest curators—who typically represent communities omitted from or misrepresented by our collections—has enabled me to advocate for interpreting our relevant holdings in new ways. We then turn that knowledge into a revised, people-centered practice that resonates within the collection and throughout our organization.

Becoming a people-centered collection means we now take a "many hands" approach to interpreting our objects. We prioritize information about the *people* behind the items in our collections. Multiple interpretations are actively encouraged. We stay away from telling a single story and instead convey how many different people would or could have used, made, or appreciated stories about the object. This has helped us broaden our audiences while maintaining our commitment to truth telling. People-centered collections empower communities and museum staff alike to tell multilayered stories about and through objects, a useful criterion for determining which objects are deemed worthy of lifetime preservation. They make room for cultural traditions and values beyond those espoused by white, Euro-American pioneers and their descendants. This practice means that we collect fewer things to tell better stories about what we do collect. When selecting what items to deaccession, we use the tiered system suggested in *Active Collections*, which proposes that collection items be ranked by significance to mission, quality, and rarity. We also consider if other local museums have similar objects we might borrow if needed, so as to avoid collecting duplicates.

When dreaming about the future of museums and their collections, I believe we are nearing the end of collecting as we know it. I'm inspired by the ideas put forth in *Active Collections* as well as the calls to abolish unjust systems in our society. Reimagining museums and their collections goes hand in hand with dreaming big about what a truly inclusive society looks like. There's no failure or victory in exploration and dreaming, only knowledge and growth. Let us be brave and willing to take risks; it is the only way forward.

Further Reading

G. Fabrikant (2009, March 12). *The good stuff in the back room. The New York Times.* https://www.nytimes.com/2009/03/19/arts/artsspecial/19TROVE.html

E. Wood, R. Tisdale, and T. Jones, 2018). *Active Collections.* New York: Routledge, 2018.

CHAPTER EIGHTEEN

Broadening the Institutional Purpose of Zoos in the Post-Pandemic Age

Scott Carter

Scott Carter, chief life sciences officer for the Detroit Zoological Society (DZS), is the executive leader of the mission of the DZS, including animal care, health, welfare, and conservation. He helped found the DZS's Center for Zoo and Aquarium Animal Welfare and Ethics and oversees its programs of science, advocacy, and training.

In the aftermath of our global pandemic, a virus likely resulting from zoonotic transmission from animals to humans, it is high time to reconsider the institutional purpose of zoos and our stewardship role. COVID has only underscored the interconnections of nature and society, of humans and nonhumans. Zoos, historically defined by collecting, owning, and displaying animals, are centers of these relationships.

Although most zoos now focus on those wildlife conservation issues that are driving animal population declines, human/wildlife conflict, and zoonotic disease, I believe that there are additional, equally significant stewardship issues that we need to prioritize.

Zoos are among our nation's most popular attractions: Attendance at accredited zoos in the United States is higher than attendance at major league baseball, football, and soccer games combined. People greatly value opportunities to see, engage with, and be entertained by animals. That hasn't changed, although there have been questions about the ethics of animal captivity.

Zoos have an important role in helping people see and understand person/ animal relationships and not only those integral to species conservation issues. Now is an opportunity for zoos to engage with our guests about additional facets of these relationships, intentionally adopting practices and programs that impact, and call attention to, the well-being of the individual animals in our care.

Our zoos, through their environments as well as the animals in our care, also provide restorative natural experiences. The pandemic underscored the importance of accessible natural spaces like zoos during times of societal unrest. Zoos have the potential to demonstrate the healing power of nature for diverse audiences, through both their natural outdoor areas and the living animals that inhabit them. Our natural environments can support peace and well-being. We saw this after we reopened during the pandemic to great public demand; people were eager to connect with animals and nature after months of staying at home.

To truly deliver on providing healing experiences, we must better align the guest experience and the animal experience by ensuring the well-being of both. Just as we strive to take care of our visitors, we must fully commit to and advance our understanding of animal well-being. How can guests have a positive, peaceful, or regenerative experience if they believe that the animals they're seeing are not thriving, or, worse, are suffering? Increasingly, therefore, zoos and aquaria are focusing on the well-being of the animals in their care. I believe that this is essential to fulfilling our mandate and mission.

Addressing animal well-being involves several dimensions, including vocabulary (how we describe animals in our care), environments, experiences, and when appropriate, when we need to remove those animals in our care (even popular ones that draw crowds) to non-zoo centers that better address their specific needs. Although many of our outward-facing public relations and marketing materials go to great lengths to personalize the animals in our care, too many of our operational, structural, and guiding principles reflect a deep human/nonhuman divide.

We must do the work necessary to understand animals' lived experiences more fully. Critics of zoos claim that animals in captivity suffer because they are in captivity, and even people who visit zoos might question what they see, up to and including claiming that animals they see are suffering. Zoos must commit to the work necessary to understand how animals experience their zoo environments, to transparency in sharing with our guests both what we know about animals' experiences and what is being done to know more, and to the hard decisions and changes that greater understanding might make necessary. Ethically, we owe this to the animals we choose to keep and to the people who visit our zoos.

The way we talk about animals, the way we tell their stories in our marketing campaigns, social media platforms, and education programming, intentionally describes animals as individuals with names, unique experiences, and intentions. This is because we know that people connect with individuals (whether human or animal), especially when they have an identity and there is a way to identify with them. The emerging zoo educational strategy of empathy building to increase visitors' conservation action is based on these potential connections.

Zoos' marketing departments have long understood this connective power, as shown by the experience of the National Zoo and its giant pandas. Knowing an animal's name is an entry point for people to feel connection; knowing an animal's story is the hook that more fully engages and potentially (and hopefully) moves people to greater learning or to action. People love details about the individual animal they're looking at more than they love learning scientific names. Knowing there's a snow monkey named Jun at the Detroit Zoo helps people understand that all the snow monkeys in the zoo are unique individuals and that when they return, they can look for Jun (or in other cities for a hippo named Fiona or a polar bear named Gus). It remains to be learned whether knowing (and potentially caring about) Jun, Fiona, and Gus leads to actions or behavior that benefits the conservation of animals in nature but making the connection is still important and is a unique opportunity for zoos.

When our visitors connect with animals, they also feel connection with us as organizations. This connection is vital to the outcomes we want zoo visitors to have in terms of understanding and respecting animals, to learning, and to potentially changing behavior. It is also vital to how they feel about (and support) our organizations.

Scientists have long resisted anthropomorphizing animals, but this practice may be important and not only for empathy building in support of conservation education. Anthropomorphizing may also develop a sense of caring for another being, which is a fundamental first step to creating the connections that may result in action.

In addition, zoos must apply what we know and understand about animals' lived experiences to avoid creating environments that privilege guests at the expense of animals. We must create environments in which animals can truly thrive. This means going beyond providing food, water, and shelter. It means providing twenty-four-hour, species-appropriate choice and control within these environments. We must consider the needs not only of the species but also of the individual animals who live in our zoos.

Prioritizing guests' experiences over those of animals—which can occur in certain handling activities and other programs—comes at a cost to animals that is still not well understood. Although zoos have used these activities to promote conservation practices among our publics, these activities could be unwelcome to the individual animals involved. And while accredited zoos claim strong impact of these conservation education programs, there is scant compelling evidence of these programs on visitor behavior.

Even though Darwinian views of ecology and traditional field conservation approaches consider the well-being of individual animals below that of populations, zoos cannot make that choice. We must ensure the physical and psychological well-being of the animals in our care, *and* we must contribute to the conservation of nature in meaningful ways. We must provide what animals need, including physical and psychological well-being, what our visitors need in our parks and campuses, and be advocates for what nature needs outside our gates.

The pandemic could and should be an inflection point for zoos. It should be when zoos broaden their institutional purposes as trusted and valued custodians of animals and stewards of nature to include and be defined as centers of both human and animal well-being. It should be when zoos continue to shape public expectations of zoos through explicit approaches to stewardship that privilege and recognize animal welfare as much as human expectations and experiences. It should be when animal welfare is explicit and visible in all our missions.

We have the authority and the ability to better understand the lived experience of the animals in our care. We must continue the scientific research needed to understand how zoo animals see their worlds, so that we can ensure that the worlds we create for them are ones in which they can thrive. We also must share this important work with our visitors and audiences. The work begins with a stewardship framework that implicitly and explicitly privileges the living beings who reside in our spaces, emphasizing our obligations as advocates and protectors of their well-being and not just custodians of their care.

This is the time to reflect on our institutional purpose and societal value. We have the opportunity for zoos to consider how we are performing with respect to the well-being of animals and of people, for the benefit of both.

PART VI

~

RETHINKING VISITORS

For more than a century, museums have seen themselves and been viewed by others as sites of entertainment, education, and public service. Over recent decades, museums have been charged to address issues of equity, internally and in their communities of service. The nested crises of the COVID pandemic have imposed yet additional responsibilities on our museums. The upheavals in our economy, society, and polity have affected the lives of nearly all Americans, inflicting trauma on individuals, institutions, and communities and forcing us to reconsider work, life, education, and leisure. The pandemic and racial reckoning have caused major changes in our behavior, including cultural presentation and participation.

In effect, the pandemic has made all of us witnesses to history and seekers of understanding. These circumstances have underscored the importance of museums as sites of meaning making, healing, and community-building. As David Carr put it, "I advocate the importance of cultural institutions helping people to increase their capacity to grasp, negotiate, adapt, and respond to change in their lives."[1]

But before museums can help people adjust to novelty, they must think about the people who come to visit, in person and online. Educators and evaluators have given close attention to different types of users, their expectations, and their needs. Study after study has confirmed that—far from arriving as empty vessels—most visitors arrive at the museum intentionally and with an array of expectations.[2] Frequent visitors, the "museum adepts," come for their aesthetic or spiritual pleasure or their enjoyment of lifelong learning.

Families and groups come to museums seeking a social experience that they can share with their familiars. Some visitors look to museums, which are widely considered to be accurate and even authoritative storytellers, as sources of confirmation for their personal views of the world and its history.[3]

As people young and old try to make sense of what is happening around them, they look to museums as conveyors of narratives that can answer their questions and restore a sense of coherence in their unsettled lives. But, as Erin Carlson Mast explains, the narratives that people discover in museums can also run counter to their values, traditions, and even their experience. When visitors arrive looking for confirmation, challenging their assumptions and expectations can be a fraught enterprise. Still, she argues, museums need to respond to the proliferation of lies and misleading narratives about the past and present that prevail in the media and current public discourse. Addressing the dissonance in our personal and collective narratives, Mast argues, will require sustained dialogue with our visitors and users if we hope to share evidence and build mutual understanding.

Given our unsettling times, however, museums may now have to assume new responsibility for the well-being of their users. One dimension of this is what Beck Tench terms "holding space," helping visitors (and staff, too) engage safely in deep exchanges within the museum's precincts. "Holding space," she argues, "is a practice of attention and emotional generosity. It is inner work that extends beyond ourselves and infuses any space, be it an exhibit hall or a Zoom room, with a sense that everyone there is worthy and welcome." At the same time, the experience of holding space can be terrifying to staff and visitors, stirring up old traumas and deep-seated fears. Learning to hold space will require museums to rethink their current praxis and acquire new skill sets that can respond to the emotional states of their audiences.[4]

Dawnette Samuels also encourages museums and museum staff to transcend their business-as-usual attitudes and practices. Instead, museum people need to be prepared for the unexpected, those moments when individuals require intense attention and engagement. Like other storytelling agencies, museums can set off powerful feelings among their users. "Finding those opportunities for personal connections is key," she writes. "And this kind of deep connection can convert an ordinary museum visit into a transformative experience, an experience that invokes inspiration, restoration, reflection, or respite." New approaches can bring together people regardless of race, gender, class, or age, Samuels suggests, by providing a sense of comfort and ease in our spaces.

We cannot hope to replicate our pre-COVID visitation: Colleen Dillen-schneider's research shows that demographic trends mean that museums cannot replace current audiences with like publics.[5] Museums will therefore need to address the complexities and contradictions of welcoming new, more diverse audiences. Like our visitors, museums and those who work in them, are themselves are on a journey, whether they know it or not. If museums want their staff and visitors and the communities they represent to benefit more fully from their mutual engagement, then museums will have to experiment with new ways to connect their respective journeys. Museums will also need to make safe spaces for visitors as they struggle for comprehension, connection, and healing. Humanizing the visitor experience, in ways that acknowledge difference and broaden understanding, will be an essential investment in future civic discourse.

Notes

1. David Carr, *Open Conversations: Public Learning in Libraries and Museums.* (Santa Barbara, CA: Libraries Unlimited, 2011), xiv.

2. See, for example, John H. Falk and Lynn D. Dierking, *The Museum Experience Revisited.* (Walnut Creek, CA: Left Coast Press, 2013).

3. A recent study conducted by the American Historical Association found that "Although museums were of only middling popularity, they took the top spot for historical dependability." https://www.historians.org/publications-and-directories /perspectives-on-history/september-2021/a-snapshot-of-the-publics-views-on-history -national-poll-offers-valuable-insights-for-historians-and-advocates

4. Carr also calls attention to "the thoughts of the user, about the interior, word-less experiences, the pauses, the interpretations, the conversations with the situation," *Open Conversations*, xix.

5. https://www.colleendilen.com/2017/01/25/negative-substitution-why-cultural -organizations-must-better-engage-new-audiences-fast-data/. See also, American Alliance of Museums/Wilkening Consulting "Audiences and Inclusion: A Primer for Cultivating More Inclusive Attitudes among the Public." https://www.aam-us .org/2021/02/09/audiences-and-inclusion-primer/

CHAPTER NINETEEN

On Bearing Witness

Erin Carlson Mast

Erin Carlson Mast is president and CEO of the Lincoln Presidential Foundation. Previously, she was the first woman to lead President Lincoln's Cottage, a National Monument in Washington, DC. She has written on living the organizational vision, museums of ideas, and transformative experiences. Her expertise includes start-ups, public-private partnerships, and strategic planning.

During the past two years, all of us have been witness to an unprecedented series of ruptures and upheavals. These nested crises have included a global pandemic, insurrection, and record-breaking wildfires. Our ability to understand those upheavals has been enriched but also confused by a multiplicity of viewpoints—each conditioned by individual experience and social situation. This idea is encapsulated in a classic scene from *Star Wars: Return of the Jedi*, in which Luke Skywalker accuses Obi Wan Kenobi of lying to him, and Kenobi counters that what he told Skywalker was true, "from a certain point of view." When Skywalker balks, Kenobi continues, "Luke, you're going to find that many of the truths we cling to depend greatly on our own point of view." Consequently, our collective understanding has been compromised and distorted by a proliferation of lies and misleading narratives about the past and present.

Amid this kaleidoscope of information and misinformation, perspectives and opinions, our museums have been thrust into prominence as potential sites of conscience and clarification. It has long been the responsibility of museums and museum people to gather and preserve evidence, identify what is authentic and accurate and what is not, and explain why we think so. In short, museums have taken on the task of bearing witness, testifying to what is real and true and sharing those testimonies with our communities.

Even in the best of times, however, there are inherent tensions in our practice. How much do professionalism and expertise matter? How do we determine who is the arbiter of truth? How can we overcome our own knowledge deficits in the face of incomplete and sometimes contradictory information? How can we assist our visitors and users to make meaning out of disruption, distress, divisiveness, and disinformation? These ongoing challenges, of course, are exacerbated in the present moment.

Here are some truths. Each of us has a point of view, a system of beliefs, a perception of reality, formed by our lived experiences. Everyone who engages with our museums and sites is bringing their own lifetime of experiences, their own beliefs, their own expertise or level of interest, however long or short their lifetime. Our core beliefs inform how we approach and think about our work and our situation; they also shape how we react to whatever we are witnessing in life—whether personal, such as an ill loved one, or communal, such as seeing police or gun violence. That is as true for our board members, staffs, donors, and volunteers as it is for our visitors.

Moreover, we practice in a continually changing environment. We uncover and piece together information, physical evidence, written record, and oral tradition, making new discoveries all the time. We interpret what we find to make sense of what happened despite gaps in our knowledge and contradictory evidence. The more information that is added, the more complex the pattern. Sometimes a subtle shift, a new take on the information, changes the pattern entirely. Based on our best information, we use our training and expertise to provide experiences for and with the public, and in so doing, we create ephemeral moments of truth, together. Ephemeral not because they lack gravity but because they are subject to nuance and perspective, to reinterpretation as more evidence is gathered over time, changing the perspective along the way to reveal different, vibrant understandings.

Bearing witness in a kaleidoscopic zone requires investment in the ability to change. If we are continually doing the work in science, art, and the humanities to learn more and add more layers, interpretation would be understood as dynamic, and methodology would needs be adaptable. And yet, we all know of museums or sites that have used the same signage for a generation or recited the same tour script for decades. Disinvestment can be viewed as disinformation by neglect. Expectations of "permanence"—permanent exhibits, monuments, holding collections in perpetuity—are unreasonable when the world around us and the people who engage, particularly visitors, are constantly changing.

Adjacent to the museums and sites that never seem to change are the ones that achieve the appearance of change on the surface by using jargon like "relevance" or cribbing trendy methodology, without addressing root issues that would result in more lasting, meaningful change. The effect is that of four-year-olds playing soccer, bunching together around the same ball being kicked here there and everywhere without much focus. When you're focused on chasing a ball wherever it goes, it's easy to avoid conversations about who is calling the plays, who is on the playing field, who has been sidelined, and why we're playing the game. In short, it's a good way to look busy without achieving meaningful change. Are we honest about the ultimate purpose and impact of our work or do we fall back on tradition, routine, and best practice without questioning who created those frameworks?

As if the challenges of interpretation and engagement were not difficult enough, in recent years Americans have been engulfed by a tidal wave of misinformation and disinformation fed from various sources. One source of this "bad" information is people opinionating from positions of collective or social influence without expertise or understanding. Another source is traditional or conventional myths and narratives that are demonstrably false yet still hold sway. And another source is political partisans seeking advantage over their adversaries. The late Senator Daniel Patrick Moynihan popularized the saying, "Everybody is entitled to his own opinion but not his own facts." Despite the logic of this pronouncement, many Americans are all too ready to embrace not only alternative facts but also alternative realities.

We can be so immersed in disinformation that even when it's causing existential harm, we refuse to accept reality and change our minds, change our behaviors. Disinformation then influences systems, including education policy and practices. How the pandemic is interpreted in the future will need to account for the fact that there has been so much disinformation in our own time, an absence of accountability, and highly divergent experiences between individuals and communities.

The result is remarkable dissonance in our personal and collective narratives. One distressing example was the phenomenon of people denying COVID-19 existed while they themselves were dying from it. There are numerous accounts from nurses who had patients that, to their last breath, insisted they couldn't be dying from the coronavirus. They had believed that the virus was overblown or, "no worse than the flu," or was a hoax. What does this have to do with our work? Quite a bit, actually.

As an exercise, replace "cause of death" with "cause of the Civil War." Anyone who works at a site touched by or a museum that deals with the Civil War knows this all too well. The overwhelming evidence, left behind in copious documentation from the Confederate leadership itself, is that the Confederacy seceded and initiated a civil war (by attacking a federal fort) to protect slavery. And yet that evidence is still refuted in the twenty-first century, thanks in no small part to more than 150 years of coordinated disinformation about the Civil War, from no less than the former leadership of the Confederacy who spun the Lost Cause narrative. There are individuals, including public figures and policy makers in recent years, who have asserted that the Civil War was caused by a "failure to compromise" or "to protect states' rights." This is perpetuation of misinformation—half-truths and euphemisms to support a false narrative.

How can our museums bear accurate and authentic witness to history and to the present moment without alienating our stakeholders and communities? Telling someone "a" truth they could perceive as denying "their" truth would likely make them become defensive. That doesn't mean we should equivocate or treat all opinions as equal; it's a reminder that beliefs are not always based on reliable evidence and facts alone are unlikely to change deeply held beliefs.

So how should we proceed? One way to achieve the goal of public trust and adaptability is through the kind of meaningful dialogue that takes place each day at so many sites of conscience. These are places that have fully embraced the power of dialogue as an effective tool for sharing evidence, building understanding, challenging confirmation bias, and grappling with cognitive dissonance. A collaborative—not competitive—approach to difficult conversations requires a grasp of complexity and nuance and the expectation of continual review and reinterpretation. We should always strive for the genuine, "I hadn't thought of it that way before now" moments, not only for our public but, if we're listening, also for ourselves.

We have little control over where we fall in a visitor's personal timeline, or how long we spend together, but if we fulfill our purpose, whatever evidence and conversational experience we provide creates an opportunity to reflect and to reconsider ideas and actions—to be vulnerable and open to change. If we wait to play clean-up, we are passing the buck to future generations. Historical disinformation and contemporary disinformation are neither separate nor sequential. We must be diligent in resisting disinformation before it can take root and spread in all directions.

Over recent decades, studies in the United States have indicated that museums and sites are among the most trusted institutions by the American people, more trusted than local news, the US government, and academic researchers. Museum professionals have celebrated that news. Although some have raised questions about how cognizant the public is about aspects of our practice such as interpretation or the negative reactions some institutions have received from audiences after incorporating previously suppressed viewpoints, a more fundamental question lies beneath: Have our organizations proven they are worthy of trust?

Now is the time to prove we are worthy of that trust. Our world is facing problems that we must solve together. That has always been the case. Each of our sites and museums bears witness to this. Solutions must reckon with humanity's difficult relationship with the "truth." Now is the time to reevaluate the truth in our work, openly, to earn the public trust every day. This will cause friction. This will cause disruption. This will create transformation. Our future depends on it.

CHAPTER TWENTY

Holding the Space We Make

Beck Tench

Beck Tench is a designer, technologist, researcher, and educator. Currently a doctoral candidate at the University of Washington Information School, Beck studies how to facilitate contemplative experience through the design of public space.

> Let no one hope to find in contemplation an escape from conflict, from anguish, or from doubt. On the contrary, the deep certitude of the con-templative experience awakens a tragic anguish and opens many ques-tions in the depth of the heart like wounds that cannot stop bleeding.

> —Thomas Merton, *New Seeds of Contemplation*

A few years ago, I attended a conference I'll never forget. It was in an idyl-lic setting. The speakers and content were exemplary. Even the food was memorable. But the reasons I won't forget it are because of the way space was held for me while I was there—the way I was held with an open heart and unconditional support—and what that enabled in and through me.

At the conference, during get-to-know-you small talk, I'd mentioned that I was getting married that summer. I'd also revealed that my father was upset to hear that his daughter was marrying a woman and offended that I'd tell him about my wedding in the first place. Moments later, I found myself sit-ting next to someone who, though we'd only just met, was crying and apolo-gizing to me. She told me that to attend the conference, she'd chosen to miss a special day at her church, one she looked forward to all year. The day was a day of atonement, and with some hesitance, she asked if she could atone for anything she might have done in her life to cause suffering in mine. I was apprehensive, but I said yes, and her tearful apology was respectful and utterly sincere. It righted something wronged in me and, in some ways, healed a wound that she had no role in creating. I felt deeply connected to her, and I am sure she felt the same.

As a participant in that moment, I look back on the experience with gratitude for the attention and care we had for one another. But as a practitioner and educator, I see it with different eyes. And I believe that this practice has meaning and resonance for our work in museums.

Before we sat down next to each other, before we boarded our planes to California, before we filled out the online registration form, the conference organizers were engaged in a process of making space, both literal and figurative. They spent months picking the right content, the right environment, and the right participants. The conference organizers set the stage, just as museums so thoughtfully do the world over. But in that moment between the two of us, those organizers were actively engaged in a different kind of work. They were *holding space* for us to fill. Had the organizers succumbed to the inevitable doubts and fears that arose for them in the moment of that conversation (and countless ones before and after), the space would have closed or been too full of other things to meet it in the way we did. It would never have emerged.

As museum practitioners, we already know how to make space, both literal and figurative, but making space is not enough. We must also hold it open, despite fear and doubt. We must trust our visitors to meaningfully fill that space, without exception. And, most challenging, we must trust ourselves to have the capacity and wherewithal to contain whatever is generated inside of the space we make.

Holding space is a practice of attention and emotional generosity. It is inner work that extends beyond ourselves and infuses any space, be it an exhibit hall or a Zoom room, with a sense that everyone there is worthy and welcome. There's no five-step framework to do it, and even if there were, it would be an iterative process riddled with doubt and mystery and require many repetitions to do at all, much less to do well. Holding space relies on tacit knowledge built over years of trying to hold space.

We've all had moments where we felt safe, even accompanied, in an experience that would otherwise be challenging for some good reason or another. Often, at the center of those experiences is an individual, or group of individuals, engaging in a particular kind of work. Perhaps you are one of these individuals, or you are attempting to be. They extend a spacious, watchful, and protective attention around the space. In that heartfelt attention, they take responsibility for the space and repeatedly show up to the difficult task of loving those within it (including themselves), moment by moment.

With words like "heartfelt" and "love," you might think this work is comforting and positive, but it isn't always so. Indeed, the experience of holding space can be terrifying and stir up old traumas and deep-seated fears. When I am teaching or running an event, I am frequently haunted by experiences of being bullied as a child. I notice a snicker between two people or a look of disengagement, and the space I'm holding shrinks to surround and protect only me. Though the work of holding space is largely invisible, it can be felt by everyone when it abruptly ends.

Holding space can also be seen in the effort we take to care for others. In my classroom, it looks like memorizing the names of my students before the first day of class. It's the questions I ask and the way I listen and care about the answers. It's generous grading policies and unearned trust. In our museums, it might look like signage, programming, spatial arrangements, policies, or email marketing campaigns. In whatever ways it manifests externally, holding space is always an internal project that ripples outward in subtle and dynamic ways. Institutionally, it is an internal project, too. It requires an institutional culture that gives staff the space, time, and permission to be reflective, generous, and observant. We cannot hold space for our visitors without having space ourselves.

Holding space requires the courage to love others, which is challenging enough, and the self-awareness to recognize when that courage comes under fire. We must continually monitor our own inner experience, notice when we've lost our confidence, and quickly repair. To do this, we must see our visitors as the warm-blooded human beings that they are. We must realize that they have rich, complicated, and important histories, just like us, that they long for friendship, want to be caring and kind, and want to be loved, just like us. We must also realize that they frequently fall short of those things and may be ashamed of that. Just like us. There is no exception because they are human, just like us. When we hold space for people we do not know, and maybe especially for people we do, we must realize and remember how messy and brave and goofy and selfish and wonderful every single one of us is. Seeing our common humanity generates compassion for ourselves and for others and fuels the work of love.

The experience of holding space in the ways I have described is a contemplative practice, by which I mean it requires us to participate in the world with our full attention and an open heart. And like all contemplative practices, the real work is noticing when you've drifted and are coming back. You may notice that holding space doesn't always look like holding space. Sometimes, it looks like failing to hold space. This is because we build strength by overcoming resistance and failing to hold space provides resistance. Trying again overcomes that resistance. When we are skilled at holding space, we are skilled at trying, again and again, to read and correct in a dynamic situation. Without moments of failure, we'd never build the capacity for attention and love that are the holding of space.

As Thomas Merton warns us, contemplative experiences "awaken a tragic anguish," and open "questions in the depths of the heart like wounds that cannot stop bleeding." Far from experiences of bliss or peace marketed to us in articles about mindfulness, cultivating open-hearted awareness means staying present to our messiness and the messiness of others. As museum practitioners, the experience of doing this will, most likely, include moments of conflict, anguish, and doubt. Most likely, too, you'll never know the true impact of the work, just as the conference organizers who made space for the stranger and me have no idea that our conversation took place. Those who are affected by the space you hold may remain grateful to you, and to each other, in ways never acknowledged or known.

Why do all this work? To that I ask, why tell a stranger about my father? Why ask a stranger to atone? We do this work because holding space for people to be messy, hurt, and beautiful invites them to see and, for a moment, perhaps love those things in themselves and each other.

In the wake of the pandemic, we are living in an especially fraught moment. If, with this book, we are each asking the question, "how do we meet this moment?" the answer is obvious to me. We meet it like we meet every moment: by paying attention to it, opening our hearts for it, and noticing when we are caught up in thoughts about moments that aren't this one. Indeed, this is as close to a five-step framework for holding space as we'll ever get. We meet this moment by holding those within it—including ourselves—with compassion, curiosity, and respect. And with full attention and a racing heart, we allow the moment to meet us.

CHAPTER TWENTY-ONE

Discovering Connections

Supporting the Quest for Meaning and Well-Being

Dawnette Samuels

Dawnette Samuels is a multimedia artist and the manager of visitor experience and interpretation at the Rubin Museum of Art, where she develops programs for gallery activities and leads guided visits for all audiences.

Museums have the means to support an individual's quest for meaning and well-being; they also have the ability to spark deeply personal and transformative experiences. Those are moments when visitors can go beneath the surface and find a deep meaning within a work of art or historical object, in an engaging activity or a compelling narrative that resonates in their lives. This kind of deep connection can convert an ordinary museum visit into a transformative experience that evokes inspiration, restoration, reflection, or respite.

I got a glimpse of this a few years ago, when I served as a docent for the Dream-Over, a sleepover-based program at the Rubin Museum of Art. Attendees get to sleep in the galleries beneath a specific work of art, participate in a discussion about dreams in the Tibetan Buddhist tradition, and listen to a bedtime story.

I was tired from a long day of work and feeling that leading the evening's program was routine. But my experience with one of the participants was extraordinary. One guest's sleeping spot was under a painting of the fierce and wrathful Buddhist protector Shri Devi, a deity who wears a crown of five human skulls, a long garland of human heads, and flayed elephant and human skin tied around her body. It is a powerful image, and for those who are unfamiliar, it might be a tricky one under which to fall asleep. So I explained the protective nature of this deity, described how wrathful deities tend to embody the fierce nature of compassion or wisdom, and read a story inspired by the painting.

The story suggested how this fierce protective nature can abide within us all. To my surprise, my guest shared with me their personal story: They had intended to come to the event with their partner of many years, but the relationship had just ended. They were anxious and hesitant to come alone but spending the night with a Buddhist protector like Shri Devi and knowing that this deity's nature can exist in everyone gave them a sense of courage and strength and the feeling they would be all right. The painting became an unexpected springboard to a level of comfort at that moment in their life. This interaction helped me understand that although this experience was unique to that program participant, the possibility of an individual's deeper connection to both art and another person is not.

I was hoping to help this person gain an understanding of this artwork and its cultural context, but I didn't anticipate the deep personal connection it evoked. Typically, visitors engage with the painting's label or a docent and learn that it is a seventeenth-century painting from Tibet. They can see and appreciate the use of red, yellow, blue, white, and gold pigments on a black background. They can notice and analyze the many fine details in the painting. They then move on to view the next object within the exhibition space. But what if we were to interject moments of possible connection between the moments of observation and learning? For the Dream-Over participant the themes of protection, strength, and overcoming adversity resonated and transformed their experience into one of comfort. But the transformative part to the experience was the opportunity to engage in a dialogue and to connect with another person.

On the surface, my interaction with the Dream-Over participant was one of teacher and student. It was formally an exchange in which I shared information and they learned something new. However, our interaction is what enabled the transformative experience. For the Dream-Over participant, I wasn't just a docent, I was a person, someone who could listen to their personal story and engage with them. We shared physical space with each other and used the art as a bridge of connection between us. That bridge created a moment of resonance that resulted in each of us discovering a deeper meaning.

That depth could not be uncovered without the connection of one person to another and the sharing of their unique experiences. One of the museum's roles is to create a space that invites this kind of dialogue and connection to others, even among strangers who have come to the museum separately.

There are, however, many barriers to making those transformative moments possible. For one thing, museums tend to focus on serving groups and communities. But how we define "communities" can be elusive. The word itself has become a buzzword rather than describing a well-defined audience. That lack of clarity hinders museum staff's ability to understand who they are really serving. Our attempts to clearly define these communities is even more difficult when you think of the many communities to which a single person can belong, each with its own characteristics and affinities.

The idea of serving the individual can also be challenging because no two people are alike. And if we focus on supporting the needs of a single person, we may be ignoring or excluding others. But one thing we have learned as we emerge from the global pandemic is that we as individuals need to connect with others, and these connections can help to link even complete strangers in a moment of camaraderie.

A third challenge museums face is how to welcome diverse visitors. Museums need to consider all the ways in which an individual navigates and connects to our collections. Race, gender, class, and age can greatly impact how welcome a visitor feels within our space. Culture and ethnicity can influence how our narratives are perceived regardless of the neutral tone and language we aspire to present.

Today, people are holding institutions more accountable. The rise in protests by marginalized communities shows many expect a higher, far more inclusive standard in all the dimensions of our museum work. Institutions that hope to become transformative, welcoming spaces for visitors need to meet that standard. As we attempt to build meaningful connections for our visitors, we should also be mindful of who might be excluded. We need honesty and deep reflection about how we may have unintentionally excluded individuals from a sense of comfort and respite in our spaces. We need to acknowledge our shortcomings.

This reflection, followed by thoughtful action, will allow space for our visitors to find a deeper connection within our museum spaces and perhaps find connections with others, whether staff or other visitors. Our job, as museum staff, is to help visitors discover those connections by creating opportunities to talk and share and by making them accessible to all.

But what role could museums play in creating connections and communities of interest? If we look back at the connection between me and the Dream-Over participant, the exhibition acted as a stage and the program provided a setting for us to engage. This combination stage and setting was vital in creating the opportunity for two strangers to interact with one an-other. Our museum's physical spaces already provide the stage, but it's the intentional creation of interpretive and programmatic settings that allow for visitors to engage not just with the art but also with their fellow museum-goers. These settings can take on the form of a program, an interactive engagement, a tour, or even simple prompts silkscreened on museum walls. What's important is that the setting is welcoming and safe and lets visitors know it's okay to interact with each other.

Museums can be seen as intimidating by many visitors and, thus, evoke a feeling of distance. We must identify and break the barriers that cause this alienation. Is the language used throughout the museum accessible or does it require prior knowledge to understand? Are the museum staff who engage with visitors welcoming or is personal demeanor devalued by their museum? For historical content, are we allowing multiple truths to surface and be in-cluded within our narratives or are we insistent in telling history from only one perspective? Through an ongoing process of candid questioning and evaluation, we can begin to identity obstacles to conversation and alter our environments, programs, and interpretation to set the stage for deeper con-nections to occur. This stage and setting will allow for genuine interactions to take place and give visitors the agency to create communities based on their encounters and shared interests.

Museums have the opportunity to play a key role in providing spaces where visitors can engage with each other on a deeper level using the mu-seum's content as a catalyst. But we first must be willing to change and to go through a transformation ourselves. We must dismantle the idea that only those of a certain status can enter our spaces and become a place where all feel welcomed. We need to become spaces in which strangers can feel com-fortable engaging in dialogue and establishing connections. Only then can we support the visitors within our spaces and foster a sense of community.

PART VII

RETHINKING LEADERSHIP

After the events of 2020, there is nary a sector in the global workplace where change has not been felt, and we still don't know how the chips will fall. In March 2021, British thought leader Margaret Heffernan dubbed uncertainty "the primary characteristic of our time." She noted that uncertainty cannot be measured, or quantified, hence responding to it requires other skills and approaches. "In the face of uncertainty, efficiency is not your friend." Complacency, and a belief that things will return to "normal," is also not an option.[1]

Museums are hardly immune from our uncertain times. From the highest leadership levels to the entire staff, they need to recruit for (and build within) the skills and competencies needed for today's volatile, uncertain, complex, and ambiguous (VUCA) environment. The challenges facing our society and our communities—from climate change to demographic shifts to economic inequality—are complex, often "wicked" problems and not solvable using technical approaches that can be found in any "best practices" playbook.

These challenges require an adaptive leadership approach that scrutinizes, revises, and likely dismantles the old hierarchies that have remained in the museum sector long after many innovative for-profits have abandoned them. In August 2021, McKinsey & Company published an article contending that "adaptability is the critical success factor during periods of transformation and systemic change," instead of a more frequent, more comfortable, default "to familiar patterns or whatever solutions worked the last time."[2]

The key ingredients for successful leadership in conditions of uncertainty are curiosity, imagination, the ability to scan the horizon for unexpected opportunities, and the willingness to experiment. Amy Gilman, director of the Chazen Museum of Art, suggests that effective leaders will define and implement a limited number of doable goals, develop a distributed and inclusive decision-making process that is "owned" by people throughout the staff, and prioritize risk-taking and experimentation to more effectively engage with the museum's publics. For Gilman, "The director's job is . . . to take a deep breath and trust this new way of working."[3]

Boards need to change as well. The 2021 BoardSource survey of more than eight hundred public charity CEOs and board chairs found boards "preoccupied with fundraising above all else," "disconnected from the communities and the people they serve," "ill-informed about the ecosystems in which their organization is operating," and "lacking in racial and ethnic diversity."

Anne Wallestad, president and CEO of BoardSource, argues that nonprofit boards need to redefine their essential responsibilities and focus on their organization's "reason for being in the world." Instead of a preoccupation with the organization's financial soundness and health, boards need to assess how the organization is contributing to the vitality of its surrounding ecosystem. How is the organization addressing and removing systemic inequities (within itself and within the community)? How is it advancing equitable societal outcomes? How is it shifting the organizational power and voice to "those impacted by the organization's work?"[4]

The contributors to this chapter advocate for the agile, responsive, human-centered dimensions of leadership that these uncertain times demand. They practice the adaptive leadership so necessary for a world of dramatic shifts and complex new challenges. They understand the importance of responding to community needs and tapping into the wisdom of the crowd, whether that "crowd" be their own staffs or voices beyond the museum walls. They are willing to experiment and support innovation; they play well with others.

Within their respective museums, Cindy Meyers Foley and Nannett V. Maciejunes, Franklin Vagnone, and Mariruth Leftwich favor forms of distributed leadership that bolster independent agency among and across the staff. Promoting the initiative of more junior staff not only empowers them but also brings new ideas and new skills to bear on the challenges at hand. Vagnone suggests that leaders need to challenge every dimension of museum structure, shape, and processes, including inverting traditional top-down decision-making. Leftwich stresses building trust throughout the staff and empowering all to embrace a sense of play and curiosity, asking "How might we?" when facing inevitable challenges. Maciejunes and Foley located leadership qualities throughout the museum staff and witnessed their "courageous imagination." Each author advocates for experimentation, shaking up the established order, and taking risks.

In the face of unprecedented change and radical uncertainty, obvious, conventional solutions—and old command-and-control leadership styles—do not apply. Museums need a generation of leaders who are committed to openness, shared authority, experimentation and next practice, and a continuous process of reflection and redirection. These museum leaders are not likely to fall into a single pattern or template. With tens of thousands of museums in the United States, varied in purpose, scale, subject matter, and programming, many different, even contrasting, kinds of leaders will have to emerge. It is our responsibility to cultivate, welcome, and support them.

Notes

1. Aspen Initiative UK, March 11, 2021 Webinar, "Embracing Uncertainty." https://www.aspenuk.org/events/embracing-uncertainty-how-creativity-and-resilience-can-help-us-navigate-an-increasingly-complex-world/

2. McKinsey & Company: August 2021. Accessed 8/4/21; https://www.mckinsey.com/business-functions/organization/). See also, Charles Conn and Robert McLean, "Six Problem-Solving Mindsets for Very Uncertain Times," *McKinsey Quarterly*, September 2020.

3. "The Era of the Visionary Museum Director Is Over . . . or It Should Be." *Hyperallergic*, July 2021. https://hyperallergic.com/665251/era-of-visionary-museum-director-is-over-or-it-should-be/

4. *Stanford Social Innovation Review* and https://leadingwithintent.org/wp-content/uploads/2021/06/2021-Leading-with-Intent_report.pdf?__hstc=166159009.78f3db711d8344acd4be324a9d82b3cc.1631206461650.1631206461650.1631206461650.1&__hssc=166159009.1.1631206461650&__hsfp=3244678409&hsCtaTracking=60281ff7-cadf-4b2f-b5a0-94ebff5a2c25%7C428c6485-37ba-40f0-a939-aeda82c02f38

CHAPTER TWENTY-TWO

Self-Worth, Trust, and Wonder

Leadership Lessons from Fred Rogers

Mariruth Leftwich

Mariruth Leftwich, PhD, senior director, museum operations and education at the Jamestown-Yorktown Foundation, has worked in museum education for twenty-five years, creating learning experiences and acting as a change maker for history institutions. Her service to the field has included tenure with the Museum Education Roundtable Board and AAM's EdCom.

The 2020 pandemic provided experiences that will be transformative as the field moves into a recovery and regrowth phase. Leaders at every level of museums looked for frameworks and models to inform how they handled those challenging times. I deepened my understanding of leadership rooted in an appreciation of people as natural learners. That model, based on the work of Fred Rogers, centers self-worth, trust, curiosity, play, and reflection in ways that could become foundational for successful leadership as the museum field evolves in the post-pandemic world.

Over the course of my years working as Director of Learning at the Senator John Heinz History Center in Pittsburgh, Pennsylvania, I found myself increasingly immersed in the world of Fred Rogers. In the cast of legendary Pittsburghers, Fred Rogers has earned a special place in the heart of the city and across the country. In recent years, his messages of love, kindness, and acceptance had never felt more relevant, propelling interest in the History Center's collections related to his life and work. Year after year, we received a growing number of requests for programs and insights to be gained from

Rogers's work. An inquiry from a school district superintendent led me to create a program for administrators that highlighted the way Fred approached teaching, learning, and challenges. This request to articulate Fred's approach led me on a path to reconsider what it means to learn and lead. It has shaped my view of leadership and my actions as a leader in a museum.

The bedrock of success in Fred Rogers's view is ensuring that people recognize and feel their own self-worth. He believed that "as human beings, our job in life is to help people realize how rare and valuable each one of us really is." In leadership roles it is important to intentionally consider the opportunities you have for instilling this self-worth in other people. When people see their own self-worth, it helps them see value in others, and this cycle of valuing yourself and others is integral to successful leadership. Valuing others does not mean perfunctory congratulations or institution-wide emails celebrating an accomplishment. It means listening carefully, recognizing the value of individuals, and supporting their needs. Museum leaders need to find opportunities to integrate the fostering of self-worth, from changing approaches to performance management to establishing ways of recognizing individual successes. Managers need to routinely, and sincerely, acknowledge people for their time, talent, and energy. Successful leadership is rooted in embracing people and understanding the multitude of ways their worth could be valued, held, and magnified.

Self-worth is nurtured in spaces where trust flourishes. Ultimately, trust is about relationships, but too often leadership is seen as power to be wielded rather than a relationship to be built. For Rogers, trust was essential for helping children navigate uncertainty and assuring them that there are people who will help, support, and listen to them. In my experience leading a team, that critical trust is built through conversations, transparency in decision-making, and consensus building. Trust-building requires leaders to prioritize relationships and be vulnerable and open to others. The ability to foster self-worth is intricately bound in the creation of trust; trust will grow when people see that you believe in them.

Over the course of the pandemic, leaders were forced to make agonizing decisions, ranging from staff furloughs to the safety of opening their institutions. The decisions that had to be made may have been unprecedented, but the opaqueness with which decisions were made was often not. Trust is cultivated in the long term, so in that moment of crisis, it was often difficult for staff to trust leadership, if such trust had not been nurtured in "normal" times. As leadership adapts to post-pandemic conditions, establishing or rebuilding trust will be essential. Although trust will look different in each organization, the hallmarks of building trust in my work have included inviting conversation and being responsive to what staff members say, following through on actions, sharing the reasoning behind decisions, and consistently showing up for staff when they need me. Importantly, trust is also about moments of laughter, sharing your own fears and worries, and being genuine.

With established trust, staff will feel more empowered to seize important moments of wonder and play that are fed by their curiosity. Fred Rogers posed the question, "Did you know that it's all right to wonder?," acknowledging how often wonder is disregarded. Early learners have a natural curiosity and Rogers recognized this should be harnessed and honed. By adulthood, that innate curiosity has often faded, and with that an aversion to risk and a fear of failure develops; people become less inclined to wonder. When embraced, curiosity can lead to innovation, changed perspectives, and acts of bravery. Asking people you lead to embrace curiosity means being willing to accept their trials, greet their failures as learning, and see their acts of experimentation as opportunities and not threats to the institution or one's authority. The pandemic forced staff across museums to become more curious about new modes of communication, interpretation, programming, and connecting. Museums could not function as they had before: Collectively, we had to wonder about how to continue our missions. New leadership models will embrace this sense of curiosity and risk-taking, prompt staff to ask questions, and try new approaches, recognizing that the future relevancy for museums will lie in our ability to wonder.

Much like curiosity, playfulness is rarely prioritized for adults, but play, according to Rogers, can be "a way to solve problems and to express feelings." Fostering playfulness in work strengthens teams, creates positivity, and allows people to let go of negative energy. Play can build trust and create moments of joy. I recently started a new leadership position and immediately began introducing play in manager meetings to better know my new team, ensure meetings begin with laughter rather than stress, and set the tone for our time and work together. Play can be a productive extension of curiosity, allowing staff to use their curiosity to solve problems and support the design thinking model that centers the question "How might we?" as we tackle a challenge, asking staff to imagine new outcomes and approaches. When problems are approached through possibility and play, the stakes seem less threatening, and the resulting solutions can be powerful and effective. In an environment where play is valued, it evokes curiosity, generates trust, and nurtures self-worth. As we imagine how museums "might be" in the future, we need leaders who push us towards collective playfulness and value its output of imagination and innovation.

Quiet times are just as important as these flurries of activity. As Rogers reflected, "It's the little quiet moments in the midst of life that seem to give the rest extra-special meaning." Even in nonpandemic times, museum work is often fast paced with a multitude of various projects to balance at any given time. It often seems impossible to slow down and pause. With an ever-growing list of projects that need to be finished and goals to be accomplished, it is easy as a leader to push from one moment to the next without stopping. Without taking time to pause, we risk losing our perspective on what gives our work meaning, to both our colleagues and our audiences. For leaders, taking the time to look and listen carefully can take on many dimensions, from beginning meetings with reflection instead of immediate action items to building purposeful breaks into programming and exhibition schedules. This practice enables deeper thought, reflection, and renewal, all of which will be critical as we imagine better museums for our audiences and the dedicated staff with whom we work.

Related to looking and listening carefully, Rogers acknowledged the need for solitude, which provides time for processing and internalizing learning. During the pandemic year we heard increasing calls for self-care and taking time to process, pieces that Rogers saw as integral to successful development. This principle can be incredibly challenging to incorporate in management. Solitude can seem at odds with creating and leading high functioning teams, primarily because it requires time away and a level of disengagement from each other. Embracing solitude is about identifying moments where people can find both focus and mental paths to wander as they disconnect from distractions that surround them. These may include flexible work hours that enable staff to leverage times where they feel most productive, providing periodic opportunities to turn on automatic email replies and not respond immediately, or committing to sending work-related communications only during work hours.

The year 2020 put museums and their leadership to the test as they grappled with what Lonnie Bunch, the Smithsonian's Secretary, described as the "dual pandemics of COVID-19 and deeply-rooted racism." As in so many facets of life, these events acted as a mirror that laid bare long-term struggles and called ideologies and belief systems into question. As we emerge from this pandemic landscape, it is important to assess the ways museum practices and systems can be transformed. One of the greatest transformations should be rooted in ways museum leadership centers staff. The work of Fred Rogers provides a model that museum leaders can draw on as we reimagine organizations, recognizing the deep need for staff to feel valued, for curiosity and wonder to be nurtured, and for relationships to be built on trust at every level of the institution.

CHAPTER TWENTY-THREE

Protect People, Not Things
Franklin Vagnone

Franklin Vagnone is a public historian, sculptor, and architectural designer who is the founder of Twisted Preservation Cultural Consulting. He is currently President and CEO of Old Salem Museums and Gardens. Among numerous articles, Vagnone is coauthor (with Deb Ryan) of *The Anarchist's Guide to Historic House Museums*.

I have imagined how museum folks felt as they stood in the gallery halls of the Louvre, the Uffizi, or the Victoria and Albert Museum moments before they started to remove the artwork from the walls or began to cover them with sandbags so they could store them safely away from the threat of World War II destruction. I try to imagine the moment of hesitation and internal dialogue that might have taken place, perhaps asking themselves whether they were overreacting?

Everything they had spent their lives protecting, interpreting, and making public now had to be removed and hidden from the public eye. Of course, in hindsight, this was necessary to protect the cultural property for the long term. The world as they had understood it up until that moment had ceased to be, and a new situation was upon them. They had to look past the boxed *Mona Lisa* and the sandbagged *David* into the future and envision a time when those objects would once again be placed openly and lovingly in public view. What a moment of sadness and at the same time a moment for powerful and proactive urgency.

Although today's context may not seem as physically devastating as war, it's proved lethal and socially corrosive. I believe we are now called on to make similar preemptive and emotionally counterintuitive operational choices. In this case, however, the future may need us to pay more attention to our human resources than to things, however greatly we prize them. The 2020 COVID-19 pandemic lockdowns have been devastating to cultural institutions in both their human cost as well as in their organizational operations. This part of the pandemic is now becoming history, yet our present situation and what looms on the horizon seem even more daunting to me. Why?

As I write this, it is spring 2021. Mass vaccinations are taking place, things are slowly opening back up, and there is noticeably more activity on the streets and sidewalks of our towns. At this pivotal inflection point, we are starting to see the sunrise, and a sense of hope might have convinced us that the storm has passed us by. So why the concern?

I believe that at this moment we are in the eye of the economic storm that has been caused by the COVID-19 pandemic. The initial shock of the storm included the many deaths and the disruption of so many lives, the fear and dread of our new day-to-day realities and how they might unfold. For cultural institutions, the stark realization has dawned that our survival depended on a new and as yet unwritten blueprint for how to operate in the aftermath of the plague.

Most cultural sites rely on various sources of earned revenue to survive, even those with sizable endowments. As someone who runs a large living-history site, I think 2021 has ushered in a different set of prevailing winds from the COVID-19 storm. "Open up!" is the increasingly vocal call heard from many sides. Cultural institutions are being thrown into this cacophonous arena, struggling to regain their footing and find balance. Persistent public calls to get "back to normal" disguise the economic realities of budgets, staffing, attendance, funding, and safety of staff.

Simply returning to normal will be a losing proposition for many.

The best-kept secret is that some cultural institutions, because of unsustainable pre-COVID operations, may in fact be in a better position when they temporarily close, using this condition to their advantage for the longer haul. They could be reimagining an operations model that is empathetic to staff, intentionally antiracist, pays a living wage, and privileges shared collaborative leadership. *Staying closed may not be popular, but do organizations really want to jump back into their outmoded top-down, financial, and attendance-driven models of the before time?*

This is a difficult opinion to voice. In fact, I haven't seen much in the public press about this perspective. We are at a crucial moment in our social and economic progress. Either we see the present moment as the end of the storm, or we see it, as I do, as merely the eye of the hurricane and a chance to prepare for the reverse winds. Now is not the time to let down our guard, removing our COVID equivalents of plywood coverings protecting our windows and sandbags protecting our cultural property. Now is the time to make sure those protections are still useful. We should reflect on our operations and policies, looking toward new organizational forms and behaviors.

Here are some urgent and important reckonings:

First, the structure and shape of our cultural organizations, how they are populated, managed, and logistically operated, need to be reconsidered. Is the corporate, top-down leadership model the best way to communicate an inclusive and collective voice? I think not. How we see ourselves informs how others see us. This self-reflection can be a powerful strategic positioning tool in transformational movements. Organizations tend to seek stasis and homogeneous demographics in staff, audience, and operations. Countering this innate systems behavior takes constant attention. No detail is too small for reconsideration.

We need to invert the traditional, top-down decision-making process and engage the frontline team members in collaborating on strategic directions. Rather than dictating to our staff, we need to see each member of the team as a fully contributing member of the overall operation.

We need to reform leadership models as collaborative teams and deeply reimagine how boards of trustees operate and in what ways they can best be used in a new collaborative process of strategy and goal discussions. The important idea here is that the logistics, sequence, and transparency of decision-making include the board of directors along with the staff team as partners not adversaries. We should consider mentor/mentee relationships with board members and staff in a way that fosters empathetic understanding of the gifts each brings to the discussion.

We should consider a smaller staff, where all would be paid a living wage. We need to stop trying to be the biggest and most powerful public institution and think in a more focused manner. What is the signature structure that best represents your mission? Figure that out and do that better than anyone else. Funders and individual contributors want to see their money go toward successful, meaningful work. I have found that reducing staff thoughtfully and consciously can bring the organization to a better financial position as well as a deeper focus on mission. Perhaps the bigger an organization becomes, the more difficult it is to remain focused on the mission. Rightsizing an organization must include serving staff and visitors before serving the buildings and collections.

As the local residential demographics change, so too must our current priority toward individual large donors be redirected in favor of larger numbers of more modest contributors. This will be a fundamental shift in how organizations behave. To achieve this rightsizing, organizations need to reconsider their physical footprint, collections size, salary scales, and development models. Most development strategies still hold close to the 1990s' model of event-based fundraising. In my experience these types of operations are costly and *performative*. I believe we have moved into an era where real tangible work is better than any gala, and modest contributions speak more clearly of a broad support system than a few large donors. We must operate within the scale that better matches our surrounding communities, economically, socially, and emotionally.

I realize that my perspective does not reflect the current "back-to-normal" zeitgeist. My feeling is, simply put: If we want our organizations to be around ten years from now, serving our communities and staff in significant ways and providing opportunities for an ever-expanding constituency, *we need to pause*. We need to think about this moment and the choice it presents.

Nothing is more important than people. Not buildings. Not collections. Not endowments. Nothing. Consider how fragile the COVID virus made us feel and recreate an organization that protects the talent that fuels your organization. That is the ultimate pivot in operations. Think of your organization as protecting people, not things.

With as much care as we gave the secret removal of the *Winged Victory of Samothrace* from the monumental staircase of the Louvre, we must plan for when the next storm arrives and reenvision a response that speaks to our higher selves.

CHAPTER TWENTY-FOUR

Courageous Imagination
Nannette V. Maciejunes and Cindy Meyers Foley

Nannette V. Maciejunes is the executive director of the Columbus Museum of Art. Under her leadership, the museum adopted the mission *to create great experiences with great art for everyone* and opened the Center for Creativity, an innovative space for visitor-centered museum experiences. In 2013, the museum was awarded the IMLS National Medal.

Cindy Meyers Foley is the Scantland Family Executive Deputy Director at the Columbus Museum of Art (CMA). She reimagined the museum and its impact on the community by situating creativity as CMA's social mission. Foley has given two TEDx talks and regularly keynotes museum and education conferences.

> If your actions inspire others to dream more, learn more, do more, and become more, you are a leader.
>
> —John Quincy Adams

For many American museums, COVID-19 and a reckoning with historic systemic racism revealed our need for deep clarity. Typically, museums spend much of their energy dealing with ongoing financial challenges and working to strengthen earned revenue, contributed income, and endowment. But what may be more important is finding new ways to articulate our beliefs, mission, and vision. For many museums, a clearly defined sense of purpose

157

will be critical in articulating a simple, compelling, authentic, relevant story that communicates who we are.

A shared sense of purpose gets us all on the same page. If our museums can develop cultures of thinking and working rooted in admiration and trust, we will be better able to take on the challenges of uncertainty, experimentation, and risk. In short, we need to enable what we might term "courageous imagination." To achieve this, we must also look to new leadership models. Here at the Columbus Museum of Art (CMA), our model of shared leadership has served us well. As we move into the future, we are even more convinced of the benefits of its intentional application.

David Perkins, Principal Investigator at Harvard's Project Zero, writes that three types of visionary leaders are needed for change to truly take hold. These leaders are the conceptual (the one proposing a new direction), the political (the one paving the way for that vision to take hold), and the practical (the one who takes the vision and says, not only can I make this vision a reality, I can take it to an even better place than imagined). Perkins's research has shown that no one leader can fulfill more than one of these roles if institutional change is the priority. Instead, the focus needs to be on the development of leadership, not individual leaders.[1]

We contend that at far too many museums, the focus on hierarchical leadership concentrates power and decision-making too narrowly. At the CMA, even before the COVID-19 outbreak, we, as Executive Director and Deputy Director, shared the roles of conceptual and political leadership. But practical leadership was widely distributed throughout our museum staff at multiple levels of authority and influence. Until the COVID-19 outbreak, when our board and staff embarked on the arduous process to develop a new framework for thinking and doing, we hadn't fully recognized the power—and the necessity—of these leadership patterns.

In the fifteen years that we had worked together, our relationship had evolved, initially as mentor/mentee and eventually as partner leaders. As we strengthened our museum's financial base, dealt with budgetary challenges, went through a major renovation and expansion in addition to seismic shifts in our approach to visitors and learning, we focused on the tasks at hand, not on the fact that we were also crafting a shared leadership model.

As we worked together to live up to our ambitious mission, we increased our appreciation for the benefits of our "push-pull" of ideas and negotiations, which reflected both our different and distinct areas of passion as well as our shared commitment to the museum. We thought and worked in a spirit of trust, respecting our individual strengths and making space for a high level of experimentation. Our shared commitment to being a visitor-centered institution and our adoption of creativity as our social mission nurtured an innovative work culture and practice. Our interactions with each other became a model for interactions with our team—and extended to our publics and our community partners.

In addition to trust and respect, we focused on intentional listening and framing better questions. We learned to ask questions that gave us insight into people's (and organizations') "why"—their hopes, dreams, motivations, and challenges. Our "better questions" led to a team approach for co-creating new initiatives, resulting in successful community partnerships that addressed mutual needs while maintaining high levels of autonomy. These practices have become hallmarks of the CMA approach.

COVID-19 sucked. It shook our foundation. Over the previous years we had learned to pivot. To change. To ask better questions. COVID-19 forced us to restructure, reimagine, respond, and re-innovate. The pandemic and racial reckoning created many simultaneous challenges that required leaders to emerge throughout the staff. COVID-19 also showed us our blind spots: the questions we had not been asking and those we had been unable to see, especially ones that address inclusion, equity, access, diversity, and belonging.

Our new strategic framework, developed and adopted during this historic moment, declares that "To Enable Courageous Imagination" is our institutional purpose. This purpose demands our continued commitment to shared leadership. Despite the turbulence and disruption of the pandemic and our national racial reckoning, we knew we needed to move beyond a clichéd image of courage. Our initial response to these crises was to tap into our core strengths—our relationship with each other and our staff, our practice of deep listening, and our belief in co-creating programs with our community partners—as we focused on the mountains of immediate and critical decisions. The weight and number of these decisions left little room for vision, for what happens next, for how we could improve.

Fortunately, we recognized that conceptual leadership was bubbling up across the institution. New voices emerged to guide us. Our "Courageous Imagination" was to make space for more leaders (political, conceptual, and practical) throughout the museum. For example, an artist and former gallery guard who managed the Visitor Experience Team suggested that we could maximize human capital, increase staff satisfaction, and save costs by combining—and reinventing—our Visitor Experience and Security teams. These staff now cross-train to function in multiple locations and diversify their skills. This innovation resulted in increased competencies, flexibility, and efficiencies, as well as enhanced levels of visitor services and safety.

Our manager of engagement, also an artist, launched Museum in Progress, a labeling, programming, and communications initiative that transparently addresses some of the ugly truths of museum history and practice, including racism, misogyny, and imperialism. During 2020, she focused Museum in Progress inward, helping to lead our efforts to "de-center" the museum, and ask, "Who is at the center of our decision making?" Do we focus on ourselves at the expense of our marginalized and suffering communities? She was heard, and heeded, by her peers, leadership, and the board, and her ideas and questions continue to reverberate in our future planning.

Prior to the pandemic, our leadership giving officer had launched, "Loud and Proud," a first of its kind affinity membership group for LGBTQ individuals. This became a signature membership program, driving a new audience, creating a space of invitation and welcome, and helping to cultivate meaningful relationships. When COVID-19 hit, our community needed safe ways to connect and experience joy, despite the museum's closure. Noting that people were desperate to come together, especially after a year of reckoning with social injustice, income inequality, and the trauma of loss, this staff member suggested the museum host an outdoor, socially distanced drag show with a hometown drag superstar. This blossomed into our extremely popular bar, art, and music (BAM) Thursdays as a safe way to gather outside, celebrate creativity, and connect across race, gender, class, and age.

All imagination requires some level of courage: You need to suspend what you know to be true to imagine what might be. You need to tolerate the unknown. You must be willing to set aside your expertise and step out of your lane. Art invites us to reimagine, to be brave, to reframe our understandings, engage with curiosity, and envision new stories and ideas. We've learned in the last eighteen months that CMA cannot merely be a place of individual growth and reflection; it must be a place of social connection and solidarity with one another and with our shared humanity.

Our innovative CMA colleagues had recognized the transformative power of art and were committed to the individual and civic potential of the museum. They were already working in the practical leadership sphere before COVID-19. What they taught us in this historic moment is that in a more fully evolved shared leadership model, they can also become effective conceptual, visionary, and political leaders. To truly achieve our purpose of courageous imagination, we must reaffirm that this vision cannot be accomplished solely by a couple of leaders at the top; instead, our museums need teams of colleagues committed to a shared vision, to each other, and to the communities we serve.

Note

1. David Perkins, "Three Visionaries for Change," PowerPoint presentation at Project Zero Classroom Institute, July 2012.

PART VIII

~

RETHINKING STRUCTURES

For decades, long before the recent crises of social protest, pandemic, and environmental degradation hit American museums, voices throughout the field argued that traditional museum organizational structures, personnel practices, career pipelines, critical skills, salary schedules, and advancement practices needed a major shakeup. Museums' organizational charts and structures have been among the most static of institutional types. Since March 2020, however, the voices and testimonies of the disenfranchised and disaffected have become exponentially louder, with individuals' dissatisfaction joining a chorus of collective accusations aimed at institutions, boards of trustees, and museum leaders. Over the past two years, these voices have aimed at nothing less than disrupting and recasting institutional culture at museums across the continent. And a growing number of museum CEOs, some contributing to this book, have taken the lead in breaking the traditional mold as they seek to respond to the dynamics of societal and cultural change.

Museums—like other kinds of nonprofit organizations—are products of a capitalist, market-driven society, and have increasingly structured themselves on corporate and business models. Especially in larger museums, power and authority are concentrated and hierarchy prevails: The board and executive monopolize decision-making about mission and other core issues; development staff focus on money; curators on managing collections; and expertise is confined to silos. In these museums, transparency and accountability are often nominal, and metrics tend to fall into a few conventional categories, associated with money, visitor statistics, and media mentions. Success is all too often equated with bright and shiny objects like "star-chitect" buildings, large donations, and multimillion-dollar capital campaigns. Yet even those smaller institutions without big budgets, staffs, or facilities often emulate, in their way, conventional organizational models and practice.

As several of the authors throughout this volume note, current crises now compel museums to reflect on the poor fit between profit-maximizing models and the production of public value. Deborah Schwartz and Frank Vagnone are among those who address necessary shifts in funding and revenue models. Schwartz argues for greatly increased public funding, assuming that museums can provide demonstrated public value. Vagnone counsels moving from a few major donors to increasing smaller donations from a greatly expanded population. Other authors throughout this volume address restructuring, silo-busting, salary inequities, and distributed leadership.

In her recent book, museum scholar Yuha Jung draws on her research to warn that unless organizational structures, institutional culture, and museum workers' mental models change, museum transformation will be limited.[1] In this section, our authors underscore the connection between an organization's structure and its culture and draw on their experience to suggest principles and processes that augur new and positive directions for museums.

As a new CEO at the Michigan Science Center when the pandemic hit, Christian Greer grasped the importance of providing some comfort for his staff in uncertain times. He understood that change—especially internal change—is never easy, but he also knew that the status quo could not be an option. Greer's essay recounts how he and his team used the science center's "self-induced coma" to establish new intra-organizational social networks through reimagining the museum as an agile, collaborative entity that responds to the unpredictable environment with innovation and experimentation. Key to the strategy has been a flatter organization chart, greater risk tolerance, and ambitious new goals and outcomes.

In another take on flattening hierarchy, Brian Lee Whisenhunt advocates for replacing a top-down management and departmental silos with a deeply collaborative, team-based organizational structure. These changes, he argues, are a prerequisite for achieving equity, collaboration, and partnership. Silos, departmental rivalries, and hierarchy limit museum effectiveness and fracture communication across an organization. Establishing working groups in the spaces between departments enhances communication that can drive the organization, its departments, and its working groups into a more inclusive and productive mode that elevates the work of the entire museum. This approach can be realized in many forms and directions, Whisenhunt observes, depending on the community and organization, but a unifying open-source model encourages a strong current of innovative thought and internal prac-tice that emphasizes people over position or hierarchy.

Breaking down internal barriers can also create new knowledge and un-derstandings. Juliana Ochs Dweck suggests that organizing discourse among interdisciplinary groupings can be used to inform and promote institutional reinvention. By fostering department and discipline-spanning conversations built on an egalitarian and dialogic framework, her museum was able to tap into the knowledge and expertise of every member, bringing existing voices into the museum's discourse in new ways. And by organizing teams around shared interests and values, rather than only around tasks, the museum was able to create communities of learning that cut across conventional depart-ments. Dweck notes that this collaborative mode of working produced new transdisciplinary ideas and knowledge that is now transforming the museum's public-facing narratives and programs as well as its institutional culture.

Sam Moore turns his lens on recruitment and professional advancement, exhorting museums to "hit the reset on hiring and advancing" by engaging in candid exchanges with new hires and providing low-cost, but significant, professional development opportunities that enable junior staff to build skills and play meaningful leadership roles. Like Whisenhunt and Dweck, Moore argues that museums need to support and encourage "staff participation in communities of practice during work hours, valuing time spent in conversa-tion with peers at other institutions." Sharing their learnings in all-hands and team meetings can, he writes, "inspire a more informed and positive workplace culture and have the potential to directly inform the reimagined work of museums in the aftermath of the pandemic."

These concrete, incremental, and achievable practices do not amount to a wholesale dismantling of the museum structure as we know it. Yet they can have profound impact, touching the lives not only of those who work within our institutions but also the publics whom we aim to serve.

Note

1. Yuha Jung. *Transforming Museum Management: Evidence-Based Change through Open Systems Theory.* (Oxfordshire, UK: Routledge, 2021).

CHAPTER TWENTY-FIVE

From Silos to Social Networks

Christian Greer

Christian Greer, EdD, president and CEO of the Michigan Science Center, is an informal STEM educator, exhibit designer, and project manager who has served in leadership positions at several major nonprofits. As a learning technologist, he explores how innovation, intrapreneurship, and collaborative culture can be cultivated using online learning circles.

When the ground is moving below your feet and the winds are swirling above your head, you can sometimes be forced—or freed—to move in unexpected new directions, and it can all happen in a moment. Like many leaders in the field, I like making big changes when the conditions are right. Unfortunately, the conditions needed for successful change are rarely optimal. Creating awareness that a change is needed, redefining the problem, expressing a sense of urgency, and giving your team the tools to make change are all part of the process. Whatever the level of difficulty you are faced with when undertaking change, it's likely not a good enough excuse to hold firm to the status quo.

Strategic internal shifts are particularly tough when they affect your organization's structure. It takes vision, courage, and sometimes even daring to initiate these shifts and see them through to completion. Leaders must also be resolute about initiating change in reporting relationships, accountability, and responsibility. They have to extol the benefits of innovative frameworks and collaborative cultures that unlock social capital and promote intrapreneurship while energizing learning potential. Of course, it's not likely that

165

everyone will be on board with the change. And you may have to live with some dissension for a while as things smooth out and people become more comfortable with various new normals. A crisis can be an excellent time to fail, though, and chaos can be the perfect cover for facilitating an empathy-based design process that gives license to creative problem-solving in an organization. Seeing over the horizon of change isn't impossible, but it may require a tall mast deeply rooted in your mission. And your mission needs to be continually calibrated for relevancy and aligned with what matters most to the communities you serve. You might not be headed in the right direction before a storm, but you definitely want to be pointed toward your north star after one.

During the past year and a half, as a freshman CEO, I experienced the ultimate leadership test for change. I was treated to two major crises: one a worldwide pandemic, and the other a racial reckoning of enormous proportions, for neither of which was I remotely prepared. In direct response to these crises, I led some major strategic shifts in my organization and made several critical decisions where the positive results ended up being inches away from total disaster. I discovered that leadership is often knowing what you're doing when you don't know what you're doing.

The risks during this moment in time were extremely high. Those critical decisions were made under a lot of stress and even confusion. Many of the decisions were already in queue before the pandemic, but our timetable was forced. I would have much preferred to make these decisions on my schedule and not because they were forced on us by an unexpected storm that made our decision-making binary. Many of the variables we were used to dealing with were all set to zero, leaving just a few terms in the equation to work out. The opportunity to change quickly was staring our leadership team in the face. So when it came to reimagining and reorganizing our internal structure with reduced staffing and missing expertise, we shifted, pivoted, and stretched. We tried to fail forward as much as possible.

After we shut down our facility and quickly transitioned into quarantine, we put ourselves into what essentially was a self-induced coma—having only meager cash reserves to carry us through. We immediately facilitated furloughs and layoffs, made budget cuts, reprioritized our program formats, designed and built new exhibits, recalibrated our mission, reconnected with our communities, blitzed local media, and went on what amounted to a gigantic fundraising-focused Easter egg hunt.

We reimagined our entire enterprise from the perspective of agility, using agile project management as a framework to reformat our structure. This meant using a temporary time horizon as the basis for our empirical approach to value delivery across a spectrum of engagement options. I was reminded during the process that risks can be relative. Leaders should be mindful of this when taking them. Some of our decisions were with eyes closed. Others needed a do-over, but collectively, they allowed us to safely reopen less than one hundred days after we closed to the public in March 2020, and we stayed open with zero COVID-19 cases behind the scenes and zero contact-traceable incidents with our guests.

However, upon reexamining our SWOT analysis, it felt as though we hardly moved the needle. By all accounts, we are stronger both technically and financially than we were before the pandemic, but we are a much smaller team and organization. Many in our field like to frequently promote the benefits of becoming leaner. Well, we should be careful what we wish for. The mountains we now must climb seem so much bigger. Perhaps change should be more aptly considered a vector quantity rather than one that is scalar. Magnitude is a great thing to have, but often it is direction that really matters.

If strategy is ultimately about positioning, your organization can either be in a position to take advantage of opportunities and avoid threats, or potentially out of position, with both your strengths and weaknesses getting in the way of your long-term success. Some of the aggressive repositionings in our field, particularly around inclusion, antiracism, and community engagement, are certainly on the road to better, more equitable futures for the field writ large. Other repositioning efforts, like many of our new business models, feel more like short-lived trends that may not be part of the new normal. Although many positive impacts of the COVID-19 pandemic and the racial justice reckoning aid us in having long-overdue critical conversations, yet there are a lot of unanswered questions about our core missions, community connectedness, and business models that leave us wondering what still needs to change.

Following a major crisis, it's often hard to tell whether your organization is running toward the future or fleeing the past. Many museums are finding themselves running in circles, especially when it comes to hitting the reset button on their organizational charts. Although we all want more equitable learning environments for our audiences and more collaborative work environments for employees, determining the right structure is challenging because of the hierarchies of the people who work within. Implicit and explicit rules and policies outline how roles and responsibilities are coordinated, controlled, and appropriately delegated. A chart can visually represent this hierarchy, showing how the flow of information, knowledge, expertise, decision-making, and other forms of social capital is channeled through organizational structure.

With decentralized frameworks, however, enterprising employees can be empowered with high degrees of personal agency; this is what we felt was needed for agility. Structures need to be able to bend and flex in response to change. We employed a distributed leadership model to address the invisible boundaries, both vertical and horizontal, within our organization. However, there can be major challenges to innovation when two or more organizational structures merge vertical boundaries, to create a phenomenon that is commonly known as the silo effect.

Silos exist for multiple reasons, and people who work in silos can be stubbornly resistant to change. Informal networks are often more democratic, and they can sprout organically and be set up by leaders at all levels. For us, a more connected, flat, and flexible structure was necessary, so we shoved all our departments, save Marketing/PR and Development, into one giant learning circle, focused on learning, and under a single leader, our COO, creating a self-organizing, autonomous powerhouse.

I believe that the success potential of an organization is a function of its ability to facilitate cross-departmental innovation projects efficiently and effectively. Leaders seeking to innovate as they adapt to volatile market conditions and dynamic business environments need to do so without being hampered by inflexible and ineffective, sometimes archaic, organizational structures. We made a dramatic shift from traditional, more methodical, methods of project management to more agile, value-based, empathy-driven approaches to getting things done. We believe this shift will lay the groundwork for enterprising team members to feel empowered to openly dismantle departmental silos and traverse functional areas to find new ways to successfully collaborate. Before the crisis, we were built on internal silos and isolated departments, often operating with little oversight and guidance. After, the vertical and horizontal barriers to the flow of social capital and collaboration had been removed. This was real.

Through learning how to create a more collaborative culture, we have come to value the following:

- the superhero abilities of each team member *over* credentials, experience, and tenure.
- coperformance of leadership *over* titles, organizational structure, and hierarchy.
- collaborative goals *over* departmental goals and individual priorities.

- creative problem solving and intrapreneurship *over* team building and consensus.
- performance and progress *over* standard operating procedures and policies.
- the growth of our guests, audiences, and communities *over* just the growth of our organization through attendance, revenue, and public recognition.

Mirroring the Agile Manifesto, we stated that although we acknowledge that there is value in the elements on the RIGHT, we value the elements on the LEFT more.

In fact, informal social networks began sprouting spontaneously and new communication back channels were forged. As noted, an online learning circle served as an intentional structure for facilitating distributed leadership. These pathways rebooted our existing meeting structures; a new collaborative culture began to emerge as we methodically moved from silos to social networks. Several social network analyses we ran previous produced sociograms that indicated due to the layoffs and furloughs a great number of structural holes had opened up. Inspired by our cultural shift toward distributed leadership, we honored our intrapreneurs by creating a statement of ideals and intentions we called the MiSci Manifesto, styled after the original Agile Manifesto drafted in 2001 at The Lodge at Snowbird ski resort in Utah's Wasatch mountains by seventeen self-described "organizational anarchists" moonlighting as software engineers. Our version paid homage to the brilliance of the Agile Manifesto's original signatories and styled values in a format like their original design.[1]

Standing firmly on these new values, we were able to redesign our internal organizational structure to be more flat, flexible, inclusive, and equitable than ever before. We're still early in the evolution of our cultural values within our MiSci Manifesto, but we expect our structure will evolve to meet future challenges. Our efforts are not necessarily a rejection of resiliency, but if resilience is about returning to the condition we were in before deformation, why would we want to do that? We had a lot of pieces missing, sure, but our new level of agility made it feel like we had the answers to the test.

Note

1. "Manifesto for Agile Software Development," 2001. https://moodle2019-20.ua.es/moodle/pluginfile.php/2213/mod_resource/content/2/agile-manifesto.pdf

CHAPTER TWENTY-SIX

Equity and Collaboration
Transforming Structure and Narrative to Center Community
Brian Lee Whisenhunt

Brian Lee Whisenhunt is executive director of The Rockwell Museum in Corning, New York, where the team is building on the museum's reputation as a leader in education; broadening the collection to include a diverse range of American perspectives; and deepening the work of the museum in the communities it serves.

To meet the needs and expectations of visitors and communities in the twenty-first century, museums must intentionally and actively evolve beyond the inherited institutional structures and processes of the past. This includes examining the traditional organizational structures and management systems to create a new philosophy based on shared leadership, collective focus, and unified vision. It also requires reprioritizing the canon, where the selection and interpretation of specific works of art are not only more representative of the community but also free of the hierarchy of authorship and biases of the past. All of this should be built on a deep collaborative structure that encompasses both internal cooperation and a continuous open dialogue with the communities that surround the organization.

Historically, community and business leaders organized many museums on business or corporate traditions and practices that permeated institutional culture—from galleries, collections, and programs to administrative offices, board rooms, and bureaucracy. These practices and policies have imbued our organizations with an inherent fealty to ideas and concepts that were not, and are not, always reflective of the needs of the people and communities we serve. These traditions often stymie the ability of organizations to achieve inherent and tangible transformation and instead lead museums down a path of saccharine superficiality that, although marketable and easily digested, provides little or no actual sustenance or connection to our audiences.

For decades, the mantra foisted onto leaders of museums and other non-profits was to be more like for-profit businesses, following their principles, values, and practices. Museum leadership was asked to *ignore* the fact they had missions focused on people and communities. Instead, leadership was charged with focusing on the bottom line. Although many of the tenets of the for-profit model never took a firm hold within the nonprofit sector, they did serve to reinforce a traditional form of leadership and organizational structure that includes top-down management of distinct silos across organizations.

In museums, the identity of departments seems to have been codified decades ago and remains sacrosanct to leadership today. Silos, rivalries, and hierarchy limit the effectiveness of these departments and prevent true collaboration across an organization, and this fractured communication model can be observed in museums across the field, regardless of size. In a post-pandemic world still reckoning with the legacy of systemic racism, museums need to dissolve these embedded concepts within their organizations. They must create new systems specific to their work, mission, and communities that emphasize an open and transparent organizational structure; increase the strength of community; and build unity and collaboration across the organization.

It is essential to consider what working groups can be formed in the spaces between departments and how these supplemental groups communicate with one another and the organization as a whole. Intentional communication can drive the work of the organization, its departments, and its working groups into a more inclusive and productive sphere that elevates the work of the entire museum. This approach can align the shared perspectives of different departments and aid in the communication among them. The conventional, pyramidal organization chart might remain in place, but flattening that structure to create a more egalitarian workplace will provide more equity to staff regardless of their position within the hierarchy. Although the possibilities of this approach include an array of forms and direction, depending on the community and organization, a unifying open-source model shared across the field could build a strong current of innovative thought and internal practice that emphasizes people over position or hierarchy.

At the Rockwell Museum, these concepts are manifested in an evolving approach to organizational structure that directly influences how programming and interpretation is developed by its teams. The museum still maintains an organizational chart with a conventional pyramidic structure but scaffolded onto that are four interdepartmental teams reflective of the cross-departmental interests of the organization. This creates a rigorous system of communication to both share information and gather feedback. Overlapping of membership across the teams allows for ideas, questions, and considerations to flow through the different areas of the organization. Although it may not be feasible to deconstruct conventional working groups, it is possible to support them more effectively with supplemental structures, communication systems, and interdepartmental teams.

How to begin to re-imagine your institutional structure and practice:

1. As a team, map all the meetings your organization holds. Discuss which of those meetings might be a topic, rather than a meeting. Consider aligning like topics to create a working group.
2. Have each department, team, or working group create a mission statement, define their focus, and craft a vision.
3. Create a transparent system that allows anyone within the organization to understand the work, processes, and dialogue of the various teams.
4. Clearly define how items and information will be reported out and shared among departments, working groups, and larger staff.
5. Clearly define how collaboration, transparency, and equity are represented in your institutional values.
6. Working with a coach or external system, investigate the work and communication styles of your teams. Use this information to bring intention to how you communicate as well how you structure your meetings.
7. Make an annual examination of your team structures, their mission, and focus a part of your professional practice.

For art museums, moving past the conventional also means letting go of accepted art histories and canons. Dissolving the canon means bringing new voices and perspectives into the galleries, not only through the choices of what is on the gallery walls but also the way those works of art are spoken about and interpreted. Institutions must create unique and compelling approaches to understanding and connecting to art that honors the perspective, voice, and experience of the visitor equally alongside those of the maker, curator, or educator. Although bringing noncuratorial voices into the gallery space may seem radical to some, this does not have to mean the removal of primary didactic information related to understanding work of art. Rather, it can allow for secondary and tertiary interpretive experiences centered on the perspective and interests of the visitor to reside in tandem with labels relative to schools of thought and established taxonomies.

At the Rockwell, some labels are crafted collaboratively by members of the Teen Council or other groups. In other cases, visitors are asked to contribute their own thoughts, ideas, or perspective. Other texts are developed by teams of staff from a cross-section of departments. Our interpretive approach sometimes considers specific works through two distinct lenses—one lens focuses on the meaning of the object in its own time and another on its implications for a viewer today. This community-first approach to interpretation works to connect people to art, rather than connect art or curatorial thesis to people.

Like the consumption of any media, visitors care about art, exhibitions, and programs that reflect and represent their identity, culture, and perspective. Aligning alternative voices within the gallery provides a gateway into an object that can lead them to deeper understanding of themselves, the people in their sphere, and the ever-changing world around them.

In many cases, museums rely too heavily on the idea, concept, or message of a single exhibition or installation that lasts only a few weeks. Using an idea across platforms and experiences at a museum allows for visitors to encounter a concept from multiple perspectives over a longer period. This serves both the organization and the visitor because it removes the pressure for one museum experience to be the end-all, be-all and creates a deeper connection through multiple visits and experiences. The special exhibition becomes one aspect of a more expansive initiative and does not have the exclusive obligation to singularly communicate a message or idea. Some museums, including The Rockwell, have begun to use an annual program theme where an idea or concept is manifested not only in the exhibition schedule but also in new interpretive materials, public programming, social media messaging, collection development, and community events. A program theme and guiding principle can also serve to connect an organization's programming to local, regional, and national anniversaries of significance to particular communities. This also creates opportunities for collaboration with other cultural organizations, civic leadership, and community groups.

Finally, museums must conduct conversations about what collaboration means to their organization and how it is activated in their practice and work within the community. Too often, collaboration is a one-way street where larger organizations present opportunities for engagement to specifically identified people or organizations. Opening the lines of communication to move in both directions, using an open call for ideas and opportunities, and saying yes when communities, people, or organizations come forward with ideas are essential to a truly collaborative museum. Collaboration is a method for sharing the position and voice of an institution and reflects an open dialogue with the community that will support the movement to honestly reflect collaborators within the museum. At the same time, authentic collaboration provides feedback to assist the organization in knowing itself and its community. This, in turn, will directly inform the decisions and direction around exhibition, collection, programming, and community activity.

To reach a place where audiences of today and tomorrow understand museums as essential and deeply connected to their lives, museums must craft new traditions that are rooted in the best ideas of equity, collaboration, and partnership. The commitment to these ideas must remain unfixed, evolvable, and responsive, allowing our museums to stay vibrant and meaningful both to museum professionals and the communities we serve. Empowering the community to be reflected within the museum will ensure that our institutions remain relevant to a society and culture in a state of rapid disruption and transformation.

CHAPTER TWENTY-SEVEN

Collaborative Knowledge Production for the Twenty-First-Century Museum

Juliana Ochs Dweck

Juliana Ochs Dweck is chief curator at the Princeton University Art Museum. An anthropologist, Dweck's career spans art, history, and identity museums; she has written about materiality, memory, and museum practice; and has curated exhibitions on subjects including African sculpture, Mexican *retablos*, and political protest.

Grappling with legacies is difficult work. To this day, museums globally continue to contend with the inheritance of a Renaissance model of *wunderkammer* or wonder cabinets, where knowledge along with rare and precious specimens were seen as things that could be amassed, classified, and owned. Likewise we continue to negotiate our roots in the encyclopedic spirit of the Enlightenment, where museums were tools for the systematic organization and diffusion of knowledge in the service of empire, and where the authority of the museum and the nation were preserved through a continual reinscribing of the boundaries around knowledge.

Although a jettisoning of this legacy might never be entirely achievable, or desirable, the upheaval caused by the pandemic and the racial reckoning facilitated by the global Black Lives Matter movement have urged American museums to reevaluate their missions, structures, and practices. As arts and cultural institutions think about power and representation, about who speaks for whom and what stories are told, museums' conversations, interpretations, and data sets are being opened up not just to new expertise, experience, and perspectives but also to multiple concurrent ones: to dynamic rather than static forms of knowledge and to polysemic ways of interpreting the world. This work to create new spaces for varied perspectives requires a rethinking not only of our structures but also our processes, the *how* of our work. This is a moment to rehearse new methods for knowledge production that are collaborative, interdisciplinary, and participatory.

At the Princeton University Art Museum, where I work, this period of reckoning coincides with a physical reconstruction. Our current building, first built late in the nineteenth century and featuring a gallery arrangement that contained vestiges of cultural and material hierarchy, will be replaced with a single floor of globe-spanning collections, presented in spaces that foster intersection and encounter. Planning for a new, pluriversal museum requires that we develop bold ways of engaging in dialogue not only with a host of communities and publics but also with each other, across areas of expertise and experience. Collaborative internal modes of working produce new kinds of knowledge and help make the museum more inclusive, multivocal, and representative.

In what follows, I offer three prompts for fostering co-creation and collaborative problem solving, each a way of mobilizing expertise and knowledge to activate multiple views and, thus, galvanize change and strengthen our organizations. This is not a proposal to restructure or undo hierarchies but a call to be self-reflexive about the interdisciplinary, participatory ways in which knowledge is made. None of the ideas is radical; all are relational. These are focused on internal participation and inward-facing practices that can, in turn, create a foundation for sharing authority with outside experts and communities in ways that are nimble and experimental as well as respectful and sustainable.

Prompt 1: Think capaciously about the diverse knowledge and expertise staff members bring to any shared project. Even in a supportive and collaborative group of colleagues, museum teams can miss opportunities to tap into the knowledge of every member. Sometimes more confident or vocal participants can drown out expertise, but a subtle intervention can create a participatory dynamic. A study that drew from social psychology and management theory found that when a project group inventoried each member's knowledge at the start, the teams were most effective at solving problems.[1] This sounds simple but it is a significant departure from the ways museum collaborations usually work, where participants tend to assume that what one's influence will be is based on title or training. In an interdisciplinary team, where the criteria for influence are defined contextually, the process can empower new voices. As we work toward thinking more creatively about the training and expertise individuals bring to their roles, shifting the criteria from status or power to informational and experiential influence can help us transform our museums.

Prompt 2: Create communities of practice centered on shared concerns or values—not just around tasks. Etienne Wenger and Jean Lave developed the concept of "community of practice" based in part on close study of apprentices in Liberia. They observed that apprentices' most transformative learning occurred not with the master but amid active, informal engagement with each other.[2] Learning happened at the intersection of the social and the individual. The communal structure facilitated the production of knowledge, and people learning together become a community.

Often, a shared institutional or global concern can better galvanize staff than a limited programmatic goal. In the wake of the social and racial justice movement of 2020, one curator at the Princeton University Art Museum organized a regular reading group to serve as a place to share learning in an informal setting. The reading group draws from all reaches of the museum staff and meets for a monthly one-hour discussion on a specific theme, such as strategies for combating a culture of white supremacy or decolonizing the museum. Even more than formal task forces devoted to diversity, this group has become a generous and valuable space for empowering staff by addressing pressing needs for change.

Unlike project teams, which are generally defined by task with responsibilities divided by roles, in this community of practice, relationships are defined by mutual engagement, joint enterprise, and a shared repertoire.[3] A common interest around which museum staff members collaborate to produce and exchange knowledge (whether on the subject of sharing authority with communities or creating an inclusive working environment) locates the production of knowledge in a social context and allows all the co-producers to be active participants in the learning community.

Prompt 3: Promote critical dialogue through collaboration outside bounded areas of expertise. Early in our planning for the collections galleries in the new museum, we created a structure of multiple concurrent working groups covering an array of periods, cultures, materials, and cross-cultural inquiries. Membership in each group drew intentionally across areas of internal expertise. Regular meetings and simultaneous cross-participation in multiple groups became opportunities to experiment, grapple with ideas, and identify synergies with each other and across our collection areas.

Sustained conversation was essential—regular and over an extended period of time—but, as for Wenger's communities of practice, diverse perspectives and the valuing of relationships enabled a high level of creative and productive engagement. These kinds of working groups are not necessarily efficient, but they are effective! Structured dialogue led to tangible recommendations for the configuration and concept of future galleries; they also facilitated a shift toward a more collaborative, dialogic working culture. Here a more apt term than interdisciplinarity is transdisciplinarity—the integration of disciplinary perspectives to work through a joint problem set. Transdisciplinarity transgresses boundaries.

Nothing about these collaborative practices is straightforward: They are complex, nonlinear, negotiated, entangled. However, it is necessary work for the long term. Collaborative knowledge production, together with the privileging of lived experience and diversification of staff, can make our institutions more resilient, accountable, and inclusive. Seemingly subtle reorientations to internal processes can facilitate and open institutions up to the broader co-creation with communities and centering of maker voices and perspectives that will generate new, multivocal narratives.

The public spaces of museums are sometimes conceptualized in the image of an ancient Greek agora—a communal gathering space in the service of democracy. An agora in this sense is neither exclusively market nor government, neither exclusively public nor private.

Similarly, modes for collaborative knowledge production in a museum might be described as an agora, that is, a forum for discourse and for creatively negotiating meaning. Unlike the traditional agora, however, this internal agora is located not in space but in a set of collective and ideally transgressive practices.

The production of knowledge, whether in an agora or a community of practice, is situated in a social context. It involves an "encompassing process of being active participants in the practices of social communities and constructing identities in relation to those communities."[4] These collaborative practices not only create the conditions of possibility for invention and transformation; they also model the kinds of relationships we want to have with our publics: relationships of co-production, transparency, and respect.

Notes

1. Bryan L. Bonner and Alexander R. Bolinger. "Bring Out the Best in Your Team," *Harvard Business Review*. September 2014. Accessed April 3, 2021. https://hbr.org /2014/09/bring-out-the-best-in-your-team.

2. Jean Lave and Etienne Wenger. *Situated Learning: Legitimate Peripheral Participation*. (New York: Cambridge University Press, 1991); and Phaedra Brotherton, "Interview with Etienne Wenger," April 19, 2011, https://www.td.org/magazines/td -magazine/etienne-wenger

3. Etienne Wenger, *Communities of Practice: Learning, Meaning, and Identity*. (Cambridge: Cambridge University Press, 1998), 73.

4. Wenger, *Communities of Practice*, 4.

CHAPTER TWENTY-EIGHT

Hitting Reset on Hiring and Advancing in Museums

Sam Moore

Sam Moore is the founding executive director of the Moonshot Museum in Pittsburgh, Pennsylvania. As a leader and teacher in museum programs and operations, his career has included senior roles with the Senator John Heinz History Center, Missouri Historical Society, the National Aviary, and the University of Missouri.

It is time for museums and museum professionals to acknowledge a simple truth of our field, one that was true before the pandemic and is even truer after a season of constriction, furloughs, and layoffs. The entry-level job market for museums is broken, and pathways to professional advancement within our organizations are, generally, hard to come by.

The dance of debt-laden emerging professionals sitting across from underpaid midcareer professionals, interviewing for jobs at nonprofits scraping by to make payroll each year, without either party having any clue what the other is looking for nor wanting to be the first to reveal their respective hands, is the stuff of dark workplace comedies on network television. It is also an unfortunate reality of our field that we should end.

The past year has further exposed a field that is financially insecure, hampered by outdated models, buffeted by political headwinds, and entirely too white, male, and cisgender/heterosexual. Recent data from the American Alliance of Museums demonstrate we're in bad shape. Some museums may not survive to see this publication, much less the last gasps of the pandemic. Many more will face the next decade with fundamentally altered strategic plans and hiring priorities as they recover from the unexpected losses of 2020–2021. This is reality, and it is grim.

But it is a moment in which we should consider a reset in our approach to hiring and professional advancement. When presented with the relatively rare opportunity to hire for a new position or promote from within, museum hiring managers should rightfully be weighing many pressing considerations, diversity and opportunity chief among them. Much timely and insightful writing has focused on the lack of diversity in our ranks and the critical need to transform the makeup of our field. This must be a real and pressing priority for institutions with any hope of relevance in a post-COVID world.

In addition to facing questions of equity in on-boarding new staff, hiring managers need to keep pace with salary and opportunity for existing positions. They must juggle the need for new perspectives alongside the institutional knowledge and continuing contributions of longtime staff. Although a substantial and across-the-field increase in the wages of our lowest-paid team members is widely agreed on as ideal, the corresponding ripple effect throughout a museum's ranks, particularly for mid- and late-career museum professionals who have dedicated their careers to a particular institution, can trigger a budgeting challenge of monumental proportions. Our shortfalls in keeping salaries on track with the world around us, particularly for longtime employees, place a salary schedule based on a $15 minimum wage far out of reach for many museums.

And as a field, we spend countless hours each year not just discussing turnover in our ranks but conducting our interviews in such a manner that directly discourages emerging and midcareer professionals from revealing their future ambitions. "Where do you see yourself in five years?" doesn't have to be a loaded question, but it is. A response of "Somewhere else, because I will have grown beyond this role" is not one to which most hiring managers are likely to be receptive.

As we seize this post-pandemic moment, our field should face these dilemmas, considerations, and questions head on.

Emerging professionals interested in advancement should further expect and plan for geographical and institutional moves. The likelihood that "the job" will be in your hometown, home state, or even preferred region was rare before the pandemic and is even less likely now. The work we do is niche, and to grow and progress in niche work requires mobility. We as a field have a responsibility to address this, early on, with students and emerging professionals interested in advancement.

As we have these frank conversations with young professionals, our field also needs to acknowledge we are not always terribly honest with emerging and mid-career applicants. Assurances that our organizations are committed to an employee's growth in responsibility and salary if they demonstrate the desire and ability are nice and certainly well-intentioned, but they generally do not pan out. Honest interview conversations should hinge less on vague promises of professional advancement and "growth" and more on straightforward conversations about the vacant position, the reason for the designated salary, and the tangible resources and development opportunities the organization can offer to the prospective employee—whether they choose to stay for two years or for ten.

The inevitable, yet frustratingly still taboo, prioritization of salary transparency necessarily follows. I have yet to encounter the museum where vacant positions are rubber stamped for hiring without first going through a detailed and potentially agonizing process of examining institutional fiscal health, overall need, and layers of approval. One can assume that a posted position has been the subject of hours of careful consideration. It is also almost certainly tied to a single salary number or tight range. Simply put, if there is a job open, there is a corresponding number in a spreadsheet somewhere close by.

I propose we do things differently as we seize this critical moment. Listing salaries is a feasible and generally simple, if in some cases uncomfortable, first step. Can't pay as well as you would like? Fine; many organizations can't. But the acknowledgment of reality is also a signal of respect for the time, efforts, and ambitions of museum applicants.

This simple change would dramatically transform the dynamics in our interview processes and our internal conversations around pay and shed light on an area that has been kept in the dark for far too long. It is also time to upend the "opportunities for advancement" conversation that happens in so many interviews. Imagine in interviews if, instead of this:

> Of course, I can't predict the future, but we prioritize upward mobility in both responsibility and salary for team members at the Acme Museum.

We said this:

> This is the position I'm hiring for at the Acme Museum and I need it to do XYZ. Here's the number I have budgeted for salary. I want this to work for both of us, and I also want us to be on the same page. Advancement is possible, but I wouldn't say it's likely. What I can do is commit that we'll support your development in every way we can for the time you choose to spend here.

A shift in how our institutions define the "professional development" nomenclature that graces so many budget lines and performance reviews should follow. Conferences are, without a doubt, powerful tools for growth and exposure to new ideas. They're also expensive, and mass sponsorship of staff to attend our field's keystone gatherings is out of reach for even the richest of museums. But all organizations can create leadership opportunities for staff who may desire them but don't personally have a leadership title. Have a Green Team or diversity, equity, accessibility, and inclusion (DEAI) council? First, give it budgetary teeth because even the smallest of allocations can have a major impact on how the team is viewed internally and signal the increased responsibility of its leader. Then vocally and visibly empower someone from outside the museum's leadership who is looking for growth opportunities to be team leader. Set them up for success by formally ensuring they have access to organizational leadership for feedback and troubleshooting as they encounter challenges in their new leadership role.

Clearly state that your organization fully supports and encourages staff participation in communities of practice during work hours, valuing time spent in conversation with peers at other institutions. Respect the space those meetings occupy on individual calendars and encourage staff to share their learnings in all-hands and team meetings. Great and innovative ideas can emerge from these collaborative conversations. Create space alongside the pressing tasks of your museum's to-do list to hear about what other organizations are up to. Make this interest a core interview question for applicants. Let them know your museum will provide support in time and calendaring resources for this participation even if you can't commit monetary resources to professional development. An investment in the time and, to a lesser extent, financial resources required for these alternative approaches to professional development can inspire a more informed and positive workplace culture and have the potential to directly inform the reimagined work of museums in the aftermath of the pandemic.

This pivot in how we approach training, hiring, and promoting (or not promoting) museum employees necessarily means we as a field should be ready for and accepting of high turnover in entry and mid-level positions. Rather than making applicants describe their five-year plan in a way that forces them to hide their interest in advancement to fit the trajectory of a particular institution, museums should zoom out and focus on investing in people, all the while expecting that they will move on in the years ahead. Truly, for our field, for museum professionals, and for our individual institutions, the best approach we can take is to hire excellent people, equip them to be even more excellent, and then wish them well as they move on to make an excellent impact elsewhere in the field. Wash, rinse, repeat.

Museums have an opportunity to do better as we hire and promote. As we ask, "Where do we see our sector in five years?" I would like to think, by then, we'd view hiring and promoting as a shared and intentional investment in our workforce for both individual professional growth and for the ultimate benefit of the entire field.

PART IX

◠

REDEFINING SUCCESS

In the wake of COVID, what, exactly, do we mean by "museum success?" Do we mean that our museum is still in business, doing mostly what we are used to doing? That we have survived most or all the social turmoil and upheaval of recent years? That no one is demanding that we do more things or other things or more meaningful things? Or do we mean something different and deeper?

If we can come to some agreement about what constitutes success for our museums, how will we measure that success? Current practice for many museums focuses on a few measures of effectiveness: meeting the annual budget; attracting a given number of visitors and users; receiving a certain number of grants and contributions; presenting several programs; adding items to the collections. These metrics are relatively easy to generate, but they are of limited help in decision-making when uncertain times require reflection, change, and renewal. If we really want to understand the efficacy of our missions and assess our success in becoming more responsive to our communities, we will need more complex, nuanced, focused metrics.[1]

Now is a good time to ask ourselves what new skills, new practices, new modalities, and new metrics we are likely to need. This means devising new ideas about what matters (e.g., partnerships and collaborations) and revising what our field considers to be significant.

Museum leaders and staff might want to begin by interrogating their existential indicators of success: If our museum were to close, who would miss it and why? Who do we care about? Who do we most want to care about us?

Who do we hope to serve but are not reaching? If we seek to expand our partnerships with community organizations, local businesses, and government agencies, or our alliances with other museums, what are the metrics we need to measure the effectiveness of our networks? If we claim to represent diversity, equity, accessibility, and inclusion, which of our policies and procedures reflect these ideals? Which are based on untested or unwelcoming, assumptions? How, in other words, do we define and measure our public value?

There are several reasons for putting these questions at the center of our thinking. We are in a moment of scarcity unlike any the museum field has experienced before. Our losses of income and support require that we reconsider our traditional funding models and what fuels those models. We tend to think about sustainability only as money, but in the long run people must believe we make a difference. For many museums, financial support already hinges on making a case for vision and impact. We must decide new ways to make our public value case convincingly. It seems unlikely the old business models will prove viable when the pandemic ends. We need different operating paradigms that bring money and mission into better alignment.[2]

But, as our contributors suggest, there are many other challenges in defining and measuring success. As Cecilia Garibay points out, evaluation is not value neutral; instead, measuring success is generally framed in compliance with pre-existing museum assumptions, using categories derived from the dominant culture and powerful groups. If we want to better understand our institutions, we need to broaden our studies to encompass those individuals and communities who do not attend our museums, we need to assess how specific initiatives reflect institutional priorities and policies, and we need, at all times, to be attentive to issues of power and influence.

Institutional awareness must go even further, as Joanne Jones-Rizzi suggests. The language we use, both in our everyday practices and in our research studies, is charged with values from existing systems. The words we use to define perspectives and world views are critical, and their connotations are constantly changing. Therefore, if we want to develop new ways of working that address inclusive practices and employ multiple perspectives, we need to ensure that our language and our categories of thought are free of the very assumptions and biases we want to discard. New terms and usages will help us to transition to new possibilities and new realities. For Jones-Rizzi, success will come when people "see themselves and their experiences represented without being made to feel deficient through words and language that do not accurately reflect the full spectrum of their experiences."

Our museums also need to adopt new systems and new structures if they are to transform themselves and their public value. In his chapter, Ben Garcia distinguishes among corporate, for-profit organizations, and those that are committed to producing social value. "We are generators of public value, not of profit," he asserts. Garcia challenges conventional leadership models, and their accompanying metrics, as mismatches for our museums. He advocates for making information more widely accessible and providing more dispersed access to decision-making. Greater investment in equitable salaries then becomes a corollary to distributed authority. He offers specific replacement metrics that are more appropriate for the public good (and for the welfare of the entire organization): from measures of transparency to percentages of staff with decision-making authority, to salary differentials between the CEO and the rest of the employees.

We are at a point when museums need to be ready to pivot in response to opportunity and open to a revised set of assumptions and conditions that define success. As Garcia concludes: "We are being called to account by colleagues and community members who believe in the value of museums and who want us to do better. Aligning our management practices, values, and metrics to a paradigm of equity is one way that we can answer the call."

Notes

1. John W. Jacobsen, *Measuring Museum Impact and Performance* (Lanham, MD: Rowman & Littlefield, 2016).

2. In 2021, Anne W. Ackerson, Gail Anderson, and Dina Bailey created a consulting service titled *The Resilience Playbook* to help museums achieve greater public impact, inclusion, and value through resilience practices, https://museum.gwu.edu /museums-today-resilience-playbook

CHAPTER TWENTY-NINE

The (Unfulfilled) Promise
of Evaluation

Cecilia Garibay

Cecilia Garibay, PhD, Principal of Garibay Group, is a leading voice in the study and development of equity-focused research and evaluation in museums. She consults with cultural institutions on equity and organizational change. In 2020, she led the first field-wide study benchmarking equity and inclusion practices in US museums.

It is tempting to look back at 2020 as an aberration—a once-in-a-century pandemic and confluence of social and political events—that although incredibly difficult also provides an opportunity to recalibrate and plan for a different future: in other words, a chance to seize the moment and look forward rather than at our past.

In principle, I agree. This moment can be an impetus to reenvision the role of museums and reenvision our practices. But my worry is that our discourse will quickly shift into phoenix-rising-from-the-ashes myth-making that allows us to avoid confronting what Hasan Kwamie Jeffries terms "hard history." That we will delude ourselves into believing that we can reimagine our institutions out of whole cloth without owning our past. But as Audre Lorde reminds us, "The master's tools will never dismantle the master's house."

We must examine the ways in which our practices contribute to social inequities. Without deep reflection and critical examination of our institutions and practices, we will slip back into our comfort zones and avoid making real change—a transformative shift in which we center equity and justice in our work.[1]

The first-ever national landscape study investigating the current state of diversity, equity, accessibility, and inclusion (DEAI) practices in US museums was released in 2020.[2] Its major finding was that museums have not taken the consistent, strategic action—at an organizational level—foundational enough to support and achieve enduring equity and inclusion. It also found that equity and inclusion efforts are not prioritized, tend to be add-ons, and that power-sharing with community members from non-dominant groups is not common. The study also pointed to a significant disconnect between the emphasis museums place on public-facing DEAI practices and their lack of focus on internal equity and inclusion practices. It also found that a major barrier to advancing equity and inclusion is the lack of focus on collecting and using data to measure progress and drive change toward DEAI.

In other words, despite several decades of talk in museums about the importance of equity and inclusion, we have not made real progress as a field. The stark gap between stated values and action raises many questions, among them whether and how museums hold themselves accountable. It is especially interesting to consider the relationship between equity and evaluation.

I recently led a workshop on culturally responsive evaluation (CRE) for a museum. As I described how this approach is grounded in critical theories, I noted that equity and social justice are central concerns of CRE. A senior staff member, perhaps taking issue, commented that the museum's internal evaluators are explicitly told that they cannot be advocates. After all, the theory goes, evaluations must be objective.

The conversation that ensued, in which we unpacked ideas about values and the assumptions of objectivity and validity, was mildly productive; the team was clearly deeply uncomfortable working through these ideas. This was certainly not the first time I had encountered this objection, but it's interesting to note that attention to equity and social justice in evaluation is almost always interpreted as "activism."

The broad field of evaluation has its own problematic history, what Caldwell and Bledsoe call out as structural racism. Although evaluation is frequently portrayed as value neutral, it advances values and specific positions through decisions about study purposes and audiences, metrics and methods used, determinations of what counts as "valid" evidence, and whose agendas are privileged. These choices are often guided by a form of what Rodney Hopson terms "epistemological ethnocentrism," meaning that they are grounded in norms and assumptions that privilege dominant worldviews and cultures and marginalize those of nondominant communities. The notion of value-neutral and objective evaluation, in fact, assumes that experiences are normative and universal—an assumption that overlooks power dimensions of race, gender, and class, among others, and disregards culture and context.[3]

Culturally responsive evaluation, Indigenous evaluation, and equitable evaluation (led primarily by Black, Indigenous, and people of color [BIPOC] evaluators), among others, have emerged in response but are still viewed as alternatives rather than the norm; these evaluation orientations are not prevalent in the informal learning field.

The issue, then, is that evaluation and museums are both historically rooted in the same white racial frame. This means that success is assessed in the context of dominant culture values and norms, which can reinforce and validate inequitable structures. Both museums and evaluators often frame equity as "optional," relegating it as something to perhaps pay attention to in special "diversity and inclusion" projects rather than as a central aspect of their work.

The purpose of evaluation is also too often narrowly framed in terms of compliance—that is, assessing project outcomes based on predefined goals set by museums or funders. In my experience, this often leads to a lack of emphasis on process and the relational power and privilege dimensions at play in a given program or initiative. Framing evaluation solely as compliance can also lead to seeing it as punitive—a pass/fail rather than as a learning tool. This is the reason that many professionals fear evaluation!

A Way Forward

I believe evaluation can be a tool for equity, but it requires us to expand our paradigms about evaluation beyond Eurocentric perspectives and broaden our vision about the role it can play in museum work. I ground my own practice in culturally responsive research and evaluation. Using this equity-focused approach, I offer the following four observations on how evaluation could be used to help drive equity-focused organizational change in the museum field.

The emphasis on conducting research and evaluation with those who already visit museums limits what we know and understand about how people perceive and experience museums. Most museum studies are conducted with individuals who are white, well-educated, and well-resourced. Focusing on this small slice of the population provides a limited—and thus distorted—view of how welcoming museums are and the effectiveness of their educational practices. The studies that have focused on "nonvisitors" from minoritized groups show that these individuals often experience museums as enigmatic, unwelcoming spaces where their experiences, knowledge, and identities are othered.[4] Such narrow focus in our studies perpetuates systemic exclusion. Part of the problem is that museums use a "client" mindset of increasing visitation and "market share." We must widen the lens.

Evaluations assess individual initiatives (e.g., programs, exhibitions) as discrete, self-contained projects but do not link or examine these efforts in the larger context of organizational change. Although many museum efforts benefit from evaluations that help improve specific project activity or assess specific outcomes, these evaluations rarely consider how such initiatives connect to and inform the organization's core work. Evaluation can and should address the effect of a specific strategy or project on the underlying systemic drivers of inequity. In other words, evaluations should examine whether and how specific initiatives are expected to inform and change the norms, policies, and practices in museums that cause or enable disparities and whether they do.

Evaluations prioritize museum perspectives and values, failing to attend to power and privilege. Evaluations most often center museum goals and use measures of success that have been predefined by museum leaders or funders. In DEAI "projects" especially, this unequally empowers some stakeholders, marginalizing community stakeholders by positioning them as passive recipients of a program or project and often presumes benefit. Evaluations should attend to these dynamics, privilege the voices of community stakeholders, and ensure that the focal community's goals and values inform and shape the evaluation. Evaluations should also examine how museum initiatives align with the values and priorities of minoritized communities involved, consider whose expertise is being privileged, and critically analyze the museum's relationships and partnerships. These questions are fundamentally about power: how evaluators and museums actively share it or do not. Does the evaluation and the museum initiative support power-building among communities, or do they instead perpetuate existing inequitable power structures?

Using an equity focus, evaluation could help museums examine their internal operations and organizational cultures to address embedded, institutional racism. Given museums' lack of focus on internal dimensions of DEAI, it is perhaps not surprising that the field has not prioritized assessing its own internal practices. Centering equity and inclusion requires organizations to think holistically, recognizing that internal operations and externally focused work are interconnected. Evaluation grounded in equity approaches could examine staff's experiences and perspectives (particularly BIPOC staff) of the organization's policies, practices, work culture, and climate and make visible the ways in which existing internal structures effectively address or perpetuate inequities.[5]

Karen Kirkhart writes that the "house of evaluation is a house of privilege." It is also certainly true that the house of museums is a house of privilege. We have an opportunity at this moment to confront this hard history and create a different future. Equity-focused evaluation can serve as a tool for informing and supporting equity-focused organizational change if museums are willing to invest in evaluation, embrace adaptive learning, transparency, and experimentation and move away from the idea that there is a "quick fix" to equity.

Notes

1. By equity, I mean fair access to resources that advances social justice by allowing for full participation in society and for self-determination in meeting fundamental needs. Achieving equity requires addressing structural and historical barriers and systems of oppression.

2. Cecilia Garibay and Jeanna Marie Olson. CCLI National Landscape Study: The State of DEAI Practices in Museums. https://www.informalscience.org/sites/default/files/CCLI_National_Landscape_Study-DEAI_Practices_in_Museums_2020.pdf

3. The parallels to the discussion in the larger field about the myth that museums are neutral spaces are striking. See the "Museums Are Not Neutral" movement cofounded by LaTanya S. Autry and Mike Murawski.

4. Emily Dawson, *Equity, Exclusin and Everyday Science Learning: The Experiences of Minoritised Groups.* (London: Routledge, 2019) and Cecilia Garibay, "Responsive and Accessible: How Museums Are Using Research to Better Engage Diverse Cultural Communities." https://www.informalscience.org/responsive-and-accessible-how-museums-are-using-research-better-engage-diverse-cultural-communities

5. For an illuminating and sobering account of BIPOC staff's experiences in the field, see the *Change the Museum* social media site.

CHAPTER THIRTY

Word Processing

Joanne Jones-Rizzi

Joanne Jones-Rizzi, Vice President of Science, Equity, and Education at the Science Museum of Minnesota, specializes in working toward systemic, ecological change within museums, expanding meaningful access through exhibitions relevant to audiences who do not think of museums as their cultural institutions. She advises museums on culture, identity, and antiracism.

I know intellectually and as a museum leader that the ways we evaluate successes and failures are critical and structural; they are built into the DNA of our institutions. There are blogs, data sets, and scorecards, all focused on informing, discussing, quantifying, and measuring "How are we doing?" We are reliant on data and metrics and standards of excellence to the point of exhaustion.

But existing metrics used to collect data in service of an increased understanding of our institutions carry layers of subtexts. Although necessary because they guide our understanding, our metrics are often self-propagating, dominating rather than revealing. While they hold institutional currency, they may not carry inclusive value.

I am immersed in equity and inclusion work, and because most museums are white-centric, supremacist organizations, the work is all about challenging the normative and decentering whiteness. I am also interested in exploring questions about language and how the words we use in museums often contradict the systemic changes and shifts taking place within our institutions.

When I think of "standards of excellence" I can't help but question who is setting the standards, determining the metrics, and defining success. Does it matter? My initial thought is that the language that we use in our work, particularly now when so many museums are paying attention to equity and inclusion in new and varied ways, shapes the ways that we think. Words can present or preclude possibilities and signal the inclusion or exclusion of who participates in imagining the future.

When we say we want new structures and new systems, why do we still rely on defining success, excellence, and performance within existing systems? Can we develop metrics that support new ways of working, that address inclusive practices, and reflect multiple perspectives? Can we dismantle white supremacy within our museums and still define metrics that are inclusive? Are we still using a model of whiteness, obscuring it by layering on a few questions or metrics that address equity work to the point of self-satisfaction?

Language is a fluid medium and new terminologies will continue to evolve as will the terms that people use to self-identify. In this moment, I am reflecting on words and phrases that are actively shifting. Each is taking on new and variable values to communicate and understand the framing of current events, the implied individual and political perspectives, individual world views, and institutional values.

For example, when people refer to the community actions and responses that took place after George Floyd's murder in Minneapolis, Minnesota, where I live, many within the media and those condemning the community response characterize those actions as "rioting" and "looting." People with greater proximity, who were more involved and supportive, and sometimes directly impacted, referred to those events as "protests" or "uprising," and lately "unrest" and "civil unrest." These varying descriptions, although seemingly similar in definition, convey completely different perspectives, framings, and values.

Language, and understanding how we use it within museums and within the strained and restructured hybrid environments many of us find ourselves in, is profoundly important. Nuanced and often coded, I check and recheck and try to learn how the terminology I use can perpetuate systems that are less inclusive, lest the language I use, unintentionally, contributes to a less inclusive meaning/reaction. I check and recheck my use of terminology for nuanced and coded language that may perpetuate less inclusive systems. I have shared with my colleagues that I don't want to be that person who corrects and chastises people for using the "wrong" word or not using the current phraseology. We are engaged in a learning process, one that reflects our growth as an institution, communicating that we are sensitive to nuance and are aware of the dynamic shifts and their correlation to the words we use and the change we are attempting to impart.

My mind keeps wandering back to the childhood idiom: "*Sticks and stones may break my bones, but words will never hurt me.*" It's a deflection, a child's way to show resistance. We all know that words can feel like slaps and can cause pain that feels visceral. The idea that words can't hurt seems ludicrous to me, particularly in the context of equity and museums. Words are how we communicate in meetings, in conversation, in memos, emails, texts, tweets, and so on. Words have power; they can feel welcoming, confrontational, invasive, soothing, inspiring, comedic. And they can hurt. How often have you opened a seemingly innocuous email that cuts you to the quick?

Language is a critical aspect of equity and inclusion in all museum work. I am struck by the convergence of the language we use to describe events now taking place in our communities and the current museum work that is centered on equity, inclusion, and dismantling white supremacy. The language that describes equity, inclusion, and antiracism has changed, particularly in the past year, and the pace of this shift in language has accelerated. A few months ago, we would not have heard the words "white supremacy" spoken in mainstream communication. Now it has entered our public discourse. Interrogating language within our political and social discourse and in our museums connects and, at the same time, for me, creates a complex disconnect.

As we learn more about ourselves, individually and organizationally, the terms we use will continue to shift. Phrases and words that were appropriate at one time become less relevant, at times incongruous, and are replaced with new terms. For example, identity terms such as people of color or POC are not obsolete, but the more inclusive term, "BIPOC," which refers to Black, Indigenous, People of Color, is in common use. Language is a living medium and will continue to evolve, as will the terms that people use to self-identify. They are also important measures of our thinking and our practice.

I've been noticing that at the museum where I work, we often use words like "deploy" and "frontline" to describe actions or staff functions, words that borrow from war and the military. Other power-laden words, such as "master" and "slave," adopted as terms in computer programming and engineering, have found their way into office functions as in "master document." When referring to community or forms of co-creative work, the word "serve" often features prominently. The power imbalance that it represents suggests we are the missionaries bestowing resources and good will from our museum on those who we perceive to be in need of what we offer. There is no sense of reciprocity in the word "serve," no sense of collaboration or working together. In my mind, words that create distance rather than closeness continue to separate us from the audiences and communities in which we are situated.

The words we use do not always convey our intention. Many are based in and support a white supremacy culture or a culture of dominance and power.

I've done a quick scan through the notebooks that I use day to day to remind myself of tasks and to take notes at meetings. They are replete with words such as *initiative, social justice, intersectionality, equity,* and *authenticity.* Although I know the context for these words, I am struck by how these terms' richness and depth are enhanced by their use internally and by how language and words can convey that richness and depth when used within a specific cultural, historical, and or social context.

I think about recent conversations with colleagues and friends about immunization shots for COVID-19. I am increasingly aware that the word "shot" has another powerful, negative meaning. When I heard on the news that Daunte Wright was shot, I was reminded of a time recently when several museum colleagues and I were preparing for a video production session, and I kept seeing emails about the video "shoot."

Every time I read the word it bothered me; finally, I wrote an email titled "The Bias Inside Us Shoot":

> This is a small thing but something I am committed to doing in the coming year—given that these two exhibitions have to do with bias, racism, law enforcement, and societal inequities—can we please call this a recording session rather than a "shoot"? In my mind there is no need to reify or bring the language of guns and gun violence into what we are doing. I know you are using "shoot" in a completely different context, but every time I read it, I am reminded of the way that the words we use are reflective of societal norms that we all can change.

Cultural shifts and power dynamics are slow to change. One way that we begin to recognize and understand the changes in motion is through the shifts in the language that we use and hear. As Audre Lorde reminds us, "What are the words you do not yet have? What do you need to say? What are the tyrannies you swallow day by day and attempt to make your own, until you will sicken and die of them, still in silence?"

There are numerous change-makers in our field; it's an exciting time as we are demanding long overdue accountability. While we work to make change, I urge us to commit to and pay attention to words like *excellence, performance, data,* and *metrics* to support inclusive growth and authentic and sustainable change. Collectively we can co-create change as we continue to work together to develop the strongest, boldest, iconic public programs and exhibitions. How will we know that we have succeeded? Every person will see themselves and their experiences represented without being made to feel deficient through words and language that do not accurately reflect the full spectrum of our experiences.

~

CHAPTER THIRTY-ONE

Measuring Our Value(s)

Let's Start with Structure

Ben Garcia

Ben Garcia is Executive Director of the American LGBTQ+ Museum in New York. He presents and publishes regularly on inclusive leadership and equitable museum practice. He worked previously at the Ohio History Connection, Getty Museum, Skirball Cultural Center, Phoebe A. Hearst Museum, and Museum of Us. He serves on the boards of the Association of Midwest Museums and Equality Ohio.

~

Over the past twenty years, I have moved from being subject to the decisions and structures of the museums in which I worked to having greater ability to determine them. The reason I chose to move away from creating programs and exhibits and into administrative roles was because I recognized a path to making more lasting change. I had seen from my various museum perches that disempowerment, inequity, and hypocrisy could be traced to organizational structures and values adopted from for-profit enterprise.

Certainly, individuals were sometimes the issue, but the organizational structure enabled, and even encouraged, dehumanizing and othering practices that led to abuse. I recently discovered the Change the Museum Instagram account (@changethemuseum). Scrolling through it is a journey into abusive relationships, with, in most cases, the organization, or a segment of the leadership, as the perpetrator. On the site, staff post their experiences of racism. In my experience, similar stories addressing gender, queerness, disability, and economic biases could fill other accounts.

I sought (and seek) new possibilities for leading museums toward greater generation of public value, toward that vision of "third space"—or fourth, depending on where you site the digital realm—where magic can happen. Lois Silverman, in an issue of the *Journal of Education in Museums*, defines museum magic as "elusive moments of insight, transformation and deep significance that help us to see the purpose and reasons for living." As a museum leader, my purpose is to connect my colleagues and the public to that magic.

Profit versus Public Good

Public value, as Carol Scott explained in her book *Museums and Public Value*, is to nonprofit organizations as profit is to private enterprise. We exist and receive benefits from taxpayers in exchange for providing value to the public realm. This is not to say that for-profit enterprise does not generate public good. It does in many cases. But the for-profit and nonprofit sectors have developed to address *different* societal needs.

Because these organizations' goals and purposes differ, their structures should reflect these differences. Yet most museums accept the inherited notion that these entities can be effectively structured in the same way. Their wholesale adoption of management and leadership forms from the for-profit sector has served to perpetuate systemic inequities in our museums.

Systemic inequities are perpetuated by systems and not by individuals or groups. At some point in the past, the biases of individuals informed the development of systems. Those biases became "invisible" as time passed; today these systems are viewed by many as "neutral." #MuseumsAreNotNeutral is a movement elevated by La Tanya S. Autry and Mike Murawski. This movement challenges the self-serving perception that museum collections, spaces, programs, and interpretation are neutral by exposing the overwhelming whiteness in mainstream museums. The concept applies as well in operations, accounting practices, and organizational structures.

This is not a broadside against capitalism. Museums have much to learn from the private sector about adopting new technologies, addressing disruption, creating greater efficiencies, improving visitor experiences, and better understanding the landscape of earned revenue and marketing/communications. Museum innovations tend to lag behind those in the private sector; even the version of corporate structure that many museums currently employ is likely an artifact of an earlier age.

The adoption of corporate structures and norms for how trustees and staff work together, of corporate hierarchies and notions of transparency, and most egregiously, of labor and compensation norms, works *counter* to goals of equity and the public good. But here's the rub: Although leadership absolutely exists at every level of an organization, undoing corporate management norms needs to be spearheaded by the CEO/ED and the board. Without leadership and buy-in there, this change will be slow (if it comes at all) and painful as recent protracted protests at the Whitney, SFMoMA, and others demonstrate.

Change is necessary to realize museum goals of achieving equity and fostering the public good. Following are three arenas for this change. Each will require buy-in from the CEO and the board. Without leadership from the top, this change will be slow, and likely painful, if it comes at all.

Board Structure and the Role of the CEO

Many trustees are recruited from corporate spaces, where the values of profit maximization predominate. Museums, on the other hand, need to educate trustees to better understand their public value purpose. Sound finances are essential, but sustainability and growth in museums, while related to those in the private sector, often look different. This disconnect contributes to the ongoing pressure to expand brick and mortar as the most common metric of successful museum leadership, a strategy that often yokes subsequent generations to support a facility rather than serve the public.

Additionally, the traditional "hourglass" form for museum structures (where the CEO occupies the narrow neck between the board on one side and the staff on the other) confers an outsized role on the CEO in determining organizational priorities, including equity practices. We need structures that ensure ongoing progress toward equity is driven by many people. The hourglass form needs to become a cylinder where ideas and leadership move back and forward between a wider group of staff and trustees.

Jim Collins in *Good to Great* defines productive ambition as ambition for ideas and the goals of the organization and not for the self. We need to apply that concept to our desire for heroic leaders. Certainly, a CEO needs to embody the vision for the museum, but so do all the staff and trustees. Sharing that generative version of ambition across the organizational chart will help ensure the legacy of any museum leader.

Communication and Decision-Making

We excel in excessive guarding and gate-keeping access to information. Although there are categories of information that need to be held confidentially (such as private personnel records, procedures for safeguarding information systems, or other assets), our propensity for safeguarding many other categories of information perpetuates hierarchy and spawns resentment and suspicion among staff and external stakeholders. In the void, imagination takes over. Poor communication (even more than poor compensation) makes staff feel disempowered. Far too often, the opacity of our management norms confers the most status on those with access to information. As people do not easily give up status, they perpetuate this practice.

Limited engagement in decision-making not only serves as a barrier to equity, but it also impacts the quality of the decisions themselves. If the big decisions (e.g., budget priorities, workplace culture changes, new organizational policies) are made by a proportionally small leadership team (1 to 2 percent of the overall staff), the number of poor decisions will be much greater than if that team consists of 5 to 10 percent of staff. We saw this at the Ohio History Connection last year when we grew the leadership team from five to twenty-two (for a staff of two hundred). The results so far, during an historically challenging year, have been promising. People around the leadership table regularly bring perspectives and ideas to bear that were absent in the original structure.

Museums need to make information available more broadly. Share minutes from leadership team meetings so staff know where the conversations are centered. Explain to all staff how leaders arrived at decisions, what values guided them, and what issues they struggled with. Report on progress against the budget, quarterly, at all-staff meetings. Not only will this empower staff; it will also teach them to think like leaders.

Economic Insecurity and Compensation

One outcome of the 2020 pandemic year has been greater awareness of the wealth disparity in our country. The ever-widening gap between executive compensation and median compensation in private enterprise is well documented. This is reflected in such nonprofits as universities, hospitals, performing arts organizations, and museums.

The pay equity issue, highlighted by such organizations as *Museum Workers Speak*, is inextricably linked to the legacies of class, gender, and racial bias in museums. While it was still an independent company, Ben and Jerry's ice cream determined that the highest paid employee would not make more than five to seven times the salary of the lowest. They pioneered in tying CEO pay raises to increases for the entire staff. This insight helped me consider what an ethically rooted differential should be in museums. How can we use a transparent, values-based process to determine our salary differentials?

Currently, we justify the shockingly high compensation of many museum CEOs as what the market requires, the cost of recruiting talent. What if a values-based compensation rubric made the minimum wage a living wage and pegged the highest wage as no greater than five to seven times that minimum? I guarantee that the many extremely talented leaders I know in the field would queue up to lead.

A living wage is defined as a wage where a full-time employee does not need a second job to pay for basic needs and is able to save for contingencies. If the minimum living wage for a museum in Columbus is about $20/hour, the CEO would earn $100-$140/hour. For New York City or San Francisco, where that minimum is arguably closer to $30/hour, the CEO salary might be up to $210/hour. And $437,000 may be half or one-third of what large museum directors earn in New York, San Francisco, or Chicago, but it is generous compensation for the head of an organization whose output is public value.

Proposed Metrics of Public Value and Equity

1. Percentage of staff and trustees that work together in working groups (number of non-C-suite staff and trustee engagements).
2. Percentage of staff who determine decisions that impact the entire organization; percentage of staff engaged with decision-making process (as advisors or influencers).
3. Number of levels between CEO and nonsupervisorial staff.
4. Types of information shared with all staff and externally (decisions and decision-making process; annual budget; leadership compensation and benefits; rubrics for staff compensation, performance evaluation, etc.). Where is that information accessed?
5. Differential between the highest paid and the lowest paid member of staff.
6. Percentage a supervisor earns over their direct reports.
7. Number of full-time staff who work second jobs in order to meet basic needs for their families.
8. Amount museum spends per staff member on professional development.
9. Amount museum spends per staff member on workplace culture improvements.

Conclusion

We are generators of public value and not of profit. This requires different structural designs and employment practices. Holding ourselves accountable for how equitable, effective, and productive we are also requires developing and implementing different measures to account for our success.

Until we transform ourselves into equitable entities, we cannot fully walk our talk of public value. We are being called to account by colleagues and community members who believe in the value of museums and who want us to do better. Aligning our management practices, values, and metrics to a paradigm of equity is one way that we can answer the call. As Toni Morrison reminds us, "Inviting compassion into the bloodstream of an institution's agenda . . . is more than productive, more than civilizing, more than ethical, more than humane; it's humanizing."

PART X

~

EXPANDING PURPOSE

In July 2019, just as the nested crises of the pandemic were beginning to disrupt the global economy, the International Council of Museums (ICOM) proposed a new and expanded definition of museums:

> Museums are democratizing, inclusive and polyphonic spaces for critical dialogue about the pasts and the futures. . . . They are participatory and transparent, and work in active partnership with and for diverse communities . . . aiming to contribute to human dignity and social justice, global equality and planetary wellbeing.

These are not entirely new ideas among American museums. Thirty years ago, the American Association of Museums (now the American Alliance of Museums) published a report charting a new course for purpose and practice in the field. *Excellence and Equity: Education and the Public Dimension of Museums* called "for museums to expand their role as educational institutions . . . to recast the definition of excellence not merely to include equity, but to require it . . . and for museums to embrace cultural diversity in all facets of their programs, staff and audiences."

Progress toward the realization of these goals has been, at best, uneven. Although museums have been largely successful in promoting themselves as public educational institutions, metrics of their educational impact have remained vague and inconclusive. As to equity, the racist, colonial origins of many museums have persisted, for the most part unquestioned and unchallenged despite repeated calls for museums to examine their own dark histories and systemic biases.

The concurrent impact of Black Lives Matter, climate change and natural disasters, and COVID-19 has forced American museums to reconsider their purposes, goals, and practices. Where silence and acquiescence once prevailed, social protest now resonates, amplified by the divisive politics of the Trump presidency and the bitterly contested election of 2020. As key players in cultural arenas locally, regionally, and nationally, museums must expand their roles to participate more fully in their communities, to protect the institutions of American democracy, and to sustain the well-being of the Earth—our common home.

In the era of the Anthropocene, humankind has the power to alter the fundamental character of our planet in ways unimaginable less than a century ago. What we now understand is that our exploitation of wildlife and landscape, watersheds and weather is creating conditions inimical to equity and in the long-term to the very survival of civilization. As Emlyn Koster argues in his chapter, we must stop denying human failure to protect the Earth System. It is now our duty—and a fundamental purpose of museums going forward—"to adopt a new paradigm that recognizes the connections between societies and environments."[1]

Simultaneously, Americans have been called yet again to a reckoning with our own histories of injustice, inequity, bias, and bigotry. Historian Alan Taylor has argued that the European colonization of America rested on two tragedies—Indian deaths and African slavery; these cataclysms still reverberate in our contemporary society, so it is our obligation and the obligation of museums to embrace social justice as a fundamental purpose. This will be neither simple nor easy: As Elena Gonzales suggests, both our environmental and sociocultural crises are the results of centuries of inequity and exploitation. But, she argues, museums have the capacity to leverage new knowledge, to tell the stories of many peoples, to refute untruths, and to "advance a more equitable distribution of risks and rewards in society."

Deborah F. Schwartz concurs that "We need models that turn our elite and hierarchical assumptions on their head and that really open us to the needs of our community." To do so, museums need to avoid a return to old, tired hierarchies, an elitist position in the community, and the elevation of expertise over community engagement. Instead, American museums must "invite fresh thinking into our inner sanctum, trust people from the community, and intertwine intellectual disciplines in new ways."

The stakes are high. The pandemic has "torn away the curtain of moral complacency," Dorothy Kosinski writes, and museums must make a decisive turn to community. Also, Kosinski suggests, "The museum cannot simply be welcoming and accessible, but rather . . . must be more for people of today rather than in service to the historical past." To reset their moral compasses, museums must become more equitable internally and more attentive to the voices and stories of their communities. "The moral center, the focal point, has shifted drastically, outside the walls," she suggests, and we need to play a larger, more fearless role "in promoting empathy, participation, good citizenship, and notions of justice."

These views, in their different ways, reflect a global reconsideration of the social responsibilities of all nonprofits that has taken center stage in recent years. Steve Dubbs, writing in the summer 2021 issue of *NPQ*, the *Nonprofit Quarterly Magazine*, asked provocatively, "Can We Reshape the U.S. Social Contract?" so as to advance a global framework that values "solidarity, participatory democracy, equity in all dimensions, and sustainability." Today, progressive museums across the continent are revisiting their ideas, reconsidering their purposes, and adopting new paradigms. With a growing sense of urgency and relevance, American museums are beginning to seize the moment.

Note

1. Museums are beginning to link their work to the United Nation's Sustainable Development Goals; see *The Sustainable Development Goals Report* 2021 https://unstats.un.org/sdgs/report/2021/The-Sustainable-Development-Goals-Report-2021.pdf

CHAPTER THIRTY-TWO

Museum Relevance in the Context of the Earth System

Emlyn Koster

Emlyn Koster, PhD, blends his geological and museological background to illuminate the Anthropocene, the new age of human disruption of climates and environments. Formerly the CEO of four nature and science museums, he is an ambassador for the International Coalition of Sites of Conscience and adjunct professor in Marine, Earth, and Atmospheric Sciences at North Carolina State University.

> We have the urgent responsibility to give voice to the Earth's immense story. . . . We are at a critical moment in the continuity of time.
>
> —Declaration at a Smithsonian Institution Convening, 2012

Between 1968 and 1972, NASA's *Apollo* missions enabled the first color photographs of the Earth from outer space. The photos revealed the stunning beauty—but also the potential fragility—of our planet with its wafer-thin, protective atmosphere. In 1970, the first Earth Day spawned an outcry over the effects of ground and air pollution on environmental and public health. Since then, mounting insights and grave warnings from scientific research have failed to generate anything close to adequate stewardship of the Earth System—the umbrella term for the Earth's enveloping shells with their interacting balance of physical, chemical, and biological processes.

In 2004, the International Geosphere-Biosphere Program published evidence for two dozen exponential trends since the mid-twentieth century of adverse environmental and socioeconomic changes. Its conclusion was clear that *Homo sapiens* have interrupted the balance of nature and altered the course of Earth history. In a geological nanosecond, the world has entered the Anthropocene, a new age of human disruption of climates, environments, and ecosystems. Needing to become a household word, the term is shorthand for the perils we face. Anxiety over humanity's course is shown by the rising frequency of mainstream news referring to the worst new trends as existential crises.

Only now are we beginning to come to grips with perhaps our greatest challenge: identifying those tipping points when a risk may switch from a gradual trend into an abrupt and major change. We know, for example, that climate change is causing a rapid, sometimes nonlinear, melting of ice sheets and glaciers. The resulting sea-level rise will cause economic dislocations and force mass migrations from low-lying coastal regions. But perhaps the most immediate hazard is that the COVID-19 pandemic is one of many diseases caused by germs passing from animals to humans. Climate change is a factor in the spread of this virus, which has caused the greatest disruption to society, its economy, and culture since World War II.

Until now, it has been possible for many people to assume that societal health is separate from, and superior to, environmental health. This form of denial has fostered impressions that nature and culture are unconnected realms. Instead, our government, for-profit enterprises, and nonprofit organizations need to adopt a new paradigm that recognizes the connections between societies and environments. The Rockefeller Foundation and the medical journal *Lancet* recently concluded that the health of human civilization depends on the health of natural systems. Environmental justice and social justice are not only pervasive concerns, but they are also conjoined imperatives at the core of progressive communities.

If museums are to become indispensable to their communities and to the nation as a whole, they need to bring forth intellectual and structural changes in their policies and practices. Apart from those about children's growth, museums are divided into aging categories—natural history, human history, art, science, and technology. These descriptors are increasingly out of sync with the need to present narratives that integrate past-present-future perspectives to illuminate the multifaceted realities of today's world. What were once different interpretive agendas for each museum category must now converge and overlap. Just as many types of museums employ interactivity in exhibition experiences and integrate audiovisual and digital media, we need to transcend outdated, and detrimental, distinctions and embrace a paradigm that places humanity squarely in both nature and society.

To do so will be a profound challenge. Changing some of our long-held beliefs about the world and our place in it raise questions of perspective, trust, positioning, leadership, and planning. On the premise that the museum sector should be doing its utmost to be a good ancestor, I offer views on each of these vital aspects from my experience as a geologist who worked in three World Heritage Sites before becoming the CEO of four nature and science museums in Canada and the United States.

The museum sector needs to distinguish the proverbial forest from the trees. The onslaught of operational and strategic challenges that confront institutions today tend to keep us focused on our particular trees. At this level, facility closure and budget turmoil have brought with them a daunting array of operational and personnel exigencies—including health safeguards, digital outreach, member retention, staff unrest, CEO turnover, and board-room conflict. Concurrently at the forest level, there is an urgent need for institutional reflection on how to respond to unfolding changes in the circumstances that surround museums. These long-view perspectives are necessary to strengthen the internal health of museums and their external value. Failure to reassess past practices or to consider alternative purposes and strategies is tantamount to sleepwalking into potentially greater challenges.

Trust in an enterprise hinges on a firm and widespread belief in its reliability and authenticity. The museum sector relies on surveys by the UK Museums Association and American Alliance of Museums (AAM) that found a high level of public trust in museums. If, however, the circumstances surrounding museums have changed—as they surely have—then so must their purpose and direction also morph if they are to remain relevant and trustworthy. Core to this new agenda is a fresh assessment of audience needs and wants. Museums, like societies, need to stay in touch with both these evolving drivers.

The recent upheaval has also intensified dialogue about the need to look more critically at structures and practices. We face a growing demand that the compositions of museum boards, CEOs, and staff should more nearly reflect our audiences and communities. Success in changing our appearance, a commendable priority, needs to pave the way for more substantial mission-advancing initiatives. The call for diversity, equity, accessibility, and inclusion (DEAI), as championed by the AAM, has quickly become popular shorthand. However, we also need to move from slogans to more profound considerations about museum philosophy and practice. An instructive comparison is provided by STEM. For years, STEM was touted as a breakthrough highlighting the topical scope of science centers. Today, as community engagement programs become the priority, STEM no longer appears in the strategic parts of the Association of Science and Technology (ASTC) website. Clearly, the highlighting of subject areas does not, by itself, guarantee new intentions.

Leadership that seeks both efficiency and effectiveness, the former defined as doing things right and the latter as doing the right things, has become more critical. Executives need a grasp of the pulse of the museum sector, detailed knowledge of and involvement with local challenges and opportunities, conspicuous appetites for new approaches, and inspiring communication skills. As the circumstances surrounding museums have become more acute, their traditionally historical focus will become a limitation and will, in all probability, seem irresponsible if not woven into contemporary contexts. Museums will need to vigorously engage their staff and stakeholders in gear-shift discussions to make them both more satisfying workplaces and, to their communities and the world at large, more relevant and worthy of support. As integral parts of social systems, museums can provide unique resources that the community will need to call on to assist with transformation efforts.

During the past year, communities have been among the loudest voices demanding attention from our museums. We need to pay close attention to the voices of the concerned public at-large. This is not a new challenge. A century ago, John Cotton Dana, director of the Newark Museum, argued that museums should know the needs of their communities and fit themselves to those needs. This was echoed in 1995 at the 150th symposium of the Smithsonian Institution, when Harold Skramstad, president emeritus of the Henry Ford Museum and Greenfield Village, urged that the mission statements of all museums specify their intended external benefits. Before the COVID-19 pandemic struck, ICOM had begun to explore a new mission statement for the museum sector, but this effort encountered a strong headwind from traditionalists. More than ever, the sector must strive to be more than the sum of its parts.

We and our museums need to think harder about how to become necessary and not just nice. As we move forward, our transformative steps must be accompanied by a shift in how we plan our way into an uncertain future. Gone are the days of nicely bound five-year plans blessed by governing boards. Strategy now needs to be an agile response to novel challenges. This entails a continuous process of planning and adjustment to align resources with solution attempts to critical problems—whether they are today's challenges or the ones likely to arise tomorrow.

We need as well to recognize that the challenges in front of humanity transcend the boundaries of conventional discipline-specific approaches. We need to embrace the idea of a holistic Earth System that encompasses nature and society. And we need to establish the Anthropocene as the prime context for museum relevance in the twenty-first century. Now is the time for museums to be innovative contributors to the collective advancement of Earth's well-being. Delay is no longer an option.

Further Reading

L. Isager, et al., "A New Keyword in the Museum: Exhibiting the Anthropocene." *Museum & Society*, 19:1 (2020): 88–107.

Emlyn Koster, "The Anthropocene as Our Conscience," in *Designing for Empathy, Perspectives on the Museum Experience*, ed. E. Gokcigdem (Lanham, MD: Rowman & Littlefield, 2019): 344–361.

Emlyn Koster, "Paradigm Shift to Illuminate this Disrupted Planet," in *Exhibition*, American Alliance of Museums, 40:1 (2021): 100–110.

Emlyn Koster, E. Dorfman, and T. Nyambe, "A Holistic Ethos for Nature-Focused Museums in the Anthropocene" in *The Future of Natural History Museums*, ed. Eric Dorfman (New York: Routledge, 2017): 9–48.

R. Nixon, "The Anthropocene and Environmental Justice" in *Curating the Future: Museums, Communities and Climate Change* ed. J. Newell, et al. (New York: Routledge, 2017): 23–31.

Sarah Sutton and C. Robinson, "The Climate is Changing, Why Aren't Museums?" *Journal of Museum Education*, 45:1 (2020): 107 pp.

S. Whitmee, et al., "Safeguarding Human Health in the Anthropocene Epoch: Report of The Rockefeller Foundation-Lancet Commission on Planetary Health." *The Lancet*, 386, (2015): 1973–2028.

CHAPTER THIRTY-THREE

Social Justice

Framework for the Future of Museums

Elena Gonzales

Elena Gonzales, PhD, is an independent scholar and curator focusing on curatorial work for social justice. She is the author of *Exhibitions for Social Justice* from Routledge's Museum Meanings Series (2019) and Curator of *Latinx Chicago* at the Chicago History Museum (fall 2023).

Museums hope to remain relevant and sustainable. Those with bright futures will illuminate the connections between environmental and human exploitation, marshal their resources in support of diverse stakeholders, and preserve, present, and interpret many stories of art, history, science, and peoples.

COVID-19 has provided a vivid, global demonstration of how our lives and fates are connected in ways that might not be obvious, illuminating the previously invisible threads connecting seemingly disconnected people all over the world. Each of us is connected to myriad other people who may seem quite distant from ourselves. We breathe together with billions of other people who look differently, believe differently, love differently, move differently, think differently, and speak or spend differently from those we think of as being "us."

The connections among strangers are not the only ones the pandemic has revealed. In *Trendswatch 2021*, Elizabeth Merritt wrote that the pandemic, the long overdue social reckoning about our white supremacist American culture, and the constant, even overlapping, natural disasters, are "deeply entangled." In our exploitation of natural and human resources, humans in general and Americans, in particular, have created a mass extinction and climate emergency. The dramatic natural disasters that are now common-place (including the pandemic) are fruits of the quest for constant growth. Our sociocultural crisis is the result of centuries of wanton exploitation in which some humans use others for the purposes of amassing and concentrating wealth.

Museums are a significant group of cultural players that have the capacity to advance a more equitable distribution of risks and rewards in society. They can illustrate and explain the connections between social and environmental crises in ways that can make them accessible and compelling to many publics. They can lead by example through their operations (by becoming carbon neutral), their cultures (by promoting equity among staff and board), and their programs (by offering safe, inclusive spaces for conversation).

Museums can also leverage their role as centers of research by contributing new knowledge. Julie Decker, Director of the Anchorage Museum, frames this obligation by saying that museums should provide "responses" instead of "reactions" to contemporary issues. Moreover, it is our obligation to provide safe and inclusive spaces for conversations around difficult topics. The Jane Addams Hull House Museum in Chicago, for example, regularly uses the site's history as a platform for contemporary discussions that center the voices of Black, Indigenous, people of color (BIPOC), queer people, immigrants, and young people. *Into Body Into Wall*, an exhibition by Maria Gaspar about the Cook County Jail, and *Aram Han Sifuentes: US Citizenship Test Samplers* are just two of their exhibitions on salient subjects.

However, most museums do not yet serve a broad cross-section of the American public. Because most museums are racist, either explicitly or implicitly, many people—the rising majority of people—have uneven, often racialized, experiences that breed mistrust of museums. There are important historical reasons for this. BIPOC folks and immigrants have experienced the tangible results of museological narratives that denigrate their cultures and spread misinformation about their histories and lived realities.

The history of disallowing touch in museums provides a telling example. In the seventeenth and eighteenth centuries, touch was a staple form of engagement with objects, Fiona Candlin writes in *Art, Museums, and Touch*. But when working-class people gained access to museums, gatekeepers became irrationally fearful. As Candlin argues, "Once the working class (whose touch had always been denigrated) gained admittance, touching became associated with damage, a lack of common sense and an absence of justice."

This is just one example of how prejudice manifests in everyday museological practice. A great deal of excellent literature documents the complicity of museums in prejudice. Museums' history of perpetuating xenophobia, and white supremacy makes them party to our exploitative culture, but they have the power to change this culture as they change themselves. Museological work for social justice begins with creating an equitable institutional culture. In tandem, museums must welcome visitors and those who don't visit with an eye toward equity, inclusion, and accessibility. This has implications for every department. Programming departments must consider whose voices their annual schedule of exhibitions and other events elevate or exclude. What local communities are not visiting and why? Welcoming those who do not yet visit begins with long term efforts to build relationships and convene equitable conversations where both parties stand to gain from collaboration. This institutional heavy lifting requires many kinds of support, including that of colleagues and members of the public who hold museums to account.

I envision museums as a global network of institutions dedicated to social justice. Encouraging tens of thousands of museums to truly act as a network, however, is a complicated and, perhaps, unrealistic proposition. There are service organizations such as the American Alliance of Museums (AAM) and its regional and disciplinary counterparts, which have facilitated professionalization and networking within the field and have helped to bring important changes into the mainstream. The International Coalition of Sites of Conscience (SoC), which has functioned as a network of institutional peers sharing resources, is perhaps a more relevant model for this discussion. However, like AAM, SoC is a membership organization and will therefore probably remain limited.

I suggest the MASS Action Accountability Project as a powerful, relevant, open, and freely available alternative that builds on a crowd-sourced format to encourage museums to stand by their words. MASS Action is a network of colleagues who have worked together since 2016 to create resources for the field, and its Toolkit has been successful and useful. The murder of George Floyd in 2020 was the tipping point that caused many museums that were previously disengaged from matters of social justice to show public support for the Black Lives Matter movement or BIPOC people more generally. But many of the statements that museums issued carried little institutional weight and did not commit museums to any practical next steps.

The Accountability Project invites museums to take responsibility for the words in their antiracist statements and offers concrete suggestions for making these statements real and actionable. Museums wishing to become antiracist or work for social justice in other specific ways need detailed plans to do so, just like the plans they use for their finances, programs, and operations. Moreover, these plans need to include long- and short-term goals that are tied to dates, dedicated budgets, and regular evaluation. In short, our institutions need to intentionally and systematically demonstrate the importance of this work with concrete steps that are visible to the public. Museums and Race has produced a new Report Card for 2021 that coaches museums through the process of attaching these types of benchmarks to their work for justice.

A large network of museums working for social justice need not require constant communication among all museums. Peer institutions and peer groups can hold each other accountable and support each other as they share their journeys toward greater equity and justice. Culturally specific institutions have been doing this for ages as they seek allies to enable their work. More than a decade ago, the National Museum of Mexican Arts (NMMA) in Chicago shared expertise with other culturally specific organizations such as the Wing Luke Asian Museum and the Arab American Museum. The Wallace Mentorship Program involved reciprocity, shared stakes, and fully funded professional development for staff members. It would be an excellent model for primarily white institutions (PWIs) wishing to learn from culturally specific institutions through respectful collaboration.

In July 2019, the International Council of Museums (ICOM) drafted a new definition for museums. The words instantly became a lightning rod for controversy, leading ICOM to shelve the revision and return to the drawing board. However, ICOM's words stayed with me. They recognized truths about the role of museums in society: the importance of including many voices in the museum and of fostering "critical dialogue about the pasts and futures;" the need for museums to "safeguard diverse memories for future generations and guarantee equal rights and equal access to heritage for all people;" and the responsibility of museums to "contribute to human dignity and social justice, global equity and planetary well-being." This was a definition whose time had come.

Making the world a better place for everyone is central to the role of museums. Museums already have a large role in society, and they already have strong voices. Recognizing the inequities of the past and present, museums must use those assets to elevate the voices of historically marginalized stakeholders, neighbors, and collaborators. Museums should *regularly* employ the stories they tell to highlight connection and to center marginalized people rather than using them for the occasional splash of color. Museums should embrace their ability to catalyze change by building relationships (between the institution and stakeholders and among stakeholders) and by calling visitors to action.

Museums have a role to play in addressing our dual environmental and social crises. If we attend to the lessons of the COVID-19 pandemic, we can see them charting museums' course for the future: embracing social justice as a guiding principle. With practice, as museums build and earn trust outside of their traditional, majority white visitors, they can offer new models of social responsibility that can encourage change in other kinds of institutions. In this way, museums can emerge as leaders in a more engaged civic domain and respectful keepers of a great diversity of culture and expertise. As the network of museums working for social justice grows, museums will make the strength of ICOM's words visible.

Further Reading

Fiona Candlin. *Art, Museums and Touch.* (Manchester; New York: Manchester University Press: Distributed in the United States by Palgrave Macmillan, 2010).
Ron Chew. "Community-Based Arts Organizations." *Americans for the Arts*, 2009, 28.
Rachel M. Cohen. "Opinion | The Coronavirus Made the Radical Possible." *The New York Times*, March 11, 2021, sec. Opinion. https://www.nytimes.com/2021/03/11/opinion/COVID-eviction-prison-internet-policy.html
Elena Gonzales. *Exhibitions for Social Justice.* 1st edition. (New York: Routledge, 2019).
"Museums and Race Report Card 2021." Accessed June 17, 2021. https://museumsandrace2016.files.wordpress.com/2021/06/mr-report-card-2021-eng.pdf
"MASS Action Readiness Assessment.Pdf." Accessed October 26, 2017. https://static1.squarespace.com/static/58fa685dff7c50f78be5f2b2/t/59dcdcfb017db28a6c9d5ced/1507646717898/MASS+Action+Readiness+Assessment_Oct17+%281%29.pdf
"Mass Action Toolkit." Accessed October 26, 2017. https://static1.squarespace.com/static/58fa685dff7c50f78be5f2b2/t/59dcdd27e5dd5b5a1b51d9d8/1507646780650/TOOLKIT_10_2017.pdf
Museums & Race. "Museums & Race." Accessed February 9, 2017. https://museumsandrace.org/

CHAPTER THIRTY-FOUR

Are We Serious about Changing the Equation?

Deborah F. Schwartz

Deborah F. Schwartz is an independent consultant focused on public-facing curatorial projects, education, community partnerships, programming, and good governance for nonprofit cultural institutions. From 2006 to 2020 Schwartz was President and CEO of Brooklyn Historical Society. Previously she served as head of education at MoMA and the Brooklyn Museum.

> We are at our best when we are restless and uneasy, testing, questioning and doubting, moving forward into an evolving comprehension in an evolving world.
>
> —David Carr

The ground under our feet has shifted. As Americans cautiously emerge from the COVID pandemic, we have an opportunity to rethink much about the life we once lived and reinvent the museums we run. I want to propose a change in three fundamental components of our museums: community-driven decision-making, interdisciplinary discourse, and public funding.

The pandemic and the BLM protests present a once-in-a generation moment in which it is possible to rework our institutions, as fundamentally as we can, so that they are imbued with democracy, transparency, community engagement, and public accountability. We have a rare opportunity to respond seriously to the dramatic events of the past two years to undo the hierarchies that have bound us to our formulas for work; to reach across disciplines for new ways to explain and explore material culture; and, above all, to listen to the folks who live across the street and down the block.

For decades our museums, regardless of discipline (art, history, science) have lumbered along, the very successful ones bustling with tourists, and others largely inhabited by energetic groups of school children. Behind the scenes our museums are run with a uniform hierarchical structure—board of trustees and CEO at the helm, a small but powerful senior staff, and decision-making driven from the top.

The leadership carries an enormous fundraising burden at every turn, with most CEOs reporting that 75 to 85 percent of their time is spent raising money. Given the pressure to keep our museums afloat, it is no surprise that community input rarely reaches the top tier of decision-making, as we push a Sisyphean fundraising rock up the hill to maintain these complicated and expensive cultural institutions.

Democracy Threatened: What Does Change Look Like?

With our country's fundamental commitment to democracy in jeopardy, now is the moment for museums to demonstrate their capacity to tend to community needs and become part of an invigorated communal infrastructure that might make a difference in the world. In the context of mutual aid and organized protests against police violence and in support of racial equity, this is not a moment to revert to a failed status quo ante. If we are to embrace the lessons of 2020 and 2021, we need to see the grave consequences of a sickly world built on inequity and deceit.

The dramatic events of the past two years require imagining how to bring the perspectives of people who generally live outside our walls into our inner sanctum and not on a project-by-project basis but, rather, to have their voices become central to our decision-making, our exhibitions, and our strategic planning efforts.

In Search of Models

We have seen glimmers of what it looks like when we invite fresh thinking into our inner sanctum, trust people from the community, and intertwine intellectual disciplines in new ways. By 2006, when I became the president of Brooklyn Historical Society (now the Center for Brooklyn History, a part of the Brooklyn Public Library). I looked first to the community for answers to guide a course correction for a disenfranchised and somewhat dusty history museum. We created *Public Perspectives*, a series based on community proposed and actualized exhibitions; and we produced oral history initiatives that demanded an interdisciplinary approach to content development and community input. In projects such as *Muslims in Brooklyn* (an initiative that includes more than fifty oral histories, an art exhibition, programs, and an award-winning interactive website), we reached a stride, a rhythm of engagement and energy within the community.

At every turn the fate of these projects was determined in major ways by private funding opportunities that were or were not available. If our institutions are to build new, less fundraising-driven structures, explore new staffing models composed of interdisciplinary teams and community voices, would we not find new ways of thinking and working together? Would we not take journeys that might lead us to unexpected turf, new knowledge, and most importantly, new relationships with and relevance to the people we serve? I can well imagine the added value of a cultural anthropologist and the long-term appointment of one of our oral history narrators to the Brooklyn Historical Society staff, both of whom would have immeasurably enhanced the long-term value of the *Muslims in Brooklyn* initiative.

For bold models the museum field should also look to the invention of unmuseums like the Laundromat Project, with its overriding commitment to "advance artists and neighbors as change agents in their own communities" and where art, interdisciplinary rigor, racial equity, and creative exuberance are sustained with minimal bureaucratic and hierarchical encumbrance.

An Institution Filled with the Voices of "Outsiders"

It is frequently suggested that far too much of our work is introverted, using language that is jargon-laden, and that our exhibitions are built on tired formulas that are comfortable only to an inner circle of museumgoers. This is less the case than it used to be. Nonetheless, our basic tools, and our approach to decision-making about what projects we bring into the public eye, have remained largely dictated from the top, discipline bound, risk-averse, and determined with little input from community.

There are exceptions to our insularity. Fred Wilson's 1992 *Mining the Museum* was the most provocative museum project of a generation. In that groundbreaking work, Wilson raised questions about the history of race and museum artifacts that continue to provoke and advance our thinking about the relationship of museums to white privilege. Our discourse about collecting and decolonizing has advanced, but our collecting and exhibition development are largely based on structures and routines that have changed little.

Meanwhile, our neighbors continue to stand outside, rarely if ever invited to pose questions about what they want from our institutions.

So, let's go back to the problem we are trying to solve: We need models that turn our elite and hierarchical assumptions on their head and that rely on the needs of our community. I am proposing that members of the community routinely become part of our staff, providing input and leadership as we plan and implement our programs. Let's give our community members, who now populate a newly established Office of Community Fellows, the opportunity to be part of the decision-making process with a mandate to ask hard questions we never seem to answer: Who really cares about these objects and what might people want to know about them?

A Call for Public Funding for Museums—Really

Bringing the community in requires a new scenario for American museums in our financial and governance structure, paving the way for institutions that are not beholden to a small group of well-heeled elite funders but, instead, accountable to the communities we purportedly serve. With a shift to public funding, our museum leaders no longer need to spend 85 percent of their time courting donors, managing fundraising trustees, and following the priorities set by foundations, nor need they spend 25 percent (or more) of their budgets on fundraising. As the needs of community become our prime responsibility, our exhibitions and our programs can be driven by the interests of the communities in which we are embedded.

Legitimate concerns about government funding should be debated, yet our current funding scenarios rely too heavily on the whims of wealthy donors who impose their own idiosyncratic preferences on our institutions. I would further argue that by putting our cultural institutions in the hands of government, the fate of our museums might reinvigorate our collective engagement in our political system, doubling down on the importance of voting rights and energizing our commitment to democratic values.

There is concern that public funding would lead to increased censorship. To this point I suggest we look to our colleagues in Western Europe, where culture is largely financed by public funds, and where I see few indications of oppressive censorship. I would also suggest that the priorities set forth in the guidelines of private foundations, a set of restraints that we are beholden to on a regular basis—not censorial, but nonetheless, restraints put on what might be considered viable projects.

Second, there is a fear that government funding will lead to a crushing bureaucracy. In response, I argue that the tilt to public funding lightens our own internal bureaucracy (we will have smaller development offices). Further, I would note some standard wisdom in the field. For those of us who have lived through the rigors of the National Endowment for the Humanities (NEH) applications (ample forms to fill out and hoops to jump through) it is a well-known fact that NEH-funded, peer-reviewed projects have clear and well-articulated goals, strong planning, impressive design elements, all sitting atop a base of diligent scholarship, generally leading to more successful work.

So, let's just put this on the table for a second: In 2018, the federal government invested approximately $393 million in cultural institutions (a combination of the National Endowment for the Arts [NEA], NEH, and Institute of Museum and Library Services [IMLS] budgets.) With a federal budget of $4.2 trillion, that comes to .009 percent of the budget dedicated to arts and culture. If you increased those numbers by a multiple of 100, you would be investing $39.28 billion in the arts. That number is still shy of 1 percent of the total federal budget. Seriously. The most enlightened and wealthiest nation in the world can't do this? It's worth noting that a recent American Alliance of Museums (AAM) study claims that museums annually generate $15.9 billion in income, $12 billion in tax revenue, and 372,000 jobs. So, remind me again, exactly why is it impossible to propose public funding for museums?

To pursue the goal of greater public funding, we need to build a sufficiently large and active constituency that cares enough about what we do. What would it take for us to reinvent our institutions so that this proposal for public funding no longer produces an eye roll, and instead, politicians were hearing regularly from their constituents about the necessity of supporting their much-loved and frequently visited museums? One sure means of continuing to have our work undervalued in the public sphere is to seek a return to the "old normal" of our tired hierarchies, our elitist position in the community, and our elevation of expertise over community engagement.

In Conclusion

If we are responsive to the challenges and needs of our communities; if we listen to those outside the museum field; if we engage a remarkable group of interdisciplinary thinkers who have long-term access to our collections and are in regular dialogue with our curators and educators; and if we develop a team of community members who are not just the ultimate consumers of our work, but who are contributors to the creative essence of the museum, then we are really getting serious about changing the equation.

With a sustainable funding model at our back, our mission to make museums accessible is now prioritized without compromise. Without consideration of fundraising, and with a shared purpose, museum leadership is no longer pushed and pulled around by funding needs that have too often kept us at odds with our community and bound by structures that are isolationist and risk averse.

With our staff now untethered from its fundraising obligations, we can begin to imagine new institutional structures in which our world becomes expansive, where the introduction of new and diverse voices is a fundamental metric built into our work plan, where the conversation among scientist, archaeologist, paintings curator, and historian takes place at the water cooler, and the opinion of our community members is always with us, just down the hall, in their own permanent staff office.

We undo some of the siloed expertise of the art museum, the historical society, the science center and replace it with interdisciplinary teams comprising artists, historians, environmental activists, geologists, urban farmers, sanitation workers, physicists, and poets. What if we were hiring under this new premise—how wonderful to imagine an interdisciplinary team at MoMA—epidemiologists, geologists, playwrights, political scientists, environmentalists, filmmakers, working alongside our art historians, conservators, and educators. One can imagine how wild and wondrous the next exhibition season might be!

Thanks to Kate Fermoile, Janice Monger, Zaheer Ali, and Fred Wilson, whose friendship and work, along with so many others, provides endless inspiration.

CHAPTER THIRTY-FIVE

Purpose Is the Only Thing

Dorothy Kosinski

Dorothy Kosinski, PhD, has served as Director and CEO of The Phillips Collection since 2008, preceded by a distinguished career as curator in museums in Europe and the United States. She serves on the boards of directors of two foundations and was appointed in 2012 to the National Council on the Humanities.

> Purpose isn't the most important thing in the museum, it's the only thing.
>
> —Stephen Weil

The sudden closure of cultural institutions in mid-March 2020 was a profound shock to the entire industry. Leadership was suddenly thrust into survival mode, grappling with diminished revenue, worries about cash flow, and federal loans, as well as decisions about cancellations, furloughs, and layoffs. All these challenges were confronted off-site via telecommunication between staff and volunteer leaders beaming in from distant locations and makeshift offices, with everyone scrambling to learn new technical skills overnight. Like the general population, leadership clung to the illusion that all of this would last weeks or at most months. Planning for reopening revolved around Centers for Disease Control and Prevention (CDC) guidelines, local health regulations, masks, hand sanitizers, social distancing, air-purification systems, temperature checks, and cleaning protocols.

In May-June there was a seismic shift of perspective, as a quick sequence of violent killings of Black individuals were thrust to the foreground of public attention. The deaths of Breonna Taylor and George Floyd tore away a curtain of moral complacency that obscured the profound systemic racism that pervades society in policing, education, economic access, housing, health, and justice. The horror of these brutal killings was compounded by the terrible toll of the COVID virus, which inordinately impacted communities of color, a fact rooted in economic inequity and long unaddressed health disparities. These crises intersect with the worldwide waves of migration and displacement, impacted by conflicts, racism, and poverty, and rooted in the global threat of climate disaster.

Where is the museum in the midst of all these crises? Quickly, the financial and managerial dilemmas of April-May shifted to a profound reckoning around the moral compass of the institution. Staff, artists, patrons, funders, and general public demanded far more than well-intended statements of support. Performative demonstrations were rejected in favor of real allyship, investment in equitable pay, diversity in staff and board, impact in community and demonstrable investment in equity in educational and cultural ecosystems. The boldest and most insistent queries unsurprisingly came from Black, Indigenous, and people of color (BIPOC) individuals and frequently from younger generations and staff who are impatient with current formulae, narratives, customs, and systems. They ask: Why do we collect those 'artists? Why do we accept that money? Why do we mount those exhibits? Why are there not more BIPOC curators? Why do you use those words? These are questions that challenge the foundational model of the museum in terms of mission, program, and funding. What does this mean for our future?

It is useful to consider the museum as a physical entity and as an institution with ethical dimensions. In an address in 2020, Secretary of the Smithsonian, Lonnie Bunch, framed the challenge in the following way: "The museum is not a community center but must be the *center* of the community." This formulation implies responsiveness, inclusivity, and an active embrace of the voices and concerns of the communities that we serve. In a white paper that was published in January 2014, I used the word "porosity" between a cultural institution and its environment, to describe the transformative impact of access, shared language, and authentic collaboration, all contributing to a sense of attachment and ownership and to the quality of place.

Six or seven years ago, porosity was adequate, today it seems more apt to borrow racial justice attorney and social activist Bryan Stevenson's term "proximity." "Our power is waiting for us, if we get proximate," Stevenson has said. "We have to get closer to those places [where people are suffering] if we're going to change to world." The museum cannot simply be welcoming and accessible, but rather more boldly out, in, and close to its communities. The moral center, the focal point has shifted drastically, outside the walls. The museum is compelled to respond with proportional force to the starkness of inequity and injustice, to the incontrovertible threat of climate destruction, and cannot realistically ignore the underlying roots in societal corruption.

The reference to space, place, focus, and margins is a useful metaphor in unpacking the need for a dramatic response to the shift in the new normal. Around forty years ago many museums were just forming education departments and official development departments hardly existed. These programmatic shifts and fundraising evolutions impacted the need for classrooms and entertainment spaces that ultimately impacted the size and scope of museums buildings. By 1992, the American Alliance of Museums (AAM) published a groundbreaking treatise, *Excellence and Equity: Education and the Public Dimension of Museums*, distilling decades–long work to shift the mission of the museum and to make service to community central. Colleagues spoke of investing their entire career in bringing the educators "out of the basement." Finally in the 2000s, museums were rewriting their mission statements in earnest, jettisoning the inward-turned traditional principles of collect, preserve, study, exhibit in favor of people-oriented goals of inspiring, connecting, igniting the imagination.

In 2021 the societal and environmental threats were so extreme that this previous gradualism is inadequate, and the change has been too incremental or even begrudging. "Proximity" implies intentionally questioning curatorial practices, welcoming in outside voices, interrogating the standard narratives, embedding generosity in sharing authority so that people who feel unheard or unseen can shape meaning. Move the center of the narrative. The museum must be more for people of today rather than in service to the historical past.

How can a museum pivot with speed and real impact? For a collection that encompasses objects that are the spoils of colonialism, the answer might be honest and efficient repatriation. For a science museum it might be foregrounding programs and exhibits that forcefully educate about the facts and immediacy of climate degradation. In an ethnic museum, centering the priorities of community will shape existing programs and make them more relevant. These self-evident solutions and responses are just one step. All institutions must center social justice in their vision and mission, and, importantly, integrate values to drive internal transformation. Everyone within the institution understands the urgency of the issues and their centrality to one's work. It is not someone else's job but rather a key measure of success.

How to confront the enormity of this challenge? There are three important levers toward success to highlight: partnerships built on mutuality;

centering contemporary artistic practice and new scholarship; and emphasizing wellness in the fullest sense of quality of being. Partnerships are transformative, widening the traditional lens of the museum to broader perspectives. A collaboration with Doctors Without Borders via augmented reality technology provides a frontline, boots-on-the-ground perspective to visitors to an art exhibit with the theme of migration and displacement, allowing an empathic dimension to the experience. Community centers, churches, advocacy groups, and social service organizations are potential partners deeply rooted in the community who can shape the priorities, the perspectives, the vocabulary, and approach of the museum's work. The museum welcomes these voices with empathy and generosity.

The artist points the way. The artists are our thinkers and disruptors, the ones who teach us to listen better, who provoke us to be open to the "unrepeatable experience." To take another instance from the world of art museums: A video installation by Belgian Francis Alys depicts children wading into the Strait of Gibraltar from the European and African shores, holding small "boats" of flips flops aloft. As they wade into increasingly deeper waters, the sense of play is overwhelmed by our growing dread as the children seem more and more endangered by the churning waters that threaten to envelope them and us. Once again, the artist engenders an empathic, personal identification with the perils of the migrant at sea. The artist Krzystof Wodiczko captures succinctly the work of the artist: "One makes democracy. We must develop the capacity for communication and for fearless listening." The artist teaches us to listen fearlessly. The museum must respond courageously and claim its partnership with the artist and its role in democracy.

We can talk of the *simultaneous* pandemics of 2020 that laid bare the intersectionality in the United States of economic, health, and racial inequities. Across the globe, the poorest are the most exposed and vulnerable to climate degradation. What strategies can an art museum embrace to keep these urgent issues centered in their mission, to avoid abdicating responsibility to specialized institutions such as natural history museums, science centers, nature centers, and history museums? A museum can embrace and foster bold collaboration between artists, scientists, and curators, and a broad range of other scholars and specialists.

We can look to Columbia University Professor of Religion Mark Taylor, or the late Bryan Rogers, former Dean of the University of Michigan School of Art and Design, for models for recapturing a *wholeness* of intellectual life, for a robust interface between art and science. At the heart of the Bauhaus aesthetic was that goal of wholeness, wherein art had both a technical and intellectual dimension, was a product of the imagination and a societal phenomenon. With every exhibition—not just those that are politically urgent or expedient—*begin* with the ideas and voices of the community. Artists partner with ecologists, clinician specialists in Alzheimer's partner with museum educators, and curators help craft virtual curricular modules to be used in K–12 classrooms. Works of art are the objects for study, passion, imagination, meditation, healing, education and training, catalysts for new conversations around new narratives. Is it possible that a meditation studio, a teaching kitchen, a library branch, become expected functions within the museum walls? Taken together these ideas imply a radical repositioning of the museum and reform of the disciplines and departments of the university as we know it.

Museums have a role to play in promoting empathy, participation, good citizenship, and notions of justice. And they will be held accountable, as Stephen Weil emphasized in 2003: "If museums are not being operated with the ultimate goal of improving the quality of people's lives, on what basis might we possibly ask for public support?" A decade later a chorus of voices insisted on the urgency for museums to make a difference in society, to articulate their purpose and engage their public as meaningful co-producers in that purpose. See, for example, Carol A. Scott's 2013 book, *Museums and Public Value: Creating Sustainable Futures.* Today major funders, traditionally key financial supporters in the museum sphere, are prioritizing social justice and racial equity issues, demanding that museums live up to the ideals they have themselves espoused for more than thirty years. Museum leaders need to keenly attend to these seismic shifts in philanthropy—from generosity to justice (to paraphrase Darren Walker, President of the Ford Foundation)—and be ready to meet this moment of challenge. Let's follow the artist; fearless listening is the way.

PART XI

⌇

VOICES FROM THE FUTURE OF AMERICAN MUSEUMS

As noted in the general introduction to this volume, we have invited reflections on the current state and future of American museums by contributors representing many ethnic, gender, and racial identities, varied professional experience and perspectives, and multiple generations of museum people. Because this book is about shaping the future of American museums, we are especially interested in the views of young colleagues who, as museum leaders, will help to reform and reshape museums in the twenty-first century. Accordingly, we have invited a baker's dozen of these emerging leaders to offer their views on the critical changes that must happen if museums are to survive as core institutions in their various communities.

Several themes run through this chorus of voices. The most obvious, of course, is that fundamental changes are warranted and necessary. The status quo is no longer sustainable, declares Karen Vidangos. "Our world has been changed forever and is never going to be the same again," writes Dejá Santiago. "We, too, will never be the same again. Our visitors will never be the same again. . . . The one thing we cannot do is remain unchanged in this volatile, unpredictable, complex, and ambiguous (VUCA) world." The necessity of change echoes through all these diverse voices.

The call for adapting to novelty is also clear. Marcy Breffle, for example, advises museums to employ "thoughtful agility" in their response to rapid social change, which will require considerable internal examination and, most likely, systemic restructuring and revision. Rebekka Parker questions the "redeemability" of the entire museum project, advocating for a radical

236 ~ Part XI

refocusing on a transdisciplinary and community-centered approach. And Rina Alfonso proposes that museum people "should be unafraid to venture into uncomfortable spaces and to embrace our discomfort in order to create truly empathetic and welcoming spaces."

Another central theme is equity, both inside our museums and in our communities. Tramia Jackson calls out white supremacy as "the water in which we swim." Rachel E. Winston challenges museums to do a better job in "bearing witness" to Black life, in ways that go far deeper than mere performative gestures, and Qianjin Montoya questions the validity of some museums' foundational assumptions, their racist hierarchies, and their colonialist structures of value that perpetuate notions of "insider" and "outsider." Jonathan Edelman contends that museums have to commit to "equity in knowledge" and proposes that museums make access to knowledge available to all. Internally, Shivkumar Desai calls for equity in compensation and more investment in the professional development of museum staff.

Greater attention to the needs and interests of the community is called for in many of these statements. Emma Bresnan poses the basic question, "Who cares?" and Kirsten McNally argues that we "need to invite our communities to dream with us at every stage." A key element of the future museum will be sustained dialogue with its communities of service, so Sara Blad calls on museums to "amplify many voices," including those of museum visitors and community members.

Today, the pace of change is accelerating, even as many museums struggle to reinstate the status quo ante. However, as the senior generation of museum leaders is beginning to fade away, a new generation is preparing for a more inclusive, equitable, accountable future. None of us in the field today is likely to see the end of the museum journey on which we are embarked, but we may at the least acknowledge—and celebrate—the new generation of museum professionals who are not tempted to return to the old normal but, instead, are crossing over Jordan to a new, more vibrant reality.

∼

CHAPTER THIRTY-SIX

Thoughtful Agility
Marcy Breffle

Marcy Breffle, Education Manager at Historic Oakland Foundation, develops programming to illuminate the multifaceted history and grounds of Atlanta's Oakland Cemetery. With passions for community building and grave humor, Marcy is a member of the Georgia Association of Museums board and the Southeastern Museum Conference's Equity and Inclusion Action Team.

∼

When reflecting on how my colleagues and peers responded to the challenges we faced during the pandemic, I am reminded of the phrase, "Move fast and break things." Infamously adopted by Facebook founder Mark Zuckerberg and modeled by startups everywhere, this motto expresses a philosophy for innovation that values tenacity, agility, and embracing failure.

During the pandemic, museum professionals reacted quickly and often without sentiment to find relevancy in a distorted reality. We shifted priorities and changed behaviors in a display of dexterity not often associated with museums. We asked tough questions and challenged widely held beliefs when confronted with limited resources and internal crises. Procedures that failed to keep up with changing conditions or buckled under pressure were discarded. We confronted policies and people when the events of 2020 illuminated inequalities and hypocrisies within our institutions.

With inquisitive minds and innovative solutions, museum staff everywhere exemplified the values of move fast and break things during the pandemic. But the phrase carries a certain stigma. Silicon Valley interpreted the motto as a call to arms to develop imperfect systems and products with the expectation that any mistakes or bugs would be fixed in the future. It was innovation without structure, change without accountability. Museums do not have the luxury, or even the desire, to present flawed products or programs to the public when community trust is on the line. Still, I believe the motto, with some slight alterations and the values it originally espoused, has a role in the future landscape of museums.

Instead of moving fast, museums must practice thoughtful agility. Our world is changing rapidly, and museums must provide perspective in meaningful and relevant ways. The flexibility and nimbleness exhibited by professionals during the pandemic show that museums are capable of quick and successful pivots. Virtual visits, digital programs, the explosive expansion of professional networks and resources, even volunteer appreciation car parades, were once novel but are now considered normal. Museums must innovate but will also require structures and frameworks to support long-term growth. Leadership must invest in people and resources. This industry cannot expect to see sustainable innovation if workers are underpaid, overwhelmed, and operating with limited resources.

When we break things, let it be the internal structures and systems that stand as roadblocks to progress. We cannot be afraid to interrogate our institutions and reexamine policies, procedures, and people. Ask "Why do we do things this way?" or "What do we believe and how might we be wrong?" That might mean parting ways with a problematic board member, eradicating silos, or cutting ties with a partner who does not share the same values. For organizations built on systems of supremacy, it will mean dismantling an entire culture. Call it a prescribed burn or an exorcism, but the work must be done and done with the support of all levels of an institution.

Once we find the rot, we must acknowledge our mistakes and outline remedial actions with transparency. Museums serve as anchors of the community, and trust is crucial to our continued existence. How many museums and cultural institutions offered mere lip service and *mea culpas* during the social protests in summer 2020, but failed to devise any action steps to address their roles in supporting white supremacy? We must do better.

My dream of the future of museums, quixotic, optimistic, with a dash of anarchy, might be considered a nightmare by other professionals in the field. But I am ready to have those conversations. Change a mind, start a revolution.

CHAPTER THIRTY-SEVEN

The Unredeemable Museum

Rebekka Parker

Rebekka Parker is an independent, Detroit-based, museum educator, artist, and writer. She has held several positions across the Detroit Institute of Arts in the curatorial, programming, and education departments, most recently as associate educator for education programs. She has also served as an assistant to the curatorial department at Cranbrook Art Museum.

The museum, the Western institution I have dedicated my life to, with its familiar Humanist offerings of knowledge and patrimony in the name of empathy and education, is one of the greatest holdouts of the colonialist enterprise. Its fantasies of possession and edification grow more and more wearisome as the years go by . . . I confess that more days than not I find myself wondering whether the whole damn project of collecting, displaying, and interpreting culture might just be unredeemable.

—Helen Molesworth

When I first read Molesworth's comments, it was challenging to even consider her conclusion that the "whole project" of museums might be unredeemable. Yet something in her statement continues to resonate. It is both deeply discerning and keenly illustrative of some of the structural challenges with which museums are faced in the twenty-first century. This resonance has been heightened during the months of upheaval caused by the global pandemic and, especially in the United States, social uprisings and racial reckonings.

What might our field look like if we collectively decided our core practices are unredeemable? Or if we acknowledged that their foundations in humanist philosophies and colonialist impulses limit possibilities for reimagining the changes museums need to make in our interconnected, dynamic, and constantly emerging present?

I believe these are crucial questions with which we must grapple now and into the future. Rather than remaining rooted in a past that is, at best, problematic and, at worst, harmful and violent, museums must do the hard and authentic work of repairing relationships with those we have harmed. We must also imagine and implement structures, systems, and practices that more readily reflect the diverse and complex world we seek to share with our publics.

If museums aim to reflect the world in which we live and the issues with which we are confronted, we must begin the work of truly understanding current realities and past transgressions. We must reimagine our shared purpose and establish new foundations and guiding principles. At the core of the most pressing concerns are issues of diversity, equity, inclusion, and access, which are themselves intimately tied to decolonial practices. The humanist lens we use to frame much of our work implies human exceptionalism and deeply embeds hierarchical thinking in our practices.

I suggest we discard the humanist lens and focus instead on the entanglements that exist among humans, the natural world, and technologies. Let's do away with silos and esoteric expertise in favor of a broad transdisciplinary and community-centered approach for creating experiences with and for our visitors. Let's radically commit to flattening our organizational structures and frame our work as a practice of learning through action and reflection.

If we aim to be responsive, continually learning organizations, then our museums need to value and respond to change, dynamism, inconstancy, ambiguity, transformation, and growth. These qualities more accurately reflect the world and the experience of living in it and can serve as an ideal for moving museums forward into the future.

CHAPTER THIRTY-EIGHT

Museums, Aesthetic Experience, and Design Justice

Rina Alfonso

Rina Alfonso, RGD, is the founder and creative director of Studio Aorta, a boutique exhibition and graphic design firm that embodies the synergy of narrative, design, and art. Studio Aorta recently completed the multisite exhibition *Shaping the Past* for the Goethe-Institut of North America, about memory work, public space, and restorative justice.

What drives my work as a museum exhibition designer is obvious to most industry professionals: the functional and aesthetic design of an experiential narrative within a museum space. As I've come to grow and evolve in my personal practice, however, I've seen the need to question and deconstruct the education and processes that have been ingrained in me to produce more meaningful work. This is primarily due to a personal reckoning. I am trying to maintain my cultural identity while acknowledging the biases that have shaped my perspective as a result of colonization.

This uncomfortable yet curious place brought me to neuroaesthetics and design justice, two emerging fields outside of usual museum practice. I came to them from totally different angles, one from technology (specifically user experience and human-centered design) and the other from art therapy (thanks to my sister who is an expressive art therapist). These disciplines led me to ask how their distinct approaches might intersect and eventually shape a new process of creating museum exhibit experiences.

Neuroaesthetics offers insights into how people respond to art and beauty. Responses "vary considerably from person to person," writes Jonathan

Fineberg. "Our perceptions are always evolving and consist of more than the sum of the parts." This insight made me think about the subjectivity of my own design aesthetic, and I began to question how we approach each project and who gets to benefit from every step of the process. I also began to question what type of aesthetic experiences I was creating—are they not only pleasing to the senses but also empathetic and accessible?

Design justice calls on us to center the marginalized in our work as designers of museum spaces. At the basic level, we can ask "What story is told? How is the problem framed? Who decides the scope? What values are built into the designed objects and processes? Who benefits? Who loses?" By analyzing our process using a design justice lens we can do more to ensure that we are not reproducing or perpetuating existing inequities.

Both emergent fields are in constant states of development, reframing, and improvement. Their experimental quality sparked my curiosity. And as I've begun to dive into them, I've discovered their potential applicability to the museum field. I came to see that there are processes in the design world that are still inequitable and could benefit from dismantling and recontextualization. We designers need to become more equitable in our practice. We also need to work more collaboratively in creating experiences that are aesthetically and emotionally engaging.

Intersectional, multidisciplinary approaches, such as co-creation, facilitation, and community-centered programming, are now more the norm than the exception in the museum field. But perhaps we still need a stronger embrace of the unknown, a greater willingness to learn from seemingly unrelated fields. We should be unafraid to venture into uncomfortable spaces and to embrace our discomfort to create truly empathetic and welcoming spaces, physically, cognitively, and emotionally.

As with anything unknown, it takes a leap of faith to get started, but as we gain experience and expertise, we can maintain what in martial arts is considered a "beginner's mind." Perhaps the museum field can start there—from a place of radical vulnerability and acceptance of the unknown—to truly create the type of experiences that enable all our community to be seen, heard, and included.

Further Reading

Sasha Costanza-Chock. *Design Justice: Community-led Practices to Build the Worlds We Need.* (Cambridge: MIT Press, 2020).

Jonathan Fineberg. *Modern Art at the Border of the Mind and Brain.* (Lincoln, NE: University of Nebraska Press, 2015).

CHAPTER THIRTY-NINE

The Water We Swim In

Tramia Jackson

Tramia Jackson is the Senior Coordinator for the Science Research Mentoring Consortium at the AMNH in New York City, which provides mentored science research opportunities for high school students from historically underserved backgrounds in STEM fields and careers. She is passionate about the intersection of learning, power, privilege, oppression, identity, and museums.

There are these two young fish swimming along, and they happen to meet an older fish swimming the other way, who nods at them and says, "Morning, boys. How's the water?" And the two young fish swim on for a bit and then eventually one of them looks over at the other and goes, "What the hell is water?"

—David Foster Wallace

In summer 2020, the horrific nine-minute video of George Floyd's murder, plus the global pandemic that disproportionately claimed the lives of African Americans in the United States, spurred an eruption of protests around the world. Museums at various stages of incorporating diverse and inclusive practices—interrogating their historic relationships to their communities, questioning their own hiring practices, widening their exhibit interpretations and the diversity of their collections and acquisitions—suddenly began crafting social justice statements on social media and speaking out against the blatant injustice of police violence against Black people. Meanwhile,

243

systemic racism still reigned in their protocols, institutional practices, and office culture. As social distancing requirements ease and vaccination rates increase, it's imperative that we as museum professionals continue to not only recognize the water of white supremacy culture that we are swimming in as a society but also aim to uproot it within our own work culture and protocols.

I currently work in the education department of a natural history museum where my primary goal is to help high school students of color gain access to science internships to deepen their sense of belonging in STEM fields and careers. During the early days of the pandemic, we noted the disparities among our students grow as access to Wi-Fi, computers, and basic needs was stratified across communities. We checked in and sent care packages to students sequestered at home as the virus spread into their communities and supported those who went into the streets to join protests against police violence.

As educators, we acknowledged these issues and talked to the students as they grappled with the world around them and brought questions into our museum spaces. We gave priority to empowering our youth by sharing knowledge and placing it in the context of science. But we also talked internally about our own personal experiences during this time and, as a staff, began questioning our own internal practices and work culture in the museum. We began really noticing the water of inequity in which we were swimming.

The pandemic highlighted inequality in job security, who got to work from home versus who had to come into the museum to keep it running and who was laid off or furloughed. These inequities exposed disparities even among staff in the same departments. Addressing these inequities is essential for staff morale and a healthy return to work as museums and cities reopen to the public.

Even as the high rates of deaths from the pandemic subside and vaccinations increase, the urgency of the need for systemic change is also subsiding. It's up to museum professionals—from the board to the frontline staff—to demand that their institutions continue to reckon with their contributions to white supremacy in society. We need to interrogate protocols, curatorial practices, and institutional legacies.

The work of holding institutions accountable can't just be the job of the most vulnerable among the museum staff. Leadership, too, must support their staff and advocate for changes in office structures and transparency of decisions, pipelines to professional growth and leadership, and clarity of goals. This pandemic has shown us that it's not enough to simply acknowledge and question the water of white supremacy we swim in but endeavor to change it and our museums for the better.

CHAPTER FORTY

More Show, Less Tell

Rachel E. Winston

Rachel E. Winston is the inaugural Black Diaspora Archivist at the University of Texas in Austin, where her work focuses on documenting the Black experience across the Americas and Caribbean. She is an alumna of Davidson College, the Coro Fellows Program in Public Affairs, and the University of Texas at Austin.

⁓

> We weren't pushing Black is beautiful. We just showed it.
>
> —Katherine Dunham

In 2009, the centennial year of Katherine Dunham's birth, the Missouri History Museum presented *Katherine Dunham: Beyond the Dance*, a full-scale exhibition to celebrate her life and legacy. I was a college student at the time, and back in my hometown of St. Louis, Missouri, over the winter break. When I entered the museum on a cold afternoon with my mom by my side, I had no way of anticipating the lasting impact this exhibition would have, and its role in my choice to pursue a career in the galleries, libraries, archives, and museums (GLAM) field.

To this day, I can recall being impressed by the exhibition's well-researched details and carefully curated objects. The dazzling costumes, so masterfully placed throughout the space, are also easy to recollect, along with the gallery lighting that was expertly designed to encourage consideration of the fragile textiles and simultaneously offer the most dramatic impact. Most importantly, I remember feeling inspired as I left the museum.

Katherine Dunham was a Black woman scholar, choreographer, and activist whose life work celebrated cultural practices rooted in African tradition. Her artistry highlighted the creative brilliance of Black people the world over. And although these practices were often expressed in the face of colonization and anti-Black violence, her work pointed to the similarities and the connections that cross international borders and lines of color. On that afternoon, I came to understand that mainstream museums were not only a place to come and bear witness to the uplift and celebration of Black life, but because these institutions can do it, it should be common practice and expected.

Now, more than a decade later, the entire museum world no longer has the luxury of looking away while members of our community grapple with the challenging legacies of the past and come to terms with the realities of the present. As sites of cultural memory and community building, museums are uniquely positioned to play a critical role in the reckoning process, especially as we collectively work to imagine the future. But to do so effectively, we must first commit ourselves to critical self-reflection, ethical collection development, and action.

Over the course of 2020, in the wake of countless tragedies and exposed social iniquities, GLAM organizations have issued public statements, fashioned new diversity, equity, accessibility, and inclusion (DEAI) initiatives and even revamped collection development policies. As this work proceeds, museums must continue to critically evaluate their internal processes and culture and the impact they have on all organizational operations. This includes embracing redescription for collection inventories and label text to ensure inclusive, humanizing language. Moreover, as cultural institutions engage visitors and welcome them back into reopened spaces, they must commit to sharing resources beyond their own physical spaces to better meet community needs. As museums work to diversify and expand their Black history collections, they need to acknowledge that documented expressions of joy, resistance, and creativity are just as important as those related to slavery and discrimination.

Though this work is challenging, it is necessary if we truly seek to best serve our communities and collections. Cultural institutions will fail our visitors and one another if we allow ourselves to be satisfied simply with statements and performative gestures. Museums must fulfill the ideals that underpin our purpose and our role within the communities we serve through internal and external actions. As we continue to charge ahead through uncertain and changing times, museums must tell us Black Lives Matter, but more importantly, they must show it.

CHAPTER FORTY-ONE

The Optics of Museum Equity

Karen Vidangos

Karen Vidangos is Social Media Strategist for the Smithsonian's *Our Shared Future: Reckoning with Our Racial Past* initiative. Known as @latinainmuseums on social media, she uses the digital space to explore underrepresented perspectives in the museum field, highlighting the Latinx community who take up space in these cultural institutions.

If you scrolled through Instagram on Tuesday, June 2, 2020, you might have noticed your feed filled with your friends, family, and preferred brands participating in #BlackOutTuesday in solidarity with the protests against police brutality and the murder of George Floyd. If you clicked on the hashtag, you would see rows of black squares numbering in the thousands, all in support of the Black community. Not to be left out, many museums across the country joined the chorus of supporters as well, but criticism came quickly, with many pointing out the hypocrisy of institutions voicing their support without having done the requisite antiracism work internally.

These concerns left many wondering if museums were serious about change or whether they were just being performative. From seeing artists of color being represented in museum collections to questioning who gets to make the decisions that guide a museum's long-term goals and strategy, both the public and museum workers have demanded their cultural institutions do better.

In an often-cited 2015 Art Museum Staff Demographic Survey by the Andrew W. Mellon Foundation, curatorial, conservation, education, and leadership roles were 84 percent white, 4 percent Black, and 3 percent

247

Hispanic white. Although the data has seen a slight uptick in the latest 2019 survey (these roles collectively are now 80 percent white), this number barely scratches the surface of the potential opportunities that museums need to make to create powerful change. We have seen small but significant steps in the right direction, but it's no surprise that after last summer's swift calls to action against museum inequity, visible change is being demanded sooner.

These numbers don't reflect a lack of interest among communities of color toward careers in the museum field (as a colleague once suggested) but a barrier of access to them. My own path has been a narrow road with few options: either take on enormous student loan debt or hope that an unpaid internship would help qualify me for a full-time position down the line. In the end, I needed both, and a lot of patience, as I landed my first full-time position after more than thirty-five job applications and interviews.

This wasn't the only barrier, of course. It doesn't consider my many encounters with microaggression and episodes of imposter syndrome, a related fear that affects marginalized communities the most.[1] We trip and stumble along this career path to museum work, encumbered for most of the way, hoping that when we have finally reached our destination, after an uphill climb that has left many of our friends and colleagues behind, we can remember why we even started this journey to begin with.

So how do we radically change a system that by its nature discourages people of color from entering the field? How do we offer more opportunities while also creating a healthy work environment? There is no single, easy solution and the work to undo decades of systemic racism within museums will be uncomfortable for some but necessary all the same. Almost every aspect of museum work needs reevaluation, but years of studies, surveys, conference talks, and an increase in dedicated diversity, equity, accessibility, and inclusion (DEAI) positions offer plenty of resources with which to start.

Change doesn't come overnight, and museums can expect criticism along the way. Now that we are all slowly moving toward a new normal and museums start to open back up to the public, we must keep summer 2020 as a reminder that what has been the status quo for decades is no longer sustainable. As art historian La Tanya S. Autry says, "museums are not neutral," and the demand for museums to better fulfill their missions and reflect their surrounding communities will not be placated by a solitary black square.

Note

1. Rebekah Bastian, "Why Imposter Syndrome Hits Underrepresented Identities Harder and How Employers Can Help." https://www.forbes.com/sites/rebekahbastian/2019/11/26/why-imposter-syndrome-hits-underrepresented-identities-harder-and-how-employers-can-help/?sh=c25a833c1cfb

CHAPTER FORTY-TWO

Will We Lose the Love
to Labor at Museums?

Shivkumar Desai

Shivkumar Desai works at the Columbus Museum as the Membership and Grants Coordinator. He received formal training from The Cooperstown Graduate Program (2020) where he focused on museum development/fundraising and administration. New to the field, he is invested in the long-term financial and programmatic success of the American museum.

Museum professionals often say, "Museums are not neutral," echoing human rights activist Desmond Tutu: "If you are neutral in situations of injustice, you have chosen the side of the oppressor." Workers throughout the museum field, especially those in art and history museums, have doubled down on their efforts to inspire radical change. They envision a field that employs diverse voices, tells diverse stories, reaches diverse audiences, and manages diverse streams of income. Even so, these workers face a great stumbling block to their goal—the museums themselves.

In thinking about the nature of museums when we collectively overcome the COVID-19 pandemic, we must consider how museums reacted to this public health crisis. The pandemic triggered an unparalleled nationwide recession, scrambling the operations and plans of public, private, and non-profit sectors alike. Museum leadership watched as earned revenue, admission tickets, and visitation plummeted to record lows. There is no doubt that they faced difficult decisions and had to balance several factors. But in many cases, their actions demonstrated their priorities: They may have believed museum education important, but they treated education staff, especially

249

contracted employees, as expendable. Thus, the staff who interact the most with the museum's constituents (read: customers) were laid off or furloughed to keep the doors open.

A 2020 American Alliance of Museums survey reported that 56 percent of responding museums had furloughed or laid off staff since March of that year, with some of these furloughs and layoffs coming as late as July and August 2020. At the same time, investments and endowments showed significantly increased returns, highlighting the twisted nature of our economic system, as unemployment reached new heights.

On social media and in public forums, we read about the frustrations and anxieties of new-to-the-field museum workers who wonder if their emotional and mental health were worth settling for below-average pay and minimal benefits. There seems to be a gap between leadership's valuation of the average museum employee and how workers value themselves.

Perhaps this is a larger labor rights issue, but the museum sector is not in a position to neglect the future talent of the field or to trivialize their problems. If museums are telling incoming professionals to "deal with" current employment conditions and practices because previous generations accepted them, then many of these young people may choose to address problems in other fields that will value and compensate them more appropriately. If museums are to be successful in the future, they must demonstrate that they value their workers, from those who clean the toilets to those who solicit seven-figure gifts and everyone in between. Although some museums may not be able to afford better pay and benefits for their employees, they can still provide value in the form of mentorships, professional development opportunities, and participation in leadership.

This trade-off is not widely in effect, at least so far. But the world around us is changing more quickly than the museum field itself. Each organization's solutions will be different, but museums can start by soliciting donors and philanthropists for funds that provide a financial cushion for their workforce. Museum leaders are used to asking for contributions for capital campaigns, expanding collections spaces, purchasing works of art, and underwriting programs, but they are not accustomed to advocating for the economic well-being of the staff who make museum operations run smoothly. The museum field faces a number of issues, but if museums do not invest in their staff, then nothing can be accomplished. Money helps the world go round, but people are moving the levers.

CHAPTER FORTY-THREE

Make Me a History Museum
I Actually Care about

Emma Bresnan

Emma Bresnan is a recent graduate of the Cooperstown Graduate Program in History Museum Studies. Her professional interests include interpretation and curation at historic sites and house museums, the interpretation of slavery in early America, textile history, and LGBTQ+ history.

Too many history museums resist change because they imagine their audiences as inherently conservative, reactionary, and likely to complain or withhold donations when museums make changes that challenge their worldviews. We must give our audiences more credit than that. It is a kind of contempt for the public to assume that people are not ready to hear challenging historical truths. It is false, a huge disservice to our communities, and a detrimental self-fulfilling prophecy to envision our primary audiences (unconsciously or not) as white, older, straight, and conservative. If small history museums are going to survive, especially small historic house museums—the most numerous type of American museums—we have to trust that our audiences want to learn about diverse historical narratives. I often hear these sentiments behind the scenes, but I rarely see them translate into action.

I know hardly anyone in my generation who would choose to donate to museums. With the exception of only a few cutting-edge projects, I would choose to give money toward feeding and housing people every time. I would, however, and I have, given money to important history projects that unearth and make visible Black history, LGBTQ history, Latinx history,

Indigenous history, Asian American history, and disability history. These are the narratives that my millennial peers and I care about. It's hard to envision history museums that don't primarily focus on these marginalized histories thriving for generations to come. Most of my peers hear "museum" and think of stolen art or racist plantation tours. Our field has some serious and radical rebranding to do.

Museum professionals are stewards of the places and objects that powerful people thought were important to preserve decades ago. Today, young people largely do not care about most of these things. Therefore, we museum professionals must constantly ask ourselves "Who cares?" as boldly and irreverently as we can.

Few people want to go to The So-and-So Plantation or The Nobody-Knows-Who-That-Is House. We can change museums' names! Give me a name that tells me what you talk about here. We can change our missions! Make it something that improves the lives of most members of our communities. We can change our hours! If it feels like most of our audiences are made up of retired people, why not open at times when more working people can come? As fewer and fewer people can retire due to devastating wage stagnation, museums will lose those audiences. If we fail to suffuse history museums with relevance and energy, they will always struggle to survive.

We need to pay our docents. Historic house museums are only as good as the person giving the tour. Docents carry the whole museum on their shoulders. The person trusted to deliver our most important messages deserves to be well paid and highly trained.

Perhaps most importantly, we need to find ways to make discussions of enslavement more than empty gestures and, instead, sources of meaningful dialogue. As a starting point, I would like to see a community-created memorial erected at every museum that was a site of enslavement. When it comes to interpreting histories of racism and slavery, we must let Black people lead the charge, but we also cannot let white museum leaders use their whiteness as an excuse for failing to make meaningful changes.

Don't you dare tell me about fancy goods imported from India or China without telling me about the exploitation and imperialism that fed the tea and textile habits of the people who lived in your house museum. When you tell me fun facts about how sugar used to come packaged in cones wrapped in blue paper, I will think about the death and pain inflicted on Black people so that sugar could reach this wealthy family. Future audiences are already thinking about this, and they are upset that you haven't mentioned it.

Give me a history museum an activist would like. God willing, future generations will know more accurate historical truths. Not only will they be able to see through your sugarcoating of history; they will be enraged by it. *They* are the imaginary disgruntled audience members about whom we should be worried, not the person who might complain on Yelp if we use the word "racism" in our tours.

CHAPTER FORTY-FOUR

Collapsing Enclosures
Qianjin Montoya

Qianjin Montoya is assistant curator at the Contemporary Jewish Museum in San Francisco, California. Focusing on institutional histories and the narratives of women and
people of color, her research and writing have been featured at the Yerba Buena Center
for the Arts (San Francisco) and the San Francisco Museum of Modern Art.

Museums are charged at this moment to reflect on the complexities of our
existence as cultural institutions, but we have heard this call before. If we are
to survive at all, this time we should respond.

The question at the core of this reflection is: With the knowledge of past
missteps and foundational inequalities within museum structures, how do we
thoughtfully proceed? The colonial, racist, and violent histories that have
made the museum a trophy case of imperialism impose a weight and scourge
we too often feel impossible to escape. And although it is a complicated
undertaking, if we are committed, we can set a course in the direction of
dialogue, transparency, and nuance—all useful and powerful shifts for our
institutions of culture to undertake—but too often wholly ignored as our
raison d'être.

Adhering blindly—or knowingly but unchanged—to our imperialist legacies reduces our current methods to a mere proliferation of enclosures. If the
only experiences and narratives discernible in our work can be contained
within colonialist structures of value, then we are perpetuating the conventional constructs of "insiders and outsiders."

255

We must reject current notions of history and who is considered a "major" or "minor" historical figure. As it is, our narratives are incomplete to the point of harm, violence, and death—literally and figuratively—for bodies and ideas. It is imperative that both our forms and functions, from our historiographies to our exhibition practices, resist the continuation of these conventional (and brutal) enclosures. As workers in art museums, we must renew our consciousness of the dark legacy and historical function of our institutional structures and use that awareness to inform our processes moving forward. Engagement with expanded sources of knowledge can call into question established Western frameworks of thought and worth.

Many Indigenous artforms, for example, illustrate embodied knowledge—the knowledge conveyed by the body in response to the ways it exists in and with the natural, social, and spiritual world. Embracing such previously ignored knowledge as an aesthetic and experiential narrative resource, can be one of many practices that break away from the singular authority of the Western canon and its hierarchical scholarship and archive. Exhibiting works of art that exist outside of the West's traditional value-systems can offer alternative, more humanized touchpoints for history and our past, as well as our present and future.

Developing institutional resources that decolonize linear time to include the personal accounts and perspectives of those figures considered on the periphery of mainstream society, as well as employing storytelling and imagination in historical accounts, offer further ways to commit to the communities we serve. For example, we can support critical engagement with speculative narratives, like those Dr. Saidiya Hartman creates to fill gaps in the archive of those who were considered less than worthy to be included wholly.

Another approach is presenting collapsed time, as manifested in the film and installations of artist Cauleen Smith, which depict astral travel and radical generosity as common and vital experiences across time, spiritual belief, race, and class. Such shifts allow for fluidity in otherwise rigid narratives and enable us to adopt new lenses through which to examine the cultural objects and concepts we present.

We, museum and arts workers, should reflect on the complexities of our participation, checking our complicities, while moving forward to offer and hold space for cultural accounts that are thoughtful and valuable, even as they are partial and permeable. We need to release ourselves from the weight of conveying a single authority or resolve in our work as cultural institutions. Doing so will allow us to center our work in a liberatory praxis and offer new opportunities for dynamic, fluid connection with artists and our public.

Attention to and engagement with complexity through nuance, dialogue, and transparency are the currencies in which we must now trade to achieve relevancy as cultural institutions. Through our actions—our investments in time, people, and resources—we must amplify our belief that what is possible through new modes of thought and practice outweighs any danger of our becoming obsolete.

CHAPTER FORTY-FIVE

A Constellation of Interpretation

Object Labels in the Polyphonic Museum

Sara Blad

Sara Blad is an emerging museum professional, art historian, and avid reader (of books and object labels alike). She has earned master's degrees in both collections management from the George Washington University and seventeenth-century Dutch art from the Courtauld Institute of Art. She is currently based in Amsterdam, Netherlands.

In July 2019, the International Council of Museums published its proposed definition of "museum." This new definition described museums as "polyphonic spaces for critical dialogue about the pasts and the futures," which I take to mean as spaces in which visitors can access many interpretations of a single object.

The object label continues to be a primary means by which museums communicate information to their publics. Other interpretive media (such as audio guides) often require self-motivated visitors to participate. Object labels, in contrast, are readily available for most sighted visitors and, thus, may be the most obvious opportunity for museums to interact with those visitors. Therefore, we must question what role object labels, and the voices they represent, can play in the polyphonic museum.

As I write this, a bold new exhibition at the Rijksmuseum encapsulates both the challenges and the opportunities at work in shaping the polyphonic museum. The exhibition titled *Slavery* (June 5, 2021–August 29, 2021), uses objects from the Rijksmuseum's collection and those of other institutions to illustrate the Netherlands' deep involvement in the trans-Atlantic slave trade.

The exhibition's interpretive framework extends beyond its galleries' walls. The Rijksmuseum added expanded texts to supplement the basic, descriptive object labels for seventy-seven objects in the museum's permanent collection. These new labels explore the historical connections between seemingly innocuous objects (such as a painting of a church's interior) and the Netherlands' major role in the international slave trade. The Rijksmuseum plans to display these "supplemental" labels for a year and will then evaluate whether it should add new information to the original labels. The outcome of this process may present a more accurate and whole contextualization of its objects, but the composite label would still present visitors with only the museum's narrative.

It is important that museums initiate more robust dialogues between their objects and publics. Kris Wetterlund recommends that object label writers adopt a concrete approach: "If you can't see it, don't write it. Never write about what the reader cannot see." But as the Rijksmuseum's new interpretive framework suggests, this descriptive approach can silence other interpretive voices that are necessary to visitors understanding an artwork's many contexts.

A plurality of labels, in contrast, can inspire visitors to connect objects with a past and future that the artist may not explicitly express but that is nevertheless present and valid. Visitors, with their unique knowledge and lived experiences, may see additional connections if the museum introduces them to competing interpretations. Yet most museums drown out those other interpretations and discourage visitors' formation of new meanings and interpretations by offering only a single label (without a byline) that carries the weight of the museum's authority (and masks the museum's awareness of other contexts and diverse perspectives).

By displaying multiple object labels, the polyphonic museum can amplify many voices in addition to its own institutional voice. I dream of constellations of labels for each object, with each label devoted to a different perspective—some written by experts, some by a variety of museum employees (not just those in the curatorial or education departments), and some by visitors and community members.

As stewards of their collections on behalf of their publics, museums should also be stewards of the infinite resonances their objects carry. I posit multiple object labels not as a practical or perfect solution—after all, the museum will still determine which interpretations to share—but as an imaginative lens through which to develop schemas that amplify a chorus of disparate, yet valid and interesting, interpretations of any given object.

Further Reading

International Council of Museums. "ICOM announces the alternative museum definition that will be subject to a vote." Last modified July 25, 2019. https://icom.museum/en/news/icom-announces-the-alternative-museum-definition-that-will-be-subject-to-a-vote/

Rijksmuseum. "Slavery: Ten True Stories." Accessed June 11, 2021. https://www.rijksmuseum.nl/en/whats-on/exhibitions/slavery

Kris Wetterlund. "If You Can't See It Don't Say It: A New Approach to Interpretive Writing." Accessed June 11, 2021. http://www.museum-ed.org/wp-content/uploads/2013/09/If-You-Cant-See-It.pdf, p. 5.

CHAPTER FORTY-SIX

"If an Object Sits on a Shelf in a Dark Warehouse, Does It Make an Impact?"

Jonathan Edelman

Jonathan Edelman is helping to create a new Jewish museum in Washington, DC, as the curatorial associate at the Capital Jewish Museum. Before earning a master's degree in museum studies, he worked for two years in the curatorial affairs division of the US Holocaust Memorial Museum.

That was the rhetorical question posed by my mentor and former boss Scott Miller as we walked through the 100,000-square-foot collections facility of the US Holocaust Memorial Museum. Since that moment, his question has stayed in the front of my mind. Most museums of any size or discipline amass collections far greater than what they would ever be able to display. There are many reasons for this, among them the limited exhibition space in our museums, as well as the high cost of building cases and displaying artifacts.

If a guiding value of the museum world is to serve the public, why are our collections so inaccessible to that very public? When I walk into a collections facility, I never lose the feeling of awe as I pass endless objects of tangible history, yet only a select few get to see these treasures. If museums truly seek to serve the public trust, should not that public get the same opportunity to browse our collections? Should they not—from their homes, schools, libraries, or community centers—be able to access and learn from that which we have so carefully preserved?

Equity in knowledge cannot occur if one is required to bear the costs of travel to access our collections in person. Even if one did have the financial means to travel to a collection and could wander through the storage areas, the vastness, variety, and complexity of our holdings make it almost impossible for any individual to properly engage with the materials. Digital access is not limited by office hours or required staff assistance. It can break down these barriers in profound ways.

My conviction that we need to make our collections more publicly accessible was reinforced by my professional experience during the COVID-19 pandemic. I spent much of that time helping to create exhibitions for the new Capital Jewish Museum in Washington, DC. With archives shuttered and libraries dark, our team had to rely almost solely on digitized materials to piece together stories for the exhibitions. We knew that materials existed in different archives and repositories, but with doors closed and materials unscanned, we often had to turn in different directions, relying on what was accessible digitally. As things begin to reopen, we find ourselves rushing to make appointments and access in person what had been closed to us during the past sixteen months. Greater digital access would have been a tremendous benefit not only to us in our research but also to the millions stuck in their homes.

A significant barrier to making collections more accessible is cost. Digitization is expensive, but we must make this work a priority. We must raise funds to help pay for this work, seeking out grants and gifts from foundations, government agencies, and individuals who understand the importance of greater accessibility. In much the same way we use docents to support our interpretive program, we might recruit volunteers to help with digitization—and for the same reasons, including involving the public in our work.

Let me be clear: Accessibility goes beyond scanning a document and throwing the PDF on a website. This is a matter of equity: Equity in knowledge requires that museums make access to knowledge available to all. We therefore need to make our collections accessible in an equitable manner. This means adding image descriptions to photographs and objects, audio descriptions to film and video, and transcriptions of scanned documents. Just as there is no impact if these collections sit on a dark shelf, impact will be severely hampered if our digitized collections are not accessible to all. As an emerging professional overseeing a collection in a new museum, I understand this work to be critically important. I know that I have a great deal of work ahead of me—we all do.

CHAPTER FORTY-SEVEN

Change and Opportunity

Resilience in a VUCA World

Dejá Santiago

Dejá Santiago is currently finishing her master's degree in leadership in museum education at the Bank Street Graduate School of Education. Her interests include exploring the role and trajectory of museums over time and their impact on Black, Indigenous, and people of color (BIPOC) communities.

Our world has been changed forever and is never going to be the same again. We, too, will never be the same again. Our visitors will never be the same again. Communities and institutions have suffered more than enough physical, social, financial, and emotional loss and will continue to face challenges. Nothing is going to erase what has happened. The pandemic is going to have ripple effects globally for a long time to come.

However, Rosabeth Moses Kanter once said: "Change is a threat when done to me but an opportunity when done by me." The persistence of change presents an opportunity unlike any other. We stand on the brink of a new era dependent on transforming our relationships to achieve greater collective impact. We need to ask ourselves: How can we better serve our communities and ourselves, and survive in this new world?

The one thing we cannot do is remain unchanged in this volatile, unpredictable, complex, and ambiguous (VUCA) world. If we do not change individually or as a field to be who and what our staff and visitors need, then museum leaders need to reevaluate and ask themselves: Whose interests are we serving? What is our purpose? What is our role?

265

Now more than ever we need to rely on each other. Museums and other cultural institutions do not exist in a vacuum but, instead, operate as part of larger ecosystems. These ecosystems consist of differing kinds of relationships across multiple sectors which support each other within communities.

Due to the exacerbated conditions of the pandemic, some of those relationships might have been strained, or even dissolved, as institutions struggled financially and adapted the best they could. But some relationships have been strengthened and transformed, and new ones have been created through programming and initiatives aimed at addressing the emerging and expressed needs of the community. Museums, like many other organizations, have come together to provide support and access to personal protective equipment, food, clothing, emergency medical attention, free virtual programming, and so much more. This kind of responsiveness is the essence of collective impact.

As Shari Werb, Director of the Center for Learning, Literacy, and Engagement at the Library of Congress, has remarked, there was no playbook on how to run a museum during a pandemic. As time goes on, any playbook we have had or created needs to be continuously evaluated and transformed at all levels if we want to survive, remain useful, and serve our communities. This might sound daunting, like more work on top of the heavy workload we already have. In fact, this may seem impossible or unrealistic.

But many institutions need to realize they have already been laying the groundwork of working toward collective impact. Diversity, equity, accessibility, and inclusion initiatives, program evaluations and institutional self-assessments, and collaboration and co-creation with the community and community-based organizations are paving the way.

We just need to transform our thinking and, in turn, become more intentional and adaptable in our partnerships. We need to take a page from systems-oriented leaders who help institutions work collaboratively to identify the needs of communities, strengthen partnerships toward a common goal or social impact, and build trust through continuous communication.

We stand on the brink of a new era. The role of museums has changed to keep up with this VUCA world. If we take this opportunity to transform how we do things, then we will not just make a greater impact on our communities, but we'll also survive.

CHAPTER FORTY-EIGHT

Co-designing the Future
Kirsten McNally

Kirsten McNally is an Education Manager at Cooper Hewitt, Smithsonian Design Museum. She has worked in both school and museum settings, formerly as the Director of Museum Programming at Children's Museum of the Arts and as a visual arts teacher at PS 20 Clinton Hill in Brooklyn, New York.

Over recent years, I've often found myself questioning the relevance of museums. My long-held belief is that we can learn much from tapping into the wisdom and insights of our communities, and it is critical that we do so. During the pandemic, I took the opportunity to design a project that engaged young adults in reimagining the museums of the future. I was not surprised when they proposed ideas and models that resonate with ideas that are just beginning to take hold more broadly among professionals in the museum field.

My museum career has enabled me to work alongside children and young people of many ages to develop programs and experiences. This has required a conscious shift in authority. As facilitator, I could choose to share the stage or step back entirely. Once a supportive structure is created, embracing a lack of control allows students to think critically and, most importantly, creates an opportunity for transformation.

In this COVID-period program, we invited students ages seventeen to twenty-two to create their ideal youth program based at my museum. Each student had a different background with museums, design, and collaboration, but the energy was palpable. In the face of a year of virtual learning, I expected some chaos (there was a lot) and some burnout (there was some), but the conversations never stopped.

Here's how we proceeded and what we learned together. One of the group's earliest endeavors was to create a mood board for the museum of the future. For the unfamiliar, a mood board is typically a collage of visuals and text that convey a vision or idea. As our virtual mood board filled with images and sticky notes, it struck me that this collective vision was not about objects, or even about physical space. It was about action: experiences, conversation, reflection, and critique. From the board:

- Museums of the future will be a mediator for the dreams of its community.
- Museums of the future will harness the power of everyday people and their stories—communities shape what stories get told and what gets archived.
- Museums of the future will share community knowledge, even if it isn't perfect or academic.
- Museums of the future will be full of sensory experiences.
- Museums of the future will avoid bureaucracy.

In many ways, the vision these students outlined in their mood board was born of 2020. The space this group created lacks walls, a collection, and structural hierarchy. According to them, it is a collection of *people* that make up the museum of the future—not its objects, not its space, but its workers, its visitors, and their conversations. These people are resilient: They organize for better workplaces, they admit their mistakes, they challenge authority, they amplify stories, and they find connection wherever they can.

The program these students built reflects their ideals, their care, and their energy. It fits into their museum of the future. I could not have done this speculative thinking on my own, nor could my institution. Although the work to change museums needs to be done from within, it is urgent that we invite our communities to dream with us at every stage.

Special thanks to the Design Collective: Aleah, Cam, Cecilia, Corina, Dahlia, Daniela, Francis, and Juddelis.

~

Postscript: What We Have Learned

Like others in the cultural sector, we share a concern for the future of museums. This widespread concern, however, is not universally matched by a conviction that changes in museums are required by the current disruptions and growing fissures in our society. As we have seen over the past two years, there can be a great deal of ruin in an institution that can still function, albeit not optimally. Relatively few museums have had to permanently close their doors and go out of business; most have been able to adapt or hunker down and survive the immediate crisis.

This so-called "resilience" did not seem to us to be an adequate response in light of social, economic, cultural, and political upheaval. For us, the nested crises of the past two years demanded more critical attention. In the months that followed the outbreak of the pandemic, the killing of George Floyd and the Black Lives Matter movement, far-right militancy and agitation, and a succession of natural disasters, we immersed ourselves in the field, talking and meeting with museum people, learning about the museum landscape, blogging and writing about museums, and convening conversations with professional colleagues across generations, regions, communities, and the wide range of subjects and disciplines museums represent.

We quickly became convinced that American museums—like other kinds of institutions—*must* change profoundly as they adapt to novel conditions and challenges. In fact, we ourselves have changed: We have been frustrated and then radicalized by witnessing the museum field's paralysis and inability to do the kinds of things that might open a different future. We recognize that we are still up to our eyeballs in crises, and it may be expecting too much to assume our organizations can pivot quickly in these conditions. But many have. Colleagues across the country have been galvanized by the myriad challenges of this moment, professional and societal, and have turned these moments of crises into times of opportunity.

To be sure, our newfound radicalism is of a particular kind. It focuses on finding ways to penetrate the museum field's pervasive inertia, its reluctance to frame missions, values, practices, and courses of action, and its hesitation to reach out to communities and partners. Like our collaborators in this book, we champion changes in thinking, mindset, and purpose, some which could, and should, lead to fundamental structural and organizational change.

All too often, we hear that utopian ideas are not realizable and that, because they are impractical, they do not merit attention. But we think that ideas are themselves transformational. One thought can be a pioneer that other ideas will follow. Breaks in the wall of change-resistance tend to grow larger over time, often more rapidly than thought possible. No one wants to be stuck in the sludge. Our imaginations and aspirations can take us to a different place, a place where we have the courage to move around and the voices to demand attention.

When we committed to this project, we had little idea of its full scope and meaning. Over the past nine months, however, we have engaged in an intensive process of learning, reflection, and growth, first among ourselves and then with our fifty collaborators. We wrestled with adequately identifying the key problems and questions. We reached out to courageous, sometimes ignored or overlooked, museum professionals, who operate on the front line of museums or are at early stages of their careers and offered space for them to speak their minds. As we heard from our authors, we had to confront our own blind spots, biases, and omissions. And we continued our own personal evolution and growth.

Along the way, we have come to new realizations and awareness, individually and collectively. Across the field, we've seen growing expressions of personal agency and a growing movement toward stronger intramuseum communities, manifested in blogs, podcasts, webinars, talking circles, websites, and publications. These have been largely the products of individual, rather than institutional, initiative, and they have created new bonds, energy, and challenges to the status quo. In these sessions, people connected, vented, envisioned possibilities, learned, and were comforted by the sense of community these trusted, safe environments provided. For all intents and purposes, these conversations have created a kind of virtual museum think tank that has grown organically and launched waves of change through the field.

Although we believe the field needs to inculcate and nourish a sense of personal agency, we should also recognize that heroic action by individuals is not enough. We need to learn how to address our collective problems as collectives—as institutional staffs united by a common purpose or vision; as transdisciplinary teams working on innovative projects; as collaborators cocreating with our communities; and as partners with other like-minded museums and organizations.

Already, a substantial and growing number of museums and museum professionals are acting on the conviction that more should and can be done to make ourselves, our institutions, our communities, and our nation more self-aware and more responsible. The chapters in this book document dozens of instances in which individuals and institutions have embraced new modes of thought, organization, and practice. We hope that these perspectives contribute meaningfully to the current vibrant debates and discussions that are roiling every part of our society. We urge our museum colleagues, and those interested in cultural matters more generally, to commit to the urgency of the task at hand, to listen to the voices of new generations of museum professionals, to expand their aspirations, and to intensify their activism and leadership.

~

Further Reading

Books and Articles

Ackerson, Anne W., and Joan H. Baldwin. *Leadership Matters: Leading Museums in an Age of Discord*, 2nd ed. Nashville: American Association for State and Local History, 2019.

———. *Women in the Museum*. London: Routledge, 2017.

Ackerson, Anne. W., Gail Anderson, and Dina A. Bailey. *The Resilience Playbook*. https://www.mountaintopvisionllc.com/resilience-playbook

Adair, Bill, Benjamin Filene, and Laura Koloski. *Letting Go? Sharing Historical Authority in a User-Generated World*. Philadelphia: Pew Center for Arts and Heritage, 2011.

Alexander, Edward P., Mary Alexander, and Julie Decker. *Museums in Motion: An Introduction to the History and Functions of Museums*, 3rd ed. Lanham, MD: Rowman & Littlefield/AASLH, 2017.

Allison, David B. *Engaging Communities in Museums: Sharing Vision, Creation and Development*. New York: Routledge, 2020.

Anderson, Gail. *Mission Matters: Relevance and Museums in the 21st Century*. Lanham, MD: Rowman & Littlefield, 2019.

Anderson, Gail, ed. *Reinventing the Museum: The Evolving Conversation on the Paradigm Shift*, 2nd ed. Lanham, MD: AltaMira Press, 2012

Betsch Cole, Johnetta, and Laura L. Lott, eds. *Diversity, Equity, Accessibility, and Inclusion in Museums*. Lanham, MD: Rowman & Littlefield, 2019.

Bunch, Lonnie. *A Fool's Errand: Creating the National Museum of African American History and Culture in the Age of Bush, Obama, and Trump*. Washington, DC: Smithsonian Books, 2019.

Carr, David. *Open Conversations: Public Learning in Libraries and Museums*. Santa Barbara, CA: Libraries Unlimited, 2011.

Catlin-Leguto, Cinnamon, and Chris Taylor, eds. *The Inclusive Museum Leader*. Lanham, MD: Rowman & Littlefield, 2021.

Decter, Avi, and Ken Yellis. "Seizing the Moment: A Manifesto for Next Practice." *Mid-Atlantic Association of Museums White Paper* (April 2021). http://midatlantic museums.org/white-papers/

———. "Straws in the Wind: Signs of Change in American Museums." *History News* 76, no. 2 (Spring 2021): 4–5.

Decter, Avi, et al. "After the Pandemic: Thinking Ahead." *History News* 75, no. 2 (Spring 2020): 8–13.

Doering, Zahava. "No Small Steps: The Time Has Expired." *Curator: The Museum Journal* 63, no 44 (October 2020): 483–96.

Falk, John H. *Identity and the Visitor Experience*. Walnut Creek, CA: Left Coast Press, 2009.

———. *The Value of Museums: Enhancing Societal Well-Being*. Lanham, MD: Rowman & Littlefield, 2021.

Falk, John H., and Lynn D. Dierking. *The Museum Experience Revisited*. Walnut Creek, CA: Left Coast Press, 2013.

Gonzales, Elena. *Exhibitions for Social Justice*. New York: Routledge, 2020.

Gurian, Elaine H. *Centering the Museum: Writings for the Post-Covid Age*. New York: Routledge, 2021.

Jacobsen, John W. *Measuring Museum Impact and Performance: Theory and Practice*. Lanham, MD: Rowman & Littlefield. 2016.

Janes, Robert R. *Museums and the Paradox of Change*, 3rd ed. London: Routledge, 2013.

Janes, Robert R., and Richard Sandell, eds. *Museum Activism*. New York: Routledge, 2019.

Jung, Yuha. *Transforming Museum Management: Evidence-Based Change through Open Systems Theory*. Oxfordshire, UK: Routledge, 2021.

Jung, Yuha, and Ann Rowson Love. *Systems Thinking in Museums: Theory and Practice*. Lanham, MD: Rowman & Littlefield, 2017.

Korn, Randi. *Intentional Practice for Museums: A Guide for Maximizing Impact*. Lanham. MD: Rowman & Littlefield, 2018.

Lonetree, Amy. *Decolonizing Museums: Representing Native America in National and Tribal Museums*. Chapel Hill: University of North Carolina Press, 2012.

Lubar, Steven. *Inside the Lost Museum: Curating, Past and Present*. Cambridge: Harvard University Press, 2017.

O'Neill, Mark, Jette Sandahl, and Marlen Mouliou, eds. *Revisiting Museums of Influence: Four Decades of Innovation and Public Quality in European Museums*. New York: Routledge, 2021.

Murawski, Mike. *Museums as Agents of Change: A Guide to Becoming a Changemaker*. Lanham, MD: Rowman & Littlefield, 2021.

Pennay, Anthony. *The Civic Mission of Museums*. Lanham, MD: Rowman & Littlefield, 2021.

Rabinowitz, Richard. *Curating America: Journeys through Storyscapes of the American Past*. Chapel Hill: University of North Carolina Press, 2016.

Raicovich, Laura. *Culture Strike: Art and Museums in an Age of Protest*. Brooklyn: Verso Books, 2021.

Scott, Carol A., ed. *Museums and Public Value: Creating Sustainable Futures*. Burlington, VT: Ashgate, 2013.

Semmel, Marsha L. *Partnership Power: Essential Museum Strategies for Today's Networked World*. Lanham, MD: Rowman & Littlefield/AAM, 2019.

Silverman, Lois H. *The Social Work of Museums*. London: Routledge, 2010.

Simon, Nina. *The Art of Relevance*. Santa Cruz, CA: Museum 2.0, 2016.

———. *The Participatory Museum*. Santa Cruz, CA: Museum 2.0., 2010.

Sleeper-Smith, Susan, ed. *Contesting Knowledge: Museums and Indigenous Perspectives*. Lincoln: University of Nebraska Press, 2009.

Smith, Charles Saumarez. *The Art Museum in Modern Times*. New York: Thames & Hudson, 2021.

Szanto, Andras. *The Future of the Museum: 28 Dialogues*. Berlin: Hatje Cantz, 2020.

Thompson, Erin. *Smashing Statues: The Rise and Fall of America's Public Monuments*. New York: Norton, 2021.

von Tunzelmann, Alex. *Fallen Idols: Twelve Statues That Made History*. London: Headline, 2021.

Winesmith, Keir, and Suse Anderson. *The Digital Future of Museums: Conversations and Provocations*. New York: Routledge, 2020.

Wood, Elizabeth, Rainey Tisdale, and Trevor Jones, eds. *Active Collections*. New York: Routledge, 2018.

Websites

Change the Museum: https://www.instagram.com/changethemuseum
Death to Museums: https://linktr.ee/deathtomuseums
The Empathetic Museum: http://empatheticmuseum.weebly.com
Hyperallergic: https://hyperallergic.com
Incluseum: https://incluseum.com
MASS Action: https://www.museumaction.org/
Museum Hue: www.museumhue.com
Museum Next: https://www.museumnext.com
Museum Workers Speak: https://opencollective.com/museum-workers-speak
Museums and Race: https://museumsandrace.org/
Museums and the Web: https://www.museumsandtheweb.com
Museums Are Not Neutral: https://museumsarenotneutral.com
Museums of the World: https://museu.ms/
Queering the Museum: https://queeringthemuseum.org

Journals and Magazines

American Archivist. Chicago: The Society of American Archivists.
Board Member. Washington, DC: BoardSource.
Collections: A Journal for Museum and Archives Professionals. Lanham, MD: Alta Mira Press.
Common Ground: Preserving Our Nation's Heritage. The National Park Service.
Cultural Resources Management: The Journal of Heritage Stewardship. The National Park Service.
Curator: The Museum Journal. New York: Wiley-Blackwell Publishers.
Dimensions. Association of Science-Technology Centers (ASTC).
Exhibition. Arlington, VA: American Alliance of Museums (AAM) and National Association for Museum Exhibition (NAME).
History News. Nashville: American Association for State and Local History (AASLH).
ICOM News. International Council of Museums (ICOM).
Informal Learning Review. Denver: Informal Learning Experiences, Inc.
Journal of Museum Education. Walnut Creek, CA: Left Coast Press.
Muse. Ottawa, ON, Canada: Canadian Museum Association.
Museum. Arlington, VA: American Alliance of Museums (AAM).
Museum and Society. Leicester, UK: University of Leicester.
Museum History Journal. Walnut Creek, CA: Left Coast Press.
Museum Management and Curatorship. New York: Routledge.
The Museum Review. Chicago: Rogers Publishing.
Museums & Social Issues. Walnut Creek, CA: Left Coast Press.

Index

AAM. *See* American Alliance of
   Museums
ableism, 86–87, 101–5
abundance mindset, 20
accessibility, 124; of building, 104; to
   community, 114, 134–35, 226; as
   equity, 105; inclusiveness fulfilled
   with, 44; of information, 203–4; of
   institution, 143, 219–20, 223–24,
   245–46; of knowledge, 263–64; of
   learning, 19–20
accountability, 143, 200, 219–20, 223–
   24, 233, 243–44
active collections, 108, 117–21
Act to Change, 82
adaptability of leadership, 11, 17–32,
   145–46, 166–67
adapting to novelty, 2, 9, 37–38, 127,
   235–36, 269–70
A + D Design Museum, 31
advancement, professional, 163, 181–
   85
afroLAtinidad (exhibition), 119
agency, 146–47, 168, 270
Agile Manifesto, 169

agility, 17–32, 166–68, 237–38
Alice Austen House Museum, 72–73
Alys, Francis, 232
American Alliance of Museums
   (AAM), 207, 213, 219, 231, 250
Anacostia Community Museum, 30–31,
   81–82
animals, 123–26. *See also* zoos
Anthropocene, 39–40, 208, 211–15
APAC. *See* Asian Pacific American
   Center
Aram Han Sifuentes (exhibition), 218
Archer, Louise, 64
art: knowledge embodied by, 255–56;
   museums, 157–60, 171–75, 229–33;
   visitors connected with, 141–44
Art, Museums, and Touch (Candlin),
   218
artists, 72, 232–33, 255–57
Asian Pacific American Center
   (APAC), 55, 79–83
ASTC (Association of Science and
   Technology Centers), 212
audiences, 127–44; museums understood
   by, 175; needs of, 66; staff engaging,

76–78; technology expected by, 71.
See also visitors
Australian Center for the Moving
Image, 47
authority, 6, 11, 25–26; of canon, 108,
171; and hierarchy, 161
Autry, La Tanya, 202, 248

Baltimore Museum of Art, 93
Barker, Holly, 112
BEHHA. See Black Education, History,
and Heritage Alliance
BIPOC (Black, Indigenous, or People
of Color), 4, 80, 86, 90, 96, 193–94,
199, 218, 230. See also Indigenous
people
Black Education, History, and Heritage
Alliance (BEHHA), 77
BLM (Black Lives Matter), 85, 90, 119,
177, 208, 223, 246, 269
"Blackout Day" (Instagram event), 90,
247
Blacks, Reggie, 72
Blk Freedom Collective, 78
Boggs, Grace Lee, 83
Bridges, William, 30
Brown, Adrienne Maree, 32
Brown, Brené, 92
building: accessibility of, 104–5;
construction, 23; hierarchy in, 178;
ownership of, 31
Bunch, Lonnie, III, xiv, 38, 152, 230
Burke Museum, 112–13
Busboys and Poets, 80

Candlin, Fiona, 218
canon, 108, 171, 173–74, 256
careers, 181–85, 247–48, 249–50
Carnegie Museum of Natural History,
39
Carr, David, 127, 129n4, 221
censorship, 226
Centering the Picture (survey), 34

Chan, Seb, 47
change, 5–12; climate, 39–40; to
collections, 109, 117–21; cost of,
2–3; crises triggering, 23; culture
galvanizing, 6; disinformation
resisting, 133; in environment,
132; toward equity, 87; with
experimentation, 66; in language,
200; leadership and, 11, 15, 158,
165; in museums, 5–7, 10–12, 31,
85–86, 133, 250; in organization,
193–94; as performance, 247–48;
resilience contrasted with, 9–10;
resistance to, 8, 12, 30, 102–3, 168,
270; risk of, 212; to structure, 11,
85; uncertainty with, 147; urgency
of, 244
Change the Museum (Instagram
account), 25, 201
children. See families
civic ecosystem, 76
Civil War, 134
closures, 13–32, 154, 229; change
influenced by, 23; pandemic
creating, 77, 85
collaboration, 117–21; with community,
2, 111–15, 174–75; by content
creators, 45; in culture, 168–69; in
deaccessioning, 119; in creating
digital content, 40; with Doctors
Without Borders, 232; outside
expertise, 179–80; expertise
mobilized by, 178; future as, 40;
hierarchy preventing, 172; labels
created by, 174; by leadership, 27,
155; silos contrasted with, 162–63;
uncertainty faced with, 27
collections: accessibility of, 263–64;
as active, 108, 118, 121; change to,
109, 117; colonialism in, 114–15;
community in, 119; decolonization
of, 109; future of, 118; Indigenous,
108, 111–15; mislabeling in, 113;

museums defined by, 107; people-centered, 120; resources maintaining, 118; of zoos, 109
Collins, Jim, 203
colonialism: in collections, 112, 114–15; in expertise, 98; impact of, 95–99; of institution, 238; in museums, 89–90, 255; Taylor, Alan, on, 208. *See also* decolonization
Columbus Museum of Art (CMA), 158
communication: to fit community, 60–61; decision-making and, 203–4; internal, 172–73; justice requiring, 217–18
communities of practice, 179, 184. *See also* interdisciplinarity
community: accountability to, 226; collaboration with, 2, 33, 55, 60, 72, 79–81, 174–75, 231–32, 270; in collections development, 118–19; customized communication with, 60–61; in decision-making, 76; empowerment of, 54, 108; engagement with, 53–54, 57–61, 81; equity in, 236; knowledge, 108; leadership informed by, 92; of learning, 28; listening to, 18; museums in, 2, 9, 12, 20, 38–39, 44, 54, 71, 143, 214; narratives of, 120, 171–75; needs of, 8, 58–59, 208, 224, 226–27, 236; science capital supporting, 64–67; staff as community members, 82–83; staff representative of, 59, 213; trust of, 59, 238. *See also* partnerships
community-centered design, 55, 80–81
compensation, 155–56, 183, 204–6, 249–52
conferences, 137–38, 184
confirmation bias, 134
content creators, 45
Cooper Hewitt National Design Museum, 47

corporation, 155, 171–72, 202–3
cost: accessibility as, 260; of change, 2–3; of recruitment, 205; of resources, 40
courage: in holding space, 139; of imagination, 159–60; structure shifted with, 165–66
COVID-19 pandemic, 1–12; building re-purposed by, 24; global connections demonstrated by, 217; disability from, 102; inequality highlighted by, 244; staff stress in, 22, 27
CRE (culturally responsive evaluation), 192–93
crises: change triggered by, 23; disruption of, 207; Edson on, 34–35; institutions in, 1; leadership in, 13–32, 165–69; multiplicity and, 131; of museum identity, 14–15, 29; museums impacted by, 10, 13–15, 29, 167–68, 220–21, 230; responsibility in, 52
culture: bias in, 86; change galvanized by, 6; collaboration in, 168–69; diversity in, 4–5; experimentation valued in, 22; of organization, 17, 19, 20, 24, 194; relationship in, 92; sites of, 154
culture wars, 7
"Culture Is Living" (exhibit), *112*
curiosity, 151, 242

Dana, John Cotton, xiii, 53, 214
Davis, Angela, 90
Dawkins, Richard, 51
deaccessioning, 107, 118–19. *See also* collections; stewardship
DEAI (diversity, equity, access, and inclusion), 28, 66, 85–86, 90–91, 184, 194, 213, 248, 266; AAM championing, 212; leadership confronting, 28; practices with,

191–95; science capital aligned with, 65; whiteness centered by, 91. *See also* accessibility; BIPOC; diversity; equity; inclusiveness

Death to Museums, 25

decision-making, 76, 86, 203–4; top–down, 155, 158–60

Decker, Julie, 218

decolonization, 95–99; authority legitimized by, 98; of collections, 109; by community, 256; Indigenizing contrasted with, 97; of museums, 86, 95–98; performative statements on, 98

democracy, 224

de Shuman, Andrea Montiel, 91

design justice, 241–42

difficult conversations, 87, 218

digitality, 33–52; COVID-19 pandemic increasing, 33, 57–58; diversity increased by, 34; information facilitated by, 39; locality compared with, 38–39; of museums, 34–35, 43–47; platforms, 41, 45, 47; social impact of, 41

Dillenschneider, Colleen, 129

disability, 101–4

disinformation, 133

disruption, 2, 61, 202, 269; by crises, 207; intentionality increased by, 65; leadership facing, 13, 15; relevance with, 7

distributed leadership, 25–28, 146–47, 158–60, 168, 224

diversity: community prioritizing, 7; in culture, 4–5; in digitality, 34; empathy and, 92; in history, 115; at museums, 81, 92, 241–42, 243–44; reflection on, 107; sites reflecting, 72; of staff, 182, 245–46. *See also* DEAI

Doctors Without Borders, 230

Dubbs, Steve, 209

Dunham, Katherine, 243–44

Dyckman Farmhouse Museum, 71–73

education, 18–19, 78, 125, 207, 239

Ellison, Ralph, 58

emerging professionals, 181–85, 235

Empathetic Museum, 89, 93

empathy, 20, 231, 233; and compassion, 83; diversity and, 92; education and, 125; performative expressions of, 90

engagement: accessibility increasing, 44; with audiences, 127–44; with community, 53–83; in COVID-19 pandemic, 26–28; using technology, 33–47

environment, 211–15

equity, 2, 85–105, 195n1, 247–48; ableism and, 104; accessibility as, 105, 264; in community, 232–33; in compensation, 204–5, 236, 249–50; evaluation as tool for, 194; in knowledge, 236, 263–64; language of, 199; metrics of, 205; at museums, 89–93, 127, 218; in professional growth, 244; and values, 206. *See also* DEAI; diversity

erasure: of BIPOC, 98; of Indigenous peoples, 113–15

evaluation, 191–95. *See also* metrics

Evolutionary Venture Fund (EVF), 14

Excellence and Equity (American Association of Museums), xiv, 207, 231

exhibitions: at Anacostia Community Museum, 30–31, 81–82; controversies over, 6–7; impact of, 245; on justice, 82; reliance on, 174; online and physical, 27–28; strategy and, 70–71. *See also specific exhibitions*

experiences: engagement influenced by, 59–60, 132; of holding space, 137–40; of visitors, 141–42, 193–94 experimentation: change with, 66; curiosity and, 242; with new identity, 30; partnerships created with, 72

expertise, 98, 177–80

exploitation: in Anthropocene, 208; history of, 69–70, 89–90; imperialism and, 252; in salaries, 249–50

families and children: 18–20, 38, 70–72, 77–78, 113–14, 139, 244, 267; feeding, 30; programs prioritizing, 57

Feed the Fridge project (DC), 81–82

Fineberg, Jonathan, 241–42

Floyd, George, 13, 198, 230, 241, 243, 247, 269

Fogarty, Lori, 39

Food for the People (exhibition), 82

fundraising, 34, 156, 226–28; boards preoccupied with, 146; by leadership, 224

future: as collaboration, 40; of collections, 117–21; of museums, 1, 4, 75, 215–33, 236; partnerships in, 76; past contrasted with, 39, 191, 238; of stewardship, 108–9; structure in, 165–69; truth in, 251–52; as virtual, 40–41

Gaspar, Maria, 218

generative conflict, 93

Gide, Andre, 10

Gilman, Amy, 146

Good to Great (Collins), 203

Gordon Parks (exhibition), 103

guests, 126

Hartman, Saidiya, 256

healing and well-being, 8, 81–82, 114; of animals, 123–26; meaning and, 141–44; responsibility for, 128

Heffernan, Margaret, 145

hierarchy: authority concentrating, 161; in building, 178; collaboration prevented by, 172; leadership and, 145, 158; structure without, 268

"Hijabs and Hoodies" (public program), 81

historic spaces, 70–72, 251–53

history: audiences challenged by, 131–35; 251; canon and, 173–74; diversity in, 115; of exploitation, 69–70, 89–90; "hard," 191; Indigenous peoples' understanding of, 111–12; of injustice, 208, 255–56; interpretations upended by, 55; museums of, 69–70, 251–53

holding space, 137–40

Hopson, Rodney, 192

hybrid museums, 37–38, 47, 198

ICOM. *See* International Council of Museums

identity: institutional, 14–15, 29–30; individual, 199

imagination, 159–60, 267–68

imperialism, 252, 255. *See also* colonialism; decolonization

improvisation, 22

inclusiveness: accessibility fulfilling, 44; in exhibitions, 82; language in, 199, 246; of leadership, 25; metrics supporting, 198

Indigenizing, 97

Indigenous people, 97; knowledge of, 256; in museums, 111–15; stewardship by, 96. *See also* BIPOC

inequality: COVID-19 highlighting, 244; impact of, 17; at museums, 120; practices contributing to, 191; in job security, 244; in structure, 255; system perpetuating, 202

innovation, 3, 22, 75, 168

insecurity, 204–6

insularity, 225–26

intentionality, 14–15, 30, 59, 64–65; disruption increasing, 65; in listening, 17–18, 159; as reflective practice, 32; words conveying, 199–200
interdisciplinarity, 8, 108, 163, 228, 240; cross-departmental, 27, 168, 271
International Coalition of Sites of Conscience (SoC), 219
International Council of Museums (ICOM), 9, 207, 220, 259
International Geosphere-Biosphere Program, 211–12
Interpretations, 132–33; multiplicity of, 120–21, 259–60; upended, 55
intersectionality, 64–67, 242
Into Body Into Wall (exhibition), 218

Jane Addams Hull House Museum, 218
Jeffries, Hasan Kwamie, 191
Jones, Trevor, 118
Jung, Yuha, 162
justice: communication required by, 220; in design, 241–42; for environment, 7, 34–35, 212; exhibitions on, 82, 218; as mission, 231; museums prioritizing, 219, 233; social, 39, 50, 192, 195n1, 208, 219–21

Kanter, Rosabeth Moses, 265
Katherine Dunham (exhibition), 245
Keza, Tracy, 81
King, Martin Luther, 17
Kirkhart, Karen, 195
knowledge: adaptability to, 54; equity in, 263–64; exhibitions framed by community, 108; of Indigenous people, 256; interdisciplinarity creating, 163; museums creating, 177–80, 218

labels: collaborative creation, 174; on collections, 113; diverse views communicated by, 259–60; erasure and, 113
language, 188, 198–200, 246
LA Plaza de Cultura y Artes, 119
Laundromat Project (un-museum), 225
Lave, Jean, 179
LBGTQ, 4, 73, 107, 160, 218
leadership, 13–28, 145–60, 161–76; Adams on, 157; adaptability of, 11, 145–47; against white supremacy, 91; change in, 15, 158, 165; collaboration in, 27, 155; command and control, 25; community informing, 92; compassion by, 83; corporate influence, 171–72; in COVID-19 pandemic, 13, 28, 150–51; in crises, 21, 25–28, 166; DEAI confronted by, 28; disruption faced by, 13, 15; distributed, 25–28, 146, 168–69; fundraising by, 224; hierarchy and, 145, 158; inclusiveness of, 25–28; incompetence of, 91; innovation sought by, 168; of institution, 159; partnerships by, 158–59; from Rogers, F., 149–52; staff and, 14, 26, 28; structure and, 168–69; success considered by, 187–89, 197; trustees, 146, 203; uncertainty handled by, 146
learning: accessibility of, 19–20; communities of, 28; from pandemic, 21–24; in solitude, 152. See also education
The Lens (exhibition), 47
Linett, Slover, 35n1
Lorde, Audre, 200
Louisiana Children's Museum, 31

management, 162, 166, 182
Manifesto for Next Practice, 4

marginalized communities, 119–20, 220
MASS Action Accountability Project,
  xiv, 219–20
Meaning-making, 141–44
Mellon Foundation, 247–48
Merritt, Elizabeth, 217–18
Merton, Thomas, 137, 140
metrics: on education, 207–8; of equity,
  205; inclusiveness supported by,
  198; of public value, 187–89, 205; of
  success, 187; subtext of, 197. *See also*
  evaluation
Michigan Science Center, 162
Mid-Atlantic Association of Museums
  (MAAM), 4
millennials, 27
Miller, Scott, 263
Mining the Museum (exhibition),
  225–26
MiSci Manifesto, 169
misinformation, 35, 31–34
mission: justice as, 231; of museums,
  177; strategy implying, 2
Missouri History Museum, 245
Molesworth, Helen, 239
Moore, Porchia, 93
moral responsibility, 208–9, 230–31
Morgan, Kelli, 91
Moynihan, Daniel Patrick, 133
museum adepts, 127–28
Museum in Progress (initiative), 159–60
Museum of Black Joy, 44
Museum of English Rural Life, 46
museum neutrality, 249. *See also*
  Museums Are Not Neutral
museums: change in, 5–7, 10–12,
  31, 85–86, 133, 250; collections
  defining, 107; colonialism in, 69–70,
  86, 89–90, 95–98; in community, 2,
  12, 20, 38–39, 44, 54, 143, 214; as
  content creators, 45, 177–80; crises
  impacting, 10, 13–15, 17, 29, 37–38,
  40, 43–44, 61, 75, 167–68, 220–21,

230, 249–50; future of, 1, 4, 75,
  121, 217–21, 235, 268, 269; ICOM
  defining, 207, 220, 259; impact of,
  51, 59, 78, 208; neutrality of, 25,
  195n3, 249; after 9/11, 51; popularity
  of, 129n3; purpose of, 5, 9, 208,
  229, 240; relevance of, 7, 237, 267;
  responsibility of, 114, 131–32, 271;
  trust in, 69, 120, 134–35, 218;
  turnover at, 184–85; whiteness
  of, 79, 89–93, 193. *See also specific*
  museums
Museums Are Not Neutral, xiv, 25, 202
Museums and Public Value (Scott), 202,
  233
Museums and Race, 220
Museum Workers Speak (organization),
  204
Muslims in Brooklyn (initiative), 225

NAGPRA, 113, 115n1
narratives, 69; community prioritized
  in, 171–75; design driven by, 241;
  dissonance of, 133; historical, 70,
  256; museums conveying, 128;
  prejudices distorting, 87
National Endowment for the
  Humanities (NEH), 227
National Gallery of Art, 103
National Museum of African Art, 102
National Zoo, 125
Native Arts and Cultures Foundation,
  31
needs: of audiences, 66; of community,
  71–72, 208, 214, 224–26, 236; of
  individuals, 143; within institutions,
  8, 26; invention spurred by, 31, 37;
  of users, 127–28
NEH. *See* National Endowment for the
  Humanities
neighborhood. *See* community
neuroaesthetics, 241–42
neutrality, 25, 30–31, 195n3, 249

new ideas and paradigms, 8, 37–38, 52, 54, 212
New Seeds of Contemplation (Merton), 137
The Next American Revolution (Boggs), 83
No Records (installation), 72
norms: disability as, 103; equity countered by, 202–3; of intersectionality, 242; museums restoring, 2; protesting against, 117; oppressive, 90; whiteness centered in, 197

objects: interpretations of, 120–21; labels for, 259–60; recontextualizing, 115
Old Salem Museum and Gardens, 30
online programming, 23, 27
organizations: change in, 193–94; culture of, 17, 20, 24, 161, 194; models of, 161; structure, 168; and uncertainty, 21–24

pandemic. *See* COVID-19 pandemic
participatory culture, 33
partnerships, 75, 83–84; adaptability in, 166; arts, 231–32; care prioritized by, 81–82; with communities, 19, 33, 55, 75–81, 231–32, 270; in COVID-19 pandemic, 19, 78; engagement marked by, 60; experimentation creating, 72; in future, 76; by leadership, 158–59; with museums, 20, 76–78; staff empowered by, 28; time invested in, 19
past: colonialism of, 96–97; future contrasted with, 39, 191, 240; history understanding, 73; museums reflecting, 111
Peale Center for History and Architecture, 39
The Pen (exhibition), 47

people-centered collections, 120–21
performative gestures, 89–93, 98, 230, 238, 246, 247–48, 252
Perkins, David, 158
Planet Word, 33–34
planning, 23, 32, 41
playfulness, 151
point of view, 131–32
polyphonic museum, 120, 260; polyvocal labels in, 173–74, 260
prejudices: in museums, 218–19; narratives distorted by, 87
Princeton University Art Museum, 178
privilege: evaluation as, 195; of guests, 125–26; literacy as, 18; of museums, 49
professional development, 181–85
programs: community framing of, 108; families prioritized by, 57; students creating, 267–68
public funding, 226–28
public value, 188–89, 202–3
purpose: of institution, 159; of museums, 5, 9, 208, 229, 240; staff united by, 271; trust rooting, 158; with uncertainty, 76; of zoos, 126

questions: Carr on, 223; listening framing, 159; of proximity, 231; by student, 244

race, 72, 103–4. *See also* BIPOC; whiteness
racism, 13, 93; in COVID-19 pandemic, 152, 156–57; equity addressing, 194; morality contrasted with, 230; in museums, 248; in structure, 192; recruitment, 163, 205
reflection: by APAC, 83; connection with, 143; in decolonization, 95–96; on diversity, 107; by institution, 255
relationships: with animals, 123–26; in COVID-19 pandemic, 166; in

culture, 92; with Indigenous people, 114; representation building, 58; resources growing, 19

relevance, 18; in community, 92; with disruption, 7; of institution, 257; of museums, 7, 237, 267; to neighborhood, 71; sustainability increasing, 217

representation: of communities, 92; of cultures, 58; of outsider voices, 225–26

resilience, 9–10, 265–67, 269

resistance to change, 8, 12, 30, 102–3, 270

resources: collections maintained with, 118; cost of, 40; museums sharing, 38; relationship grown by, 19

responsibility, 209; in crises, 52; MASS Action Accountability Project inviting, 219–20; of museums, 114, 131–32, 271; in stories, 211; for well-being, 128

restorative justice, 31

revenue, 154. See also fundraising

rightsizing, 156

Rijksmuseum, 259–60

risk and risk-taking, 13, 166–67, 212

Rockefeller Foundation, 212

Rockwell Museum, 172–74

Rogers, Bryan, 232–33

Rogers, Fred, 149–52

Roy, Arundhati, 37, 41

Rubin Museum of Art, 141

Ryan, Deb, 153

safety, 138–39

San Diego Natural History Museum, 21–24

scarcity, 188

science capital, 63–67

Scott, Carol A., 202, 233

silos: change resisted by, 168; collaboration contrasted with,

161–63, 172; interdisciplinarity contrasted with, 228, 240

Silverman, Lois, 202

sites: of culture, 154; diversity reflected by, 72; of enslavement, 252; of history, 69–73, 132–35

Skramstad, Jr., Harold K., 214

Slavery (exhibition), 259

SmartMuseum, 47

Smith, Cauleen, 256

Smithsonian Institution, 21, 49, 51, 102, 211

social media, 40–41

social justice, 8, 50, 192, 195n1, 217–21

society: colonialism in, 99; health of, 212; impact in, 52; museums in, 220

STEM (science, technology, engineering, and mathematics), 17–20, 63–67, 213, 244

staff: agency of, 146–47; as community members, 82–83; cross-training, 24; in decision-making, 11, 26, 28, 155, 157–60, 168–69; diversity of, 8, 178; empowerment of, 28, 151; fundraising burden of, 224, 228; and Indigenous people, 112–13; professional development, 181–85, 164; recruitment, 181–85; responsiveness, 38; turnover, 182–85; unity, 22, 271

Stevenson, Bryan, 53, 230–31

stewardship, 107–26, 252, 260; future of, 108; by Indigenous people, 96; objects recontextualized with, 115; at zoos, 123, 126

stories: of community, 120; of Earth, 211; engagement with, 46; museums telling, 43; relevance of, 71–72, 251–53; speculative, 256

strategy: exhibition and interpretive, 70–71; fundraising driving, 22; positioning in, 167; re-defining,

153–56, 165–69, 171–75; roadmap
  for, 21–22. *See also* leadership
students: and families, 19–20; programs
  created by, 267–68; questions by,
  244; teacher with, 142
success, 187–206
sustainability, 217, 235, 248
Sylvester Manor Educational Farm, 72

Taylor, Aja, 29
Taylor, Alan, 208
Taylor, Breonna, 230
Taylor, Mark, 232–33
team process, 8, 171–75, 177–80
Tech Museum of Innovation, 47
technology, 50; ambivalence to, 52;
  audiences expecting, 71; centers for,
  10; in COVID-19 pandemic, 39;
  engagement and, 33–34; museums
  updating, 33. *See also* digitality
Tech Tag, 47
Tisdale, Rainey, 118
transdisciplinary. *See* interdisciplinarity
transformation: art creating, 160; with
  decolonization, 99; of values, 188–89
transformative listening, 14, 17–18
transparency, 183
trauma, 81–82, 111–12, 114–15, 137–40
trust, 50, 54; of community, 134, 238;
  in museums, 69, 120, 134–35,
  218; purpose rooted in, 158–59;
  and reliability, 212; and self-
  worth,150–51
trustees, 11, 146, 155, 203
Tutu, Desmond, 249

UK Museums Association, 213
U.S. Holocaust Memorial Museum, 263
uncertainty, 7, 9, 21, 24, 145, 150, 162;
  leadership responses to, 146; and
  partnerships, 76. *See also* VUCA
unemployment, 85, 250
unions, 3

urgency, 11
users, 127–28, 129n4. *See also*
  audiences; visitors

vaccination, 154
Vaccines and Us (organization), 40
values: and activism, 192; change in,
  91; in communities of practice, 179;
  and compensation, 250; and equity,
  206; in language, 188. *See also* public
  value
violence, 82, 97. *See also* Floyd, George
virtual museums, 41–44
visitors: changes in, 129; expectations
  of, 127–28, 131–35; experiences
  of, 141–44, 193–94 viewpoints of,
  131–32. *See also* audiences; users
VUCA (volatility, uncertainty,
  complexity, and ambiguity), 34–35,
  235, 265–67. *See also* uncertainty

wages. *See* compensation
Wallestad, Anne, 146
We Are Nature (exhibition), 39–40
Weil, Stephen E., 53, 233
Well-being. *See* healing and well-being
Wenger, Etienne, 179
Werb, Shari, 166
Wetterlund, Kris, 260
whiteness: of audiences, 44; DEAI
  centering of, 91; in evaluation, 193;
  of museums, 30, 79, 89–93, 181–82,
  193, 252; in narratives, 69–70, 120,
  256
white supremacy: in American culture,
  217–18; in museums, 89–93, 98,
  197–200, 244; protests against, 91
"wicked" problems, 145
wildlife conservation, 123, 126
Wilson, Edward O., 10
Wilson, Fred, 225–26
Wodiczko, Krzystof, 232
Wong, Alice, 101

Wood, Elizabeth, 118
World War II, 153
Wright, Daunte, 200

zoos, 123–26
Zuckerberg, Mark, 237

About the Editors

Avi Decter, Managing Partner of History Now, is especially known for programs and exhibits interpreting difficult subjects, including labor unrest at the Boott Cotton Mill Museum in Lowell, Massachusetts; civil war at the National Civil War Museum in Harrisburg, Pennsylvania; and genocide at the U.S. Holocaust Memorial Museum. Over the years, he has helped to plan new museums in six states and the District of Columbia. His projects have been honored by the American Alliance of Museums (AAM), the American Association for State and Local History (AASLH), and two Dibner Awards for Excellence in Museum Exhibits. Decter is the coauthor and coeditor of numerous exhibition catalogs. He is the coauthor of *Ten Years: Remembrance, Education, Hope* (2006); author of *Interpreting American Jewish History at Museums and Historic Sites* (2016) and *Exploring American Jewish History through 50 Historic Treasures* (forthcoming). With Ken Yellis, he is the author of numerous blogs, a manifesto for next practice (published by MAAM), and the "History in Progress" column in *History News*.

Marsha L. Semmel is an independent consultant working with cultural and educational organizations on leadership development, strategic planning, and partnerships. In 2019, she published *Partnership Power: Essential Museum Strategies for Today's Networked World*. An adjunct faculty in the Bank Street College of Education's graduate program in museum leadership, Semmel is a founding faculty member for the Southeastern Museums Conference's Executive Leadership Institute. She's served as Senior Advisor to SENCER-ISE, a project of the National Center for Science and Civic Engagement, and the Noyce Leadership Institute, a global program for science museum leaders. Previously, Semmel headed the Division of Public Programs at the National Endowment for the Humanities. She also held the President and CEO posts at Conner Prairie and the Women of the West Museum. In her decade at the Institute of Museum and Library Services (IMLS), Semmel led such projects as *Museums, Libraries, and 21st Century Skills* and served as Director for Strategic Partnerships; Deputy for Museum Services; and acting IMLS director.

Ken Yellis, Principal of Project Development Services, is a historian with nearly fifty years in the museum field. He served fourteen years at the National Portrait Gallery and has worked at Plimoth Plantation, the Yale Peabody Museum of Natural History, and the International Tennis Hall of Fame. Ken has developed many innovative programs and major exhibitions, among them the eleven-year run of *Portraits in Motion* events at the National Portrait Gallery and the acclaimed exhibition, *The Brooklyn Navy Yard: Past, Present and Future*. Most recently, his project on *Seeking Shelter: A Story of Place, Faith and Resistance* has traveled to fourteen community venues. He has consulted for the Brooklyn Historical Society, the Penn Museum of Archaeology and Anthropology, and the Loeb Visitors Center at Touro Synagogue National Historic Site, among many others. With Avi Decter, Ken is coauthor of a dozen blogs on post-pandemic museums and a manifesto on next practice. A longtime editor-in-chief of *The Journal of Museum Education*, Ken has written for museum, scholarly, and popular publications. His book, *The Museum Journey*, is forthcoming.

About the Artist

Bill Brookover (Cover Art) uses pattern and geometry to express the tension between chaos and harmony in modern life. GRAND DISSIDENCE, shown on this book cover, is part of his *Dissonance* series of screenprints begun in 2019. As we emerge from the pandemic into an ongoing crisis of racial and economic inequity, he continues to explore visual metaphors for our unsettling times. His printmaking practice is grounded in his training in architecture and design. He has shown his work in solo, curated, and juried exhibitions. His portfolio can be seen at https://billbrookover.com/.